Modern German Drama

A Study in Form

C. D. INNES

Associate Professor, Department of English
York University, Ontario

CAMBRIDGE UNIVERSITY PRESS

Cambridge
London   New York   Melbourne

Published by the Syndics of the Cambridge University Press
The Pitt Building, Trumpington Street, Cambridge CB2 1RP
Bentley House, 200 Euston Road, London NW1 2DB
32 East 57th Street, New York, NY 10022, USA
296 Beaconsfield Parade, Middle Park, Melbourne 3206, Australia

First published 1979

Printed in Great Britain at the
University Press, Cambridge

Library of Congress Cataloguing in Publication Data
Innes, C. D.
Modern German drama.
Bibliography: p.
Includes index.
1. German drama–20th century–History and criticism. I. Title.
PT666.I5   823'.9'1409   78-26597
ISBN 0 521 22576 0 hard covers
ISBN 0 521 29560 2 paperback

Modern German Drama

Contents

Illustrations

Acknowledgements

I wish to express my gratitude to the Canada Council and to York University, who aided me in the preparation of this book with Research Grants, and to the dramaturgical staffs of various German and Swiss theatres, without whose assistance and co-operation this study would hardly have been possible. In particular I am grateful to Peter Palitzsch and Claus Peymann for drawing certain productions to my attention and answering my questions, to the various actors who gave me details of their roles, and to the colleagues and friends who offered me encouragement and advice: among others Professor Ann Saddlemyer, Dr Walter Huder, Dr Gilbert Mackay, and Diane Speakman. I would also like to thank the librarians of the Taylorian Institute in Oxford and the Akademie der Künste in West Berlin, David Hamer and Gabriele Engelmann who acted as my research assistants, as well as Ilse Buhs, Rosmarie Clausen, Günter Englert, Werner Schloske, Daisy Steinbeck and Hildegard Steinmetz for giving me permission to use their photographs as illustration. Last, but by no means least, my sincere thanks go to my wife for her criticism, patience and support.

January 1978   CHRISTOPHER INNES

1. *Introduction*

As a cultural institution the German stage suffers from the same malaise of rising prices and falling audiences as the theatre elsewhere. But it has an intellectual vitality and imaginative force that continues to give it significant social influence of a kind that recent English and American drama has only achieved in such isolated instances as Osborne's *Look Back in Anger* or Miller's *Death of a Salesman*. German dramatists become centres of public controversy, premières of Dürrenmatt and Hochhuth have attracted press conferences, performances Dorst, Weiss and Kroetz have provoked riots and public demonstrations, while the work of a writer like Wallraff is reported in the news columns of the daily press rather than the book review sections, and the influence of Brecht could be said to have set the tone and standard for much of modern drama in a way comparable to Ibsen fifty years earlier. Partly this importance comes from the traditional German view of the stage as a 'moral tribunal', a political forum – and if one were cynical it might be possible to put the status of German theatre down to a national failing, as indeed Friedrich Wolf has (extending Marx's comment that in politics 'the Germans have *thought* what others have done'): 'We have not translated our political passions and perceptions into deeds, rather we diverted them into the realm of the intellect and the theatre.'[1] Certainly the German playwright can count on a national enthusiasm for drama and the arts which immediately after the war put plays and music above comfort and even at times personal security, and which has since led to a massive public investment in rebuilding theatres and concert halls. Carl Ebert, for instance, touring Germany for the Allied Control Commission in 1945, reported packed audiences standing for over two hours in freezing cold in a ruined stock exchange or in the windowless auditorium of Frankfurt university to hear musical recitals, while the critic Friedrich Luft has given a graphic account of what Berlin theatre-goers risked to attend performances. Crossing the city to the reopening of the Deutsches Theater he had to clamber over a canal on two unsafe conduits, had to run from looters, and on his way home was knocked unconscious and robbed: 'It was the next day before my family saw me again and they had just about written me off, imagining that I could even be on my way to Siberia. Theatre-going was dangerous.'[2] If pre-formed public support or an escapist tendency to substitute art for life explained the prominence given to German playwrights, their work would be only of limited or academic interest. But the real reasons for their position relate to the choice of material, the exploration of new techniques of presentation, the consistent attempt to develop styles to express contemporary modes of perception – and these stake a claim for wide attention to their work, in particular to its dramatic form.

Even on a basic level of subject-matter German drama can be seen as seminal since the German experience of total war, communal guilt feelings, the student riots of the 1960s and the pressures of urban terrorism in the 1970s mirrors English and American experiences in a more extreme form. Where we have a general awareness of the cold war and the social problems caused by prosperity (the 'you never had it so good' syndrome) – in Germany, the Berlin wall and the scale of the transformation from ruins to a dominating industrial position within a single decade have intensified the political and economic stresses on contemporary society, putting the disruptive effects of a nation divided against itself, the reaction against purely materialistic values, or the strains of accelerated social change in a sharp perspective where the fundamental issues appear clear-cut. The themes in which these issues are embodied may seem at first glance to have a limited and specifically German relevance. Auschwitz is not our guilt, the short-lived Bavarian communist republic of 1919 or the events of 17 June 1953 are not our history. On looking closer we find that these concentration camps or revolutionary situations are not the subjects of the plays but symbols, examples through which general questions can be analysed: the nature of capitalism; whether personal responsibility can exist in a context where the individual is powerless; the function of art and its relationship to effective political action. Indeed a striking characteristic of recent German drama is the way the issues that arise from specifically national experience are translated into global terms – Vietnam, Cuba, or Dürrenmatt's paradigmatic model countries – even to the extent that the details are too alien for the immediate audience to understand and the meaning becomes so generalised that special techniques are required if German spectators are to apply the points to their own context.

More important in its implications for modern drama as a whole is the way German artists have been forced to confront aesthetic issues by the extreme nature of wide-spread social problems. With these problems being seen as of immediate and overwhelming relevance playwrights have had to try to deal with them directly, which has meant formulating new methods of representation. In this they have been following the lead of Brecht whose starting point a generation earlier was the conviction that

Just the grasping of a new range of material requires a new dramatic and theatrical form. Can we speak about finance in heroic couplets?... Petroleum struggles against the five act form... The dramatic technique of Hebbel and Ibsen is totally insufficient to dramatise even a simple press release...
... Indeed one no longer dares to offer [drama] in its old form to grown-up newspaper readers.[3]

So the postwar stylistic concern as such was hardly new to German theatre. In the 1920s Brecht had remarked (unfavourably) on the 'Babylonian confusion' of styles, a point echoed – but as a positive value – in the sixties by Dürrenmatt, who commented that the eclectic borrowing of stylistic elements from every conceivable theatrical period made the playwright aware of 'all the potentialities of theatre, opens the theatre of our time to all experiments'.[4] Indeed, practically the only approach not evident in serious German drama of the last twenty years is the conventional naturalistic form. With the possible exception of Walser's *Home Front* (*Die Zimmerschlacht*, 1967) which is closely modelled on Albee's *Who's Afraid of Virginia Woolf?*, work like Terence Rattigan's well-made problem plays, or Tennessee Williams' 'corn-pone melodrama' are no longer viable on the German stage as vehicles for addressing significant contemporary issues.

On a general level the kind of themes that seem to require stylistic experiment could even be called traditional to German drama. The radical challenge to social structures in much of documentary theatre, for example, can be traced back to revolutionary plays of bourgeois emancipation like Schiller's *The Robbers* (*Die Räuber*, 1781). Already in Büchner there is the same questioning of the point at which revolution becomes repression in the name of freedom and the same tragic conflict between ideology and humanity as in Brecht's 'teaching play' from the 1930s, *The Measures Taken* (*Die Massnahme*), or in Weiss' *Marat/Sade* and Dorst's *Toller*. The equation between extending the range of subjects open to the theatre and stylistic innovation may be a familiar one; what is new in the voice of postwar German drama is the attempt to develop a specifically contemporary stage vocabulary. At the turn of the century the misery and poverty of Silesian weavers could be represented by Hauptmann's amalgamation of Greek choric effects with the new naturalistic form that expressed the environmental determinism, the social perception of the time. Today a similar treatment – Wesker's working-class trilogy or O'Neill's version of *The Lower Depths* – seems dated. It may be exciting as theatrical entertainment, but it does not correspond to our perception; and in their attempts to portray social deprivation, to rouse public opinion by showing the social causes of exploitation and its individual effects in contemporary terms, German dramatists have explored different possibilities. At one end of the spectrum is a new version of the 'folk play', adapting its traditional ironic ambiguity to present apparently simple situations from multiple viewpoints, and extending its oblique presentation of social analysis in a linguistic form to the point where the quality of the characters' speech makes overt commentary unnecessary. At the other is a complex adaptation of 'the happening', where actual events and situations are structured so that those involved become aware of the true political nature of what they usually accept unconsciously – an integration of performance and reality which moves outside any normal definition of theatre.

Because of the pressure of twentieth-century social changes in the German context which has magnified and exacerbated them, the German artist has been forced to respond to the challenge of Hegel, who concluded in his analysis of history that the era of art was at an end; of Adorno, who stated that poetry, the creative imagination, could only be seen as illusory escapism in light of Auschwitz and was therefore impossible to justify. The effect has been a search for new forms and a decisive break with the conventional dramatic approach, which remained basically unchanged from Lessing's *Hamburgische Dramaturgie* of 1768 to Lukács (who in 1909 could still state that 'modern drama is the drama of the bourgeoisie', based on a particular definition of individuality and 'historical consciousness')[5] and which still essentially holds the Broadway and West End stages today. To some extent this stylistic search, the concern for modernity and the sensitivity to changes in perception, is as traditional to German theatre as its characteristic themes. Hofmannsthal had noted it in 1926, expressing a widespread feeling that the concept of individuality, created by the Renaissance and reaching its fullest form in the nineteenth century, was basically responsible for the catastrophe of the First World War, and that: 'I would even go so far as to say that all the ominous events in Europe which we have experienced in the last twelve years are nothing else but a very circumstantial way of burying the life-weary concept of the European individual in the grave that it has dug for itself',[6] – a viewpoint that forms the theme of Handke's most recent plays. In the 1920s this revolution in consciousness lay behind expressionism, Brecht's epic theatre and Piscator's experiments with a multi-media, mechanised stage. In the postwar period it has produced documentary and 'dialectical' theatre forms, the new 'folk play' and Handke's linguistic drama. On one level all these theatrical approaches have their roots in the 1920s and 1930s, particularly the 'folk play', which derives from Horváth, and the documentary, which can be seen as realising the aims of the '*neue Sachlichkeit*' (new objectivity) movement – the qualities of which were summed up in 1928 in terms accurately describing the documentary drama of forty years later:

The term '*Sachlichkeit*' is no longer...a simple translation of the term 'Realism'. It signifies: the object itself replaces the work of art: the thing itself, life itself, the authentic subject...In the theatre? It means the direct presentation of contemporary life and its forces, not humanised; without artistic structuring and harmonising...[A 'problematic' age needs] direct theatre; theatre of statement and actuality.[7]

In fact it is arguable that without this prewar background contemporary German dramatists would have been unlikely to reach their high level of formal achievement. However, with the complete break in artistic continuity represented by the twelve years of fascist rule they were forced to formulate their own approaches, and the distinctive postwar styles are therefore more radical, based more on contemporary experience than on examples from the past.

Experiments with form then are not simply arbitrary or personal choices, for novelty as such is self-defeating and conventions only communicate effectively when they are accepted as natural and therefore unnoticed. This, for instance, is one of the basic flaws in expressionism: the means of expression that theoretically transmit immediate experience on a subliminal level in fact obtrude because they are based on a too simplistic equation between the artist's personal imagery and the symbols common to the public at large, with the result that the means attract our attention at the expense of the meaning they are intended to express. So innovations are only valid (even by the very basic test of stage-worthiness) when they correspond to the audience's perception of life, and might be said to be most effective when they give meaningful shape to perceptions which have been widely accepted without being fully recognised. As a generally accepted view, this explains German dramatists' at first sight paradoxical rejection of the 'avant-garde' label as 'conservative'. To be avant-garde is 'apolitical' in the sense that style which lacks any social correlative cannot heighten or change the audience's awareness.[8] To another generation, of course, much of what is most contemporary in German drama may seem as dated as those characteristic styles of the 1920s, expressionism, futurism, vorticism, do to us. Which theatrical forms will survive? It is still too early to say, but what is of immediate interest is the way these new styles reflect or formulate modern experience, adapting the theatre to suit new social conditions, making it capable of handling new subject matter.

Literary and dramaturgical criteria (whatever the claims of critics) are at best relative. If the actor's name, as Garrick remarked, is written on water, the same is true of theatrical values which depend on changing public expectations, technical or philosophical advances, even fads. But there are certain basic questions that any study such as this must attempt to answer, at least provisionally. One is the relationship between form and content. Another is the way the difference in effect between various styles can be defined, for which one needs to determine how to treat that amorphous abstraction, the audience. Equally, it is a mistake to assume that a particular range of subject-matter limits the exploration of theatre as an art form, or that political commitment rules out stylistic advances – an all too common view in the light of British or American experience and one argued, for instance, by Marowitz, who has claimed that

contemporary theatre in Germany is fixated on politics, while the important developments in theatre today are occurring elsewhere. The most advanced phenomena are neither literary nor political, but formal. If the middle of the twentieth century is going to be remembered, it will

6

be for the ensembles of the Living Theatre, the Open Theatre, Café La Mama and Grotowski, whose common factor is a physical, unnaturalistic theatre-language, spiritually revolutionary and standing in opposition to...psychological realism, Aristotelian time-structure.[9]

It is certainly true that every significant contemporary German dramatist, apart from Bernhard and possibly Dorst, must be counted as politically committed. Grass and Kroetz have fought elections, for the socialists and communists respectively; Hacks, Wallraff and Weiss are professed Marxists; even Dürrenmatt's anti-ideological stance is a highly political protest. But none write in a 'realistic' mode, whether psychological or social, and as we shall see the nearer their plays approach documentary fact the more aesthetic or purely formal structures are emphasised. Not only has a fairly narrow and intense political spectrum produced a wide variety of styles, but (with the exception of the rather suspect Brechtian assertion that epic techniques embody dialectical materialism) there is no discernible link between particular styles and political principles.

Equally it is all too easy to talk about style as if it were something separable, applied independently, and Dürrenmatt has given a neat example of how a dramatist might treat the same subject – Scott's death in the Antarctic – in different ways. As a tragedy in the Shakespearean mould, where the pride of the protagonist leads him to attempt the impossible and the jealousy or treachery of members of the expedition is responsible for the catastrophe: from the epic perspective (on analogy to the changes Brecht made in his adaptation of *Coriolanus*) where Scott is presented as a product of his society, so that 'class thinking' caused him to buy ponies instead of the more efficient dogs, and the disaster illustrates the evils of a particular social structure: as an existential symbol *à la* Beckett, with Scott and his companions as blocks of ice carrying on echoing, isolated monologues: or as a paradoxical farce in which Scott comes to be 'shut in a cold-store by mistake while buying the necessary food-supplies for the expedition', freezing to death with an incongruous heroism.[10] The McLuhanesque medium-equals-message formula is an oversimplification. As Walser has put it, representational forms 'have to be such that they do not simplify what is complex, and so that the means is not taken for the thing itself'.[11] But even Dürrenmatt's deliberately facetious flight of imagination indicates the way stylistic choices define subject matter. The starting point may be the same, the statement is not. A style then represents a perspective, and changes in theatrical convention should express new criteria for defining reality. Conversely, any theatre-goer associates certain forms of presentation with particular types of dramatic experience, so that a play's style has to be appropriate to the author's intention in the sense that it keys in the desired range of expectations.

The minimal requirements, then, for evaluating style are coherence and contemporaneity: that there is a harmony between the theme and its treatment, and that the approach provides a perspective in which the modern world becomes more comprehensible. This is not to say, however, that there is such a thing as a specific 'modern' style. The limitations of such an assumption can be seen in certain German critics who claim that only the 'comic' approach or 'open' dramatic forms are valid because these correspond to 'democratisation', represent the mobility of industrial society or 'emancipate the audience'.[12] Rather than any direct analogy between social and dramatic structures, new conventions would seem to be developed by taking elements from previously discarded or foreign theatre forms, as Brecht borrowed from Elizabethan and Chinese drama or as the modern documentary play is based on Piscator's early, partially-unsuccessful experiments. The modernity lies in the way stylistic elements are altered by being used in unusual combinations or gain fresh significance in the context of untraditional dramatic material. In one sense there is no such thing as a 'new' theatrical element – the revolutionary innovations have come from social changes, architectural or technological advances that occurred independent of the stage – and the basic difference between theatrical styles comes from the relative weighting of mimesis and abstraction.

As for the audience, on whom the effectiveness of any particular approach depends, generalisations are bound to be inaccurate. Not only can the composition of different audiences significantly alter the apparent meaning of a play, but any major public event can give a play a totally unintended reference or remove its immediate relevance, causing completely different but equally legitimate responses on different dates.[13] From Aristotle's discussion of catharsis to Brecht, all drama theory has been based on the spectator, and even the apparently purely formal concerns of the neo-classicists (such as the unities or the use of heroic couplets) are in fact means of heightening the intensity of response on a specific, elevated emotional level. Thus techniques of representation are at bottom justified by the kind and degree of audience participation; and it is this that really distinguishes different dramatic forms, defining classical tragedy (emotional sublimation, evoking pity and fear as a form of psychiatric purgation) or traditional satire (focussing peer-group pressure through ridicule, 'vicious people' in Congreve's model being shamed by the laughter of others who are 'both warned and diverted at their expense') or contemporary epic drama (rational perception and objective judgement, creating 'a theatre full of experts' by enforcing 'a smoking-observing attitude'). As Handke has put it, plays have only a putative existence without a public, and 'therefore need a *vis à vis*. At least *one* person who listens.'[14] The problem is to determine exactly what an audience's reactions might or should be. Here external evidence can be drawn on, reports of specific public responses or personal evaluations; but only to indicate the range of possibilities. Since conditions outside the theatre and quite unrelated to the play can change its effect, all that such evidence can define is a variable. In addition, where there have been clearly defined reactions such as the occupation of the stage by the audience, a street demonstration, vocal expressions of disappointment or approval, these may be due to a homogeneous but unrepresentative group within the audience, such as members of a student organisation, or to the playwright's reputation rather than the performance itself, as in demonstrations *before* the opening of Kroetz's plays or the rejection of Hochhuth's second play simply because of the unrealistic expectations generated by his first. Similarly, a professional critic's opinion may not reflect the general public's, and the gap is indicated by the performance/spectator ratio. In 1968–9, for example, there were 508 performances of Handke's highly praised *Kaspar*, while Miller's *The Price*, which critics generally disparaged as conventional, was given 418 German performances in the same season – yet only 54,868 people saw *Kaspar* as compared to the enthusiastic 154,348 who went to the Miller play. It would seem appropriate then to treat the audience as neither a collection of independent individuals nor an anonymous and unified totality, but as a socially variable group whose reactions are the sum of personal responses, these being to some extent conditioned by those around them.

This leads to a third problem area, performance. A play only reaches its full expression on the stage, but obviously each production is a different interpretation and a director can materially alter the dramatist's intended effect by imposing his own style. Where the differences in production are marked, however, it is frequently a sign that the original stylistic concept of the play is unsatisfactory, as with Handke's *They Are Dying Out* (*Die Unvernünftigen sterben aus*, 1974) which was played in Düsseldorf as a realistic analysis of a monomaniac, demonstrating the psychological effects of capitalism, as a slapstick farce performed by clowns in Zürich and as a Daliesque, surrealist dream in Frankfurt. An even more extreme example is Hochhuth's *The Representative* (US title: *The Deputy/Der Stellvertreter*, 1963). With its controversial theme and momentous subject it was a play that no major theatre could ignore, but the monumental length of the text with its weight of unassimilated factual detail meant that it was unperformable without radical cutting. There is also an uneasy jumble of styles in its various scenes ranging from vulgar naturalism, through static argument between embodiments of moral principles rather than individualised characters, to symbolic monologues; and the different attempts to resolve the stylistic conflict together with a wide range of cuts produced essentially different plays. In the Bern production, for instance, *The Representative* became a symbolic passion-play. Almost all historical references, facts and statistics were omitted and it was staged in an abstract setting of six plain white, moveable screens with symbols marking each scene – immense antlers for the *Jägerkeller*, a barbed-wire cross for Auschwitz – while the order of episodes was changed to create parallels between the Nuncio's moral abdication and the vacuous materialism of the Nazi revellers, between the Pope's betrayal of humanity and the daemonic nihilism of the Doctor, so that the action was one of redemptive sacrifice and the guilt universal. By contrast, in Düsseldorf the play became a Brechtian parable, with a bare stage, visible machinery and lights. Placards announced time and place, while the cuts gave a typically 'epic' focus by turning the positive moral position of Riccardo and Gerstein into a short-sighted error – the Church being a political institution and religion a form of propaganda, it is simply unrealistic to expect ethical action. Other interpretations varied from a neo-classical drama of ideas in which all Nazi figures and the concentration-camp scenes were cut, the conflict was purely intellectual, and the play ended with a monolgue put together from Riccardo's final speeches of self-justification which followed directly on the Pope's rejection of his plea (in Bochum), to a naturalistic study of Christian conscience, which emphasised psychological pathos and personal dilemmas, and cut almost all the political reference (at Essen). No analysis of theatrical styles can be valid without taking preformance qualities into account, yet with this kind of possible variation any conclusions drawn from a single performance would be deficient and any generalisations based on several productions contradictory. The only practical solution is to use the première as the basis for discussions of staging, since this is the one production in which the playwright is commonly involved. Alternatively, an author may have singled out a particular production as corresponding to his aims. In either case the performance must be measured against internal evidence in the text itself, since stage-directions and even dialogue are frequently changed following the playwright's experience of his work in rehearsal.

These are the principles on which this study of German drama is based. Since the questions of drama's social function and the nature of stage illusion have been widely argued by the various playwrights, these are our primary focus, and the theatrical forms will be discussed both as modes of perception and as techniques for manipulating audiences. Novelty itself is not a value. Any form has advantages in one area that are inevitably paralleled by limitations in another. Documentary drama tends to sacrifice audience involvement on a personal level for a broad historical picture; Handke's 'speaking plays' gain linguistic depth at the expense of other dramatic elements such as characterisation or plot, naturalistic plays substitute empathy and the illusion of reality for factual accuracy – swings versus roundabouts. So 'realism' cannot be defined by the qualities of any one type of drama. Each stylistic innovation raises different critical issues and to some degree sets its own standards and expectations, which means that any evaluation must be relative. In some cases the influence of other artistic genres is the most important element in the formulation of new stage conventions, as in Peter Zadek's use of Pop Art. In others, external social pressures or the demands of unusual subject-matter are the decisive factors. But in each the same basic requirement applies. A form which has been given no theoretical definition or justification and exists only in terms of isolated performances may be of interest in understanding the work of a particular director or playwright, but is likely to be transient. Decisive innovations which have general applicability normally seem to occur today through defining specific goals, usually by contrast to an accepted idea of traditional or commercial theatre. Only when there is some form of programmatic declaration, by the artist or occasionally by critics or philosophers, do the performance qualities gain a general validity because then they can be clearly identified and interpreted in different ways. As Brecht put it in an essay 'On Subject and Style', there are three interrelated steps in creating new artistic approaches: 'discerning new material', 'giving shape to new relationships' through formulating the theory that explains them, and finally 'practical examples' derived from this.[15] It is a commonplace that Brecht's own work is more complex than his theory, indeed bears little relation to it; yet without the clarification of his thoughts his plays would probably lack their distinctive intellectual consistency, while (perhaps unfortunately) outside Germany it is his theoretical essays rather than his stage work which has had the widest influence.

Brecht himself falls outside the scope of this study, since almost all his creative work and most of his theory had been completed before his return to Europe in 1947, although as the most significant catalyst and example for postwar German dramatists his name constantly recurs. Our boundaries are chronological, 1945 to the present, but the major part of the dramatic material comes from the second half of this period. Even when the theatres had been rebuilt there was at first relatively little new German drama. On average there are some 2,500 productions each year in Germany, Austria and Switzerland, of which approximately 1,600 could be called 'serious' plays. Ten years after the war, in 1956–7, no more than 150 of these were plays by living Germans, and over half were of plays by only four authors. In 1962–3 the number had increased to 285, but 128 of these were productions of just two plays, Dürrenmatt's *The Physicists* (*Die Physiker*) and *Andorra* by Frisch – and it was only in 1963–4 that there was a sudden upsurge with *The Representative*, Weiss' *Marat/Sade*, Kipphardt's *In the Matter of J. Robert Oppenheimer* (*In der Sache J. Robert Oppenheimer*) and plays by over thirty other authors, all in multiple productions.[16] Since then there have been between sixty and seventy new German plays performed each year and over 200 plays by more than fifty authors have been published, quite apart from adaptations of classics.

As a panorama this creative ferment, covering the whole spectrum from glittering stylistic exercises to political agitation, appears chaotic; and no study could possibly be comprehensive. But a closer examination shows six quite distinct forms of theatre emerging, plus others which are carry-overs or imports – socialist realism in east Germany, for example, agitprop or 'the Happening' in the west – and some more minor plays which do not fall into any category or mix elements from the different styles. A separate analysis of each of these six forms seems the clearest way of giving shape to developments in the period as a whole, although this may lead to some chronological confusion since at least four are more or less contemporaneous and means, where some of the more eclectic authors like Weiss are concerned, that their plays have to be treated under different headings. Conceptual labels such as 'epic', 'absurd' or 'documentary', however, can have a procrustean effect, and it seems reasonable to attempt to redefine them in analysing the plays, deriving their qualities from specific works rather than applying them as pre-set categories. At the same time, since any given theatrical style can include variations and should be seen as a developing rather than static formula, the discussion of each is based on the work of at least two complementary playwrights.

A final note: it has been customary for critics to divide German drama along frontier lines, treating work in the Federal Republic and the Democratic Republic separately and distinguishing both from Swiss and Austrian writers. This seems arbitrary since most significant influences are shared while both directors and playwrights cross borders. West Germans such as Peter Stein direct plays in Switzerland, an Austrian like Hans Hollman works in west Germany and Palitzsch has crossed from east Germany. Hacks left the west for the east, Müller lives in the east but is practically only performed in the west, while Kipphardt began his career in east Berlin. Handke is Austrian even though he has made his reputation in Germany; Dürrenmatt too, the epitome of Swiss drama, has had his major success on the German stage. So examples of the different theatrical ways of representing reality will be drawn from all four German-speaking areas, and unless otherwise specified the term 'German' will be applied impartially to all.

2. The starting point

1945 – the German stage was, literally, an empty space. Many of the theatres had been gutted or destroyed, the theatre centre, Berlin, isolated and condemned to provincialism. More significant still, the cultural focus had gone. Tradition had been broken. Theatre buildings were already reopening by the autumn of 1945 – at least in the eastern sector where the Russians, with a proper appreciation for art as the new opiate of the people, ordered all actors in Berlin to rejoin their acting companies or face imprisonment – but German drama as such had ceased to exist. The closing of all theatres by Goebbels, the official 'Patron of German Art', which followed his declaration of 'total war', symbolises the artistic void that the twelve years of fascist domination represented. Unlike the end of the first world war which had acted as a creative catalyst by destroying an authoritarian society without damaging cultural institutions, in 1945 almost all the established German authors were dispersed or dead, while the younger generation had been cut off from international trends and the mainstream of drama since 1933.

Very little had been achieved by the exiles. Toller had committed suicide in despair, Zuckmayer and Friedrich Wolf had written little and had no work performed. The only play written by Brecht in America, *Galileo*, was a collaboration which owed so much to Charles Laughton that Brecht later revised it extensively to bring it into line with his own ideas, while the last work from his time in Finland, *Puntila*, only reached the stage in 1948. Of all the arts drama is most closely integrated with society, and although the stage may indeed signify the world, to do so it must be rooted in specifics. In particular the nuances of speech by which characters are created come from the way the people who form the audience express themselves. A dramatist cut off from his language is crippled, however universal his themes and, equally important, the exiles were cut off from their potential public. Apart from Switzerland there was no German-speaking population sufficiently concentrated to provide a theatre audience, free from Nazi censorship. The Zürich Schauspielhaus was the one open stage, and since the only new German plays produced there during the war were *The Good Person of Setzuan* (*Der Gute Mensch von*

14

Sezuan, 1940) and *Mother Courage* (*Mutter Courage*, 1945) Brecht's influence was the first to cross the cultural divide of fascism. But even that had no immediate effect on the wider theatre scene.

Not surprisingly, when the theatres in Germany reopened it was with classics such as Shakespeare or Schiller, traditional works ranging from Ibsen and Strindberg to Hauptmann and Shaw, the expressionists whose work had been banned, Kaiser, Sternheim or Wedekind, and above all foreign plays. The first need was to catch up on twelve years of development outside: Cocteau, Eliot and Lorca, Anouilh, Giraudoux and Sartre, O'Neill, Odets and Elmer Rice – none of whose work had been seen on the German stage – and Thornton Wilder, whose experiments with stage convention, open form and theatricality represented all the innovation they had missed. *Our Town*, for instance, was the first play put into rehearsal at the Deutsches Theater in Berlin in 1945, although the Russians forbade the performance on the grounds that Wilder, as an American, was an enemy of democracy: an early indication of the differences in development between the socialist section of Germany and west German drama. Later on, in the east Brecht, who opened his Ensemble in 1949, provided the dominant example for new playwrights and directors, while in the Federal Republic, where Brecht's work was effectively banned until the 1960s, the influences were initially American and French, with Beckett, Ionesco, Adamov, Miller and Tennessee Williams being performed as soon as their plays appeared.

However, new influences take time to mature, and playwrights who had not experienced the oppressions of dictatorship, the communal guilt of aggression and atrocities, or the devastation of defeat and occupation could only offer stylistic models based on very different norms of experience, not a framework for dealing with the traumatic German situation. For the first decade after 1945 there were few new theatrical initiatives, apart from the plays of Dürrenmatt and Frisch, who had been insulated from the direct effect of the war in Switzerland and not cut off like their German and Austrian contemporaries from the work of Brecht, Wilder and the expressionists. Instead the tone was set up to the late fifties by two very different attempts to translate pre-war German theatre to the contemporary situation.

In the east: Brecht, whose creativity was mainly channelled into production and whose post-war writing was almost entirely limited to adaptations. His theories, for the first time, were tested consistently in practice, which led him to revise some of his premises – for instance substituting the concept of 'dialectical drama' for 'epic theatre' and re-evaluating the function of emotion in his work. He produced definitive productions of his major plays, among them *Puntila* and *Mother Courage*, publishing *Modellbücher* to document 'alienating' techniques of presentation, episodic structural patterns and ways of achieving the right objectivity in characterisation. These were intended as examples of his approach for other companies performing his plays, while within his own Ensemble he trained younger directors, notably Benno Besson, Manfred Wekwerth and Peter Palitzsch. His success can be indicated by the way his version of Shakespeare's *Coriolanus* came to epitomise his style of theatre. His adaptation, started in 1951, was abandoned unfinished, and it was only after his death that his Ensemble began to work on staging *Coriolan*. Working in rehearsal they filled out the uncompleted dialogue and restructured the action so that the battle scenes, abstracted to a ritualised ballet of slaughter, became the central sequence in the play. First performed in 1964 and still in the repertoire of the Berliner Ensemble, this production is generally recognised as the culmination of Brecht's theatrical approach, even though he had no hand in its direction. Brecht's training and example established his theatre as a model, his adaptations acted as illustrations of how traditional dramatic forms and themes might be appropriated for reflecting contemporary issues, and his work has become a force that no modern dramatist in Germany can ignore. But it was only in 1953 with Erwin Strittmatter's *Katzgraben*, which was revised following Brecht's suggestions when produced by the Berliner Ensemble, and in 1956 with Peter Hacks' arrival on the stage that his example began to provide significant results in the form of new plays.

The other major influence in the first decade was the work of Gustaf Gründgens, which set the standard for theatre in the Federal Republic up to his death in 1963. If Brecht represented the carry-over of the radical side of prewar theatre and the updating of approaches developed in the Weimar Republic, Gründgens stood for the continuity of tradition and the transformation of classical style. His aim and excuse in the Third Reich, where he acted as the chief Intendant of the Berlin Theatre, was the preservation of (apolitical) art. But his experience showed him that situations from Schiller and Lessing, or even single lines which overlapped the contemporary context, gained an immediate relevance; and he began to choose plays with such parallels and to emphasise them in his acting until

By the end there was hardly a play which didn't violate one of the laws of 'total war'. With the instinctive certainty of growing hate and despair there was no situation on the stage which could not be made to serve as occasion for a spontaneous expression of opinion by people who had been condemned to silence.[1]

Oblique reference remained Gründgens' principle when he became resident director at Düsseldorf in 1947 and Hamburg in 1955. During the war it had been impossible to produce plays which dealt openly with political realities – even such an established classic as *Nathan the Wise* was too dangerously direct – and afterwards there were at first few topical plays of any quality available. His 1952 production of Pirandello's *Henry IV* is a good example of his approach. He emphasised the themes of guilt and evasive self-deception by setting the action in Henry's memory, so that it became the story of a man who some years before had committed murder and escaped justice by claiming madness as a excuse – a situation which he saw as exactly that of Germany at the time.

The second principle Gründgens developed during the Nazi era was that of overt theatricality, a stress on style and form which can be seen as another aspect of his defence of art in a context where 'art' was his only defence. Exactness, precision, clarity of line and expression defined his productions, which began with technical considerations, establishing patterning before allowing emotion to enter the portrayal of a character – the opposite in every way to Stanislavski's 'method'. This was rhetorical rather than psychological theatre, an actor's theatre in the traditional sense of displaying the performer's skill instead of presenting character based on emotional identification. Gründgens' mistrust of 'everything uncontrollable, introverted, dark that goes with us by the beautiful word "feeling"' resulted in an aversion to vagueness or imprecision.[2] At the same time he liked to stress that his approach, both as an actor and director, was naive, not intellectualised. The result was to accent rhythms in movement, musicality in speech and balanced structure, all of which distanced the stage from everyday life. Theatre was to be played as theatre, and one sign of this anti-illusionism was his cutting of stage properties to a minimum. Every element in his productions was heightened, transformed, simplified, and he deliberately avoided naturalistic drama. This was not simply a retreat into aesthetics. Rather it was based on a perception of the potentially trivialising effect of make-believe, of the problems inherent in representing contemporary events on the stage; and his concern was summed up by a rhetorical question which he posed in 1948 and which was to become a keynote in discussions about the function of drama: 'would it not be terrible if the tragedies of recent years were to be cut down to three acts?'[3] In his view the theatre could only deal with reality indirectly.

Just as *Coriolan* illustrates Brecht's theatre, so one of Gründgens' productions, the Hamburg *Faust* of 1957, is recognised as epitomising his approach. It was with his performance of Mephistopheles in 1922 that Gründgens had made his reputation, and *Faust* was to him *the* German drama, but his production was no museum-piece. Traditional interpretations simplified the play by concentrating, like Max Reinhardt, on the conventionally dramatic Gretchen story. Instead Gründgens used the Faust–Mephisto relationship as the focus, transforming the play into an interior monologue in which the affirmer and the eternal denyer were presented as two sides of a single personality, and where the ghosts of *Walpurgisnacht* were shadows of the modern imagination: Rock-and-Roll and the atomic bomb. How contemporary the basic concept was can be indicated by the way this dualism echoed the existential division of the main figure in Borchert's picture of immediate post-war Germany, *The Man Outside* (*The Outsider* /*Draussen vor der Tür*, 1947) and looked forward to the daemonism of Hochhuth's depiction of Auschwitz. At the same time the play was presented as theatre, a performance, by acting it on a stage within a stage, without scenery and with the actors seated on a bench watching the action or revising their parts when not required in any particular scene, and by including Goethe's *Vorspiel auf dem Theater*. This preface, almost always omitted in production, underlines the symbolic nature of the action by stripping away illusion. A poet, a ham actor and a second-rate director discuss theatre and the play they are about to present, and Gründgens slid from this satiric introduction into the main action without a break by having the director hook a beard over his ears to step forward as God. This open theatricality was not just a superficial framework but the key to the interpretation, allowing

Gründgens to explore the traditional image of the devil as an actor – and giving the characterisation a striking immediacy through the double exposure of Mephisto-as-actor with his own persona as Germany's most famous performer.

In spite of a real difference in intention (there is no sense here that character is provisional, the situation changeable) Gründgens' insistence on clarity, precision and rational naivety, and his use of theatricality for distancing parallel Brecht in a striking way. Both worked for a metaphoric relationship to reality, rejecting naturalism for earlier dramatic forms, and Brecht recognised this relationship by asking Gründgens to direct the première of *St Joan of the Stockyards* (*Die heilige Johanna der Schlachthöfe*) in 1949. The original première had been cancelled by political developments in 1933, but Brecht obviously did not consider Gründgens' subsequent career to have disqualified him, even though when the play was finally performed in 1959 the interpretation was very different from Brecht's intentions. This production sums up the distinctions and similarities between their two approaches. The bare stage and simple props which allowed no distraction from the actors' exhibition of their art also avoided surface illusion so that the action was naturally 'alienated'; the strong rhythms that Gründgens favoured not only created the emotional involvement of a boxing ring in the stock-market scenes but focussed on Brecht's model of economic relationships as a demonstration of the laws of supply and demand; Gründgens' heightened style of performance suited the parody of Schillerian pathos. But Pierpoint Mauler was a character caught up in and trapped by an adopted role, not an actor exposing the essence of capitalism; and Johanna was a girl with a gospel, driven to despair by ignorance and indifference, in no sense a revolutionary. In short, Gründgens' techniques were comparable to Brecht's, but divorced from the political philosophy that Brecht had designed his 'epic' effects to express, they turned a teaching play illustrating a specific social point into a theatrical statement about human nature. Gründgens' aim of creating a theatre 'appropriate to the time in which we live' is no different to Brecht's, but he did not define the age as 'scientific', and rejected dogmatic drama no less than the pure aestheticism of 'esoteric embroidery'.[4] Thus he is certainly not the exponent of anachronistic traditions and outdated values that he is commonly thought to be,[5] and although he saw himself as re-establishing the 'grand forms' of 'classical humanism' his perspective gave a modernity to his repertoire of classics that made his work relevant as a model. His influence in the west is by no means as clear as Brecht's in the east, but he set the style for a decade with guest performances in most major centres, productions in Düsseldorf and Hamburg, and it is arguable that some theatrical elements which are not found in DDR drama can be traced to his example. Hildesheimer, for instance, whose development led him to the absurdist position, was one of the new playwrights he encouraged.

Both Brecht and Gründgens represent bridges over the cultural divide, attempts to build a basis for new work by reintroducing established forms from the pre-1933 theatre. But neither approach could be simply transferred to the new context. The overwhelming impact of the immediate past on the artistic vacuum of the present made it necessary to reinterpret conventional perspectives – hence the way Brecht concentrated on adaptations rather than writing new plays (though the use of familiar scripts also had a value in providing one constant factor for his experiments). This reinterpretation of styles, which after a twelve-year break were already historical, was characteristic of initial attempts to deal with the war on stage.

Apart from occasional revivals of agitprop technique – slogans on placards, black and white caricature and choral commentary in a revue structure with the by now obligatory ending, a cathartic tableau of red flags and triumphant revolutionaries – which were embarrassingly anachronistic since the idealism of the 1920s appeared empty declamation in the 1940s,[6] serious plays about relevant themes fell into three main groupings. The most popular, and most conventional, were such basically naturalistic portrayals of war situations as Zuckmayer's *The Devil's General* (*Des Teufels General*, 1946). Then there were adaptations of the expressionist approach, the most significant of which was Borchert's *The Man Outside*. The third group, for which Frisch's *Now They've Started Singing Again* (*Nun singen sie wieder*, 1945) provided a model, is in some ways a new stylistic initiative; but conceptually it turns back to religious forms and mixes mystery-play elements with Thornton Wilder. Together these plays represent the most productive stylistic trends in German drama in the first decade after the war. They also demonstrate the problems of treating new material from a traditional perspective – as contrasted to Brecht's or Gründgens' practice of using traditional material to formulate new perspectives.

The choice between a mimetic or expressive (or in Nietzschian terms apollonian as against dionysian) approach is basic to all art, and the general qualities can be found in any period; but Zuckmayer, Borchert and (to a lesser extent) Frisch were basing their work on the forms that had been dominant, particularly in Germany, from the turn of the century to the thirties. Naturalism, originally a development from the bourgeois tragedy represented in Germany by Lessing and Hebbel, is characterised by specific techniques, which express a set of philosophical assumptions that can be summarised as Darwinian materialism. The primary criterion is physical accuracy and the comprehensive descriptions of stage properties, the three-dimensional illusionistic settings and the attention to authenticating detail imply that personality is determined by environment. The economy of statement imposed in the theatre by the limitations of stage space and performance time makes the dramatist's every choice a thematic statement, and giving weight to a localised social context – the naturalist scene is almost always the interior of a house – signifies automatically that circumstance determines character. Another aspect of this specificity relates to the selection and treatment of dramatic figures. The protagonists are typically a single family or close-knit social group, drawn fully rounded, normal not exceptional, but individualised rather than typified and with a personal history extending outside the frame of the stage play that makes them seem independent of the dramatic scheme. Their past, progressively revealed, either shapes the action or is given such importance that its discovery is the action, and their future (if they survive) can only build on or repeat the present of the plot. All this implies that the essential fact about man is not his class nor his immortal soul but his individual psychology, and what is significant about the social structure is its molecular unit, the family. It also presupposes that men are motivated by their personalities, rather than having their actions determined by an external fate in the form of economic laws, historical forces, a divine plan or the *deus ex machina* of the playwright, and are therefore responsible for their own actions. Cause and effect works on a personal level and social problems are explored in terms of individuals. The perspective is objective, without moral prejudgements or direct authorial comment; the material is drawn from observation or experience; and the appeal is emotional, based on identification with characters whose problems are sufficiently similar for the audience to relate to their own concerns.

21

Naturalism carries in it the ideas of Darwin and Taine, the sociological premises of the nineteenth century and an individualistic humanism; and those are still reflected in today's entertainment theatre which applies naturalistic stage techniques uncritically and perhaps unconsciously. In Germany these ideas, as interpreted by Ibsen and Zola, entered the theatre with Gerhart Hauptmann whose *Before Dawn* (*Vor Sonnenaufgang*, 1889) shows strong traces of *The Wild Duck* and *The Master Builder*, and Zuckmayer acknowledged Hauptmann as his artistic 'father'.[7] The majority of Zuckmayer's plays are basically naturalistic, and *The Devil's General* is no exception.

This play, written between 1942 and 1944 while Zuckmayer was in America, attempts to come to terms with the realities of the Nazi experience by exploring the moral conflicts of ordinary people. A range of moral attitudes is presented; from the war hero Eiler's desperate faith in the rightness of the fascist cause to the secret resistance-fighter Oderbruch's belief that his country can only be saved by defeat. Harras, the devil's general, stands in the middle as an individualist who trusts only in himself. The corruption of the dictatorship is portrayed in a young girl, Pützchen, who is introduced as a normal if amoral member of the younger generation. The links between the major characters are all on a personal level; each relates to Harras, either as a lover, a comrade in arms or a protégé; and even Schmidt-Lausitz, the Gestapo spy, has an emotional bond with his victim: hate. The settings for these characters are detailed, realistic, with the description 'solid' repeatedly used in the stage directions; the wider milieu is suggested by searchlights outside the window or sound effects – sirens, dance music, aeroplane engines – and the dialogue is individualised by slang and different dialects. Schmidt-Lausitz's dramaturgical function is that of the conventional naturalistic outsider (Hauptmann's Stranger, Ibsen's Gregers, Chekhov's Trigorin) whose intrusion disturbs an apparently normal social surface and precipitates the process of self-revelation and discovery; and the traditional nature of Zuckmayer's techniques can be seen in his use of the 'two-servant exposition' to build up the main character.

But the naturalistic conventions, which are so suitable for exploring private suffering or exposing the personal deception behind a respectable façade, continually break down in this attempt to deal with the experience of fascism. Naturalism assumes the existence of social norms and the possibility of solutions on an individual level, but the monstrous inhumanity of the Third Reich is hardly comprehensible in psychological terms. Average standards of behaviour are inapplicable to a situation so extreme that murdering comrades can be defended as an ethical act, and although Zuckmayer conceived his characters to be free-acting, morally responsible individuals, 'reaching their own decisions, which the author can no longer prescribe for them', the proper naturalistic objectivity is not there. Metaphysics replaces milieu: 'in hell there are no angels and, as the title already says, the circumference of this play is dominated by hell on earth'.[8] An airfield is not simply concrete and steel but Hades, 'blueprint of the underworld...Damnably rational – and utterly fantastic. Buzzing, whirring, shaking with fantasy',[9] while the pattern of five searchlights over Berlin is the hand of Hitler strangling Germany. Similarly the plot works on two contradictory levels. The surface situation, in which Harras is given ten days to find the underground opposition who are sabotaging aircraft, is arranged in a conventionally dramatic way to reveal how the protagonist's personality develops under pressure in a sequence of one-to-one challenges – to save a Jewish friend, to survive by compromise, to affirm his integrity in love or to sacrifice his principles for power and take over the leadership of the Nazi party, to join the resistance and, finally, to atone for the death of his protégé. But the underlying structure of the play is iconological and apocalyptic, with the central motifs announced in the title to each act and repeated in the dialogue: 'Infernal Machine', 'Stay of Execution', 'Damnation'. Naturalistically conceived individuals are unequal to the weight of such an escatalogical context. Either, as with Karl Kraus' attempt to deal with the first world war in *The Last Days of Mankind* (*Die letzten Tage der Menschheit*, 1922), the incongruity results in parody where 'operetta figures play out the tragedy of mankind',[10] or the characters have to become symbolic universals; and the problems inherent in using naturalistic techniques to present such material can be clearly seen in Zuckmayer's treatment of his main character.

Harras, drawn from Zuckmayer's personal observation in an approved naturalistic way, is loosely based on a friend, Ernst Udet, a first world war fighter pilot who headed the technical division of the German aviation ministry in 1936 and was promoted to General in 1938. At the time the play was written, Zuckmayer apparently only knew that Udet was dead, not that he had committed suicide after being held responsible for the failure of the German airforce in the Battle of Britain. If Zuckmayer's comment on the Udet/Harras relationship seems ingenuous, being written after the truth about Udet's death was generally known, it is because the way it points out that an imaginary plot corresponds to unknown facts implies that Zuckmayer's perception of character was accurate enough to extrapolate a man's real actions from a knowledge of his personality. In effect it is a claim to authenticity:

In December 1941, not long after the United States' entry into the war, a short notice appeared in the American papers. Ernst Udet, the German airforce general, was killed in an accident while testing a new weapon and was buried at a state funeral. Nothing else. There was no commentary, no speculation on his death. Accidental death, state funeral...Again I saw him as I had seen him in my last carefree visit to Berlin: 1936. We met for a meal in a small, little known restaurant. 'Not at Horchers' he had said – that used to be our meeting place – 'the party bosses roost there now.'

He was in civilian clothes even though he already had a high rank in the airforce. 'Shake the dust of this land from your shoes', he said to me. 'Go into the world and don't ever come back. There's no human dignity here anymore.'

'And you?' I asked.

'I', he said casually, almost in passing. 'I have become addicted to flying. I can't do without it any more. But one day the devil will come for us all.'[11]

The news report provides the final, ironic words of the play, and the elements of Harras' character are all in the brief personal sketch. But so is the daemonic context which transforms Harras from an individual case-study to a tragic hero and ultimately a religious symbol. His name, taken from Schiller's *Wilhelm Tell* where Harras is the only member of Gessler's retinue to show sympathy for the rights of the people, has connotations of romantic tragedy which are underlined in the byplay of Act 1, with Harras cast in Tell's role to shoot a wine-glass off a young officer's head. On this level Harras is very close to Zuckmayer's prewar hero figures and shares his vitality with the Robin Hood robber of *Schinderhannes* (1927) whose career of crime is the expression of unrestricted self-realisation. Harras' justification for serving the Nazi war-machine is the same: 'Nowhere else in the world would I have been given these possibilities – these unlimited resources

– this power' (p. 362). But already in Act II this faustian Hero-of-Nature is heightened into a Christ image, offered the kingdom of the world from 'the peak of a high mountain', (p. 413) and the figures who surround him are symbols. Eiler's wife becomes 'the Black Angel from the depths. From the kingdom of death' (p. 449); Pützschen, introduced as a shallow and amoral but average member of the younger generation, is revealed as the devil in person, 'evil-itself. The incarnation of evil in sex. Uniform over the body – vagina naked in the face.'[12] Oderbruch is not an individual but a collective, 'without personal motive. No – human explanation' for resistance:

Our names – we have forgotten. Some of us had centuries-old coats of arms. Others only names on wage-slips. That doesn't count any more. For one hour of the world – we have become equal. Classless.[13]

This melodramatic characterisation is highly effective theatrically. Harras' courage, sexual vitality and sense of humour – particularly his ability to laugh at the heroic image of himself, as when striking a pose: 'Please do not touch. Protected monument' (p. 353) – is sympathetic and attractive. So much so that the play was banned in Germany until 1949 for fear it would arouse militaristic, nationalist sentiment or might created a new *Dolchstosslegende* (the right wing propaganda that helped to discredit democracy in the Weimar Republic by the myth that the front-line soldiers had been 'stabbed in the back' by politicians). Harras is an empathetic figure, audiences were drawn into the moral conflicts of the play, and Zuckmayer received several hundred letters beginning 'I am your Lieutenant Hartmann' – the youth who searches for death in battle, sensing the falsity of Nazi ideals, and is forced into passive resistance by his horror at witnessing atrocities. But critics found the success suspect because the poetic treatment made the political and economic causes of fascism mystical and therefore mysterious.[14]

In fact the flaws are inherent in the stylistic approach. Issues are repeatedly reduced to 'a personal question' (p. 364), 'a private matter' (p. 422), 'a question of honour' (p. 424), 'me personally. I carry the direct responsibility' (p. 363–4); and since conventional naturalistic techniques present social problems in terms of the individual, Zuckmayer can only give the issues wider significance through a form of heightening which empties the characters of meaning as people by inflating them to symbols. But the central questions are still limited to a psychological level, so that emotional statement replaces analysis – for example the only motivation attributed to the Nazis is envy, 'that's why they always want to make war and mark down great men, simply repressions' (p. 412), while 'the German madness' is the one explanation that can be offered for events: 'the death wish, the schizophrenic inner life' (p. 427). When the questioning goes beyond this it becomes abstract and unconvincing. Oderbruch can only answer in generalities when asked about the specific tactics of the resistance because the basis for economic and social enquiry is not contained in the play, and the dedication to the first version typifies the stylistic problem: 'to the unknown fighter'.

Most of the other naturalistic war plays of the 1940s and 1950s show the same failings. The issues are oversimplified, the problems are dealt with in moral terms, the characterisation tends to melodrama. The central conflict is frequently similar, as in two plays about the officers' uprising in 1944, *The Fortress* (*Die Festung*, 1950) by Claus Hubalek in which a Russian general is torn between his oath of loyalty and justice, or *The Conspiracy* (*Die Verschwörung*, 1948) by Walter Schäfer where an SS officer chooses to join the condemned Generals on the scaffold. It quickly became a stock approach, and critics complained of set patterns and type characters – the corrupt General, the young liberal officer as his antagonist, the half-Jewish family friend – all following Zuckmayer.[15]

Zuckmayer himself was aware of the limitations of naturalistic techniques, and his next attempt to explore a similar subject, *Song of the Fiery Furnace* (*Der Gesang im Feuerofen*, 1950) is framed in a very different and for him untypical style. The plot is sequential, again explores an individual's motives for betrayal in Louis Creveaux who leads the Gestapo to a French resistance group, and like *The Devil's General* was based on a news report. As the newspaper pointed out, this was material for a tragedy: the French, all young, were burnt alive by the Germans in an old chateau where they had gathered for a formal dance. What made it particularly impressive was the timing – Christmas Eve – and the apparently willing atonement of the betrayer who admitted his guilt and was condemned to death. But Zuckmayer deliberately avoided in-depth characterisation. There are thirty parts, the Gendarmes and the German soldiers are played by the same actors and called by the same names, the Chaplain and a young girl

double as angels, and the costumes are bare indications – hats, a
soutane, a police cape 'as for a rehearsal or an improvised
performance'.[16] The action is framed and broken at key points by
reflective scenes in highly poetic verse where angels or personifi-
cations of Nature mingle with the human characters, so that the
story is seen in retrospect and from a universal perspective.
Unfortunately this does not make it a better play. It is an uneasy
mixture of elegiac pathos and conventional dramatics; the naturalistic characterisation is only sketched in, but is still present with
the result that the motivation for betrayal is reduced to the cliché
of sexual jealousy; the symbolism moves on two conflicting levels.
The influence of Frisch's *Now They've Started Singing Again* is
unmistakable, and not only in theatricality *à la* Thornton Wilder
and the echoing of a song that Frisch's victims sing as they die.
Zuckmayer's themes too are identical – the establishing of a
common humanity between murderers and victims in death:

Let us make peace, with ourselves and with those we have fought... It
was our duty to be enemies. Now it is our right to be brothers (p. 571).

and the power of the dead who

	...are not absent
CLEAR VOICE:	You see them not
CHOIR:	But they regard you
VOICE:	They stand above pain and joy
	...above appeal and fear...
	They grow. They wait. They stand
	In the light of transformation (p. 574).

(In an earlier version of this scene the correspondence is even
stronger, and we are told that the dead, whose song is 'silent',
'know/No revenge/The dead help God'.)[17] But Frisch is not the
only model. The mix of metaphysical and human figures, and the
pathos of the imagery has a strong resemblance to Borchert's *The
Man Outside*, as does the challenge to the audience to accept the
guilt of 'the other':

> ...Do not say:
> That was others. Do not say:
> That was another nation. Never say:
> That is the enemy.
> Always say: that am I' (pp. 578–9).

Unlike Zuckmayer, the exile whose hero Harras was an integral
part of the Nazi system, Borchert, who had been directly involved

– on the Russian front and in a Gestapo prison – made his protagonist an anti-hero and an outsider. In doing so he was following an established formula: the returning-soldier or *Heimkehr*
pattern developed by the expressionists, Toller, Hasenclever,
Werfel, after the previous war – and it is no accident that his
protagonist was named after Beckmann, an expressionist whose
paintings depict men as distorted puppets, empty carnival masks
engaged in murder. The original radio version of *The Man Outside*
(1946) was written in a single week, and the speed of composition,
which is still betrayed by uneven tempo and contradictory details
in the stage play, could only have been achieved by working within
a familiar tradition.

Borchert's early poetry and short prose pieces, which portray
the world in terms of feelings, are firmly in the expressionist
school. The style is typical of the 1920s. Words are used conno-
tatively for their emotional associations, syntax is telescoped into
telegrammatic sentences, and as stream of consciousness the
structure is an emotional unit not a logical sequence of actions.
Night and death, hunger and cold are recurring motifs, and the
titles clearly signal the expected levels of reader involvement. *The
Victims* (*Ausgelieferten*), *The Lost* (*Verlorenen*), *The Deceived*
(*Belogenen*). The generalisation implies a universality of experience, the emotive anonymity channels empathy to the human
situation instead of the individual, and the tone is passive.
Suffering replaces action. The same qualities, basically lyrical
rather than dramatic, are characteristic of Borchert's play.

As with naturalism, these stylistic techniques embody a philosophic viewpoint that can be traced back to the nineteenth
century, in this case to Schopenhauer, Nietzsche and Heidegger.[18]
The world is conceived as the dynamic projection of the mind, and
reality, that ambiguous justification for art, is located in the
subconscious with the result that dreams take precedence over
rational perceptions of causality. Hence the apparently arbitrary
structure of events in expressionist drama and the juxtaposition
of contrasting impressions, farce and pathos, caricature and ideal.
The most obvious distinction to naturalism is in characterisation.[19]
Instead of personalities explained in terms of their environment,
the expressionist figure becomes a symbol in a symbolic context
whose traits tend to the universal – all mankind, not an individual.
Just as Toller's typical hero, derived from the 'Unknown Man'
of Strindberg's *To Damascus*, is the human being *per se* ('der

Mensch'), Borchert's Beckmann is introduced as simply 'a man' because from the expressionist standpoint what defines people is what all have in common, the emotive and instinctive psyche (by definition pre-rational and in some ways equivalent to the Romantic 'night-side' of the mind), while social individuation is superficial and illusory. Similarly the short, episodic scenes and the compression of sentences into single images reflect the belief that 'intensification and condensation...appear to be the funda- mental laws of the mind'.[20] Direct visual presentation replaces intellectual analysis, emotion substitutes for events and distortion is used to show moral essence under the logic of appearances, because the stage scene is a mindscape. In an extreme form the expressionist action becomes a dream, and Borchert sets his play in a visionary frame pointedly titled 'The Dream'. Stage direc- tions describe Beckmann as 'drunk with sleep, dream-like', 'in a trance, haunted', 'dazed' or 'in sleep'.[21] And the initial comparison of the play to 'a completely incredible film' (p. 8) – which is hardly incidental since the fluidity of film, its ability to transpose or collate through montage, and the hallucinatory effect of close-up or changing camera-perspectives made it a model for expressionist drama in the twenties – implies that the performance should give the effect of *déjà vu*. The classic definition of this type of dramaturgy is, of course, Strindberg's introduction to *A Dream Play*:

the Author has sought to reproduce the disconnected but apparently logical form of a dream. Anything can happen; everything is possible and probable. Time and space do not exist; on a slight groundwork of reality, imagination spins and weaves new patterns...The characters are split, double and multiply; they evaporate, crystallise, scatter and converge. But a single consciousness holds sway over them all – that of the dreamer.[22]

Strindberg believed that the 'pain' of the dream state made life desirable by contrast: 'the sufferer awakes – and is thus recon- ciled to reality'.[23] For the German expressionists of the 1920s dream-drama was even more positive, it could transform reality by transfiguring the audience. For Borchert in the psychological trauma of total defeat, having been forced to fight for a false cause that had condemned him to death as subversive, the dream could only be a recognition of reality as a nightmare, and Beckmann's awakening is an accusation. But the structural principles are the same.

Another aspect of the expressionist world view is indicated by the name of the movement itself. It is the expressive quality of the approach, both in its choice of material and stylistic techniques, which is significant. The structures of action not only embody the laws of the mind, but in doing so communicate to the audience on a subconscious level. Franz Marc's belief that certain colours automatically trigger specific emotional associations is like the reduction of dialogue to key words – Life, Death, Love, Brother, Money, Atonement, Sunrise, Resurrection; always capitalised and followed by two, sometimes three exclamation marks – in a play like Hasenclever's *Humanity* (*Menschen*, 1918), or the symbolically charged gestures in expressionist film. All are designed to arouse responses subliminally (even if it sometimes seems as though the expressionists lacked faith in the sensitivity of their audience's subconscious, since many of the techniques are used with less subtlety than sledgehammers). Directness, immediacy and intensity are the basic criteria, and ideally the play or painting should be a transparent conductor which transfers the artist's subjective vision directly to the audience's mind, not the creation of an objective reality to be observed.[24]

This approach contains certain inherent weaknesses. The trend to abstraction in the use of symbolism and distortion, together with the presentation of subjective experience in universal terms and the heightening of emotion all assumes that what is significant in a statement is communicated on a subconscious level. In effect this substitutes means for meaning. The attempt to reproduce the workings of the mind overshadows the thoughts themselves, so that the intention of many expressionist works is unclear except on the most general (and therefore platitudinous) level. Borchert's techniques are by no means so irrational and encapsulated as some of the more extreme examples of expressionism, but his play is still open to considerable misunderstanding. It has been read as both a realistic psychological study of an exhausted soldier and as an inverted passion-play, with Beckmann as a Christ figure who chooses to die as the only way of saving himself from a damned world. Alternatively, the play has been seen as a document of the frustration of post-war German youth, or as a personal cry of despair in which Beckmann as Borchert's *alter ego* expresses his own self-hatred and guilt. There is no critical agreement even on a very basic level of comprehension. In one case the whole play has been interpreted as a dream, with the title of the second episode being used as a subtitle for the whole; in another the human encounters have been seen as realistic, Beckmann's peregrinations being on the same waking level as his final speech and the only dream scenes being the episode 'in the Elbe' (specifically listed as such) and the penultimate section of the final scene between the stage directions 'he falls asleep' and 'wakes up' (pp. 44–58); in a third, where the whole play is presented (on analogy to Golding's novel *Pincher Martin*) as a sequence of memories in the mind of a man on the point of drowning, the prologue is taken to be real while the whole of the play itself is interpreted as an extended hallucination.[25]

In traditional or mimetic drama the level of reality is established immediately and held throughout, and where there are to be shifts in image (a play-within-a-play, the mingling of men and supernatural beings, an epilogue) those are signalled by clearly-defined conventions. By contrast the expressionist stream of consciousness makes for ambiguity, and since it excludes the network of motivations and environmental constants which link scenes together in other dramatic forms, its images can only be correctly interpreted if the personal symbols happen to mean the same to the audience as to the author.

The surface action of Borchert's play is deceptively simple. The prologue and the following dream set the tone: an old man and an undertaker, who reveal themselves as 'the God in whom no one believes any more' and Death, 'the new God', watch an unknown man jump in the river. Beckmann is 'only one of those who can't go on' (pp. 10–11), but the Elbe (personified as a rough-tongued fishwife) rejects his plea for death as the only escape from an intolerable life, and washes him up on the sand. The central scenes, with a girl who finds him by the waterside, at the family dinner-table of the colonel who had commanded his old regiment, with a cabaret producer, and at the house that used to belong to his parents, form images of different aspects of society – a personal relationship, the bourgeois ideal of family life, the wider public, roots in the form of the parental home – and the scenes are linked simply by recurrent motifs (the one-legged man, the spectacles that everyone wears) and by the ubiquitous 'Other', who prods Beckmann into each move. Finally, when Beckmann reawakens after another dream in which all the figures (including God and Death) reappear, the audience are challenged to deny the indifference that made their social representatives (Colonel,

Producer, Mrs Kramer) murderers. The economy of each short scene, the onomatopeic language and the vividness of the verbal images – death as a belching, overfed undertaker; as a general, sweating blood that runs down to form the two red stripes on his trousers, who plays on a xylophone made of bones; as a civil servant, the street-sweeper whose broom wheezes like a dying man's last gasps – even though these may be merely left over from the original draft as a radio play, gain an emotive intensity that makes the final rhetorical questioning of the audience highly powerful. But this impact is achieved at the expense of consistency. Not only, as in Strindberg's *Dream Play*, is there an uneasy mix of allegorical and human figures, but the social criticism is weakened by the subjective nature of Borchert's vision.

There are clear links between Beckmann and his author, who was also wounded on the Russian front, returned to Hamburg and, though seriously ill, worked in cabaret from 1945–6. These autobiographical parallels authenticate the emotions in the play, but they are also indicative of the way situations are presented solely through Beckmann's eyes. He is the dreamer. He is also the only character with any depth or sensitivity. We are forced to identify with him not only because of the dubious status of the other figures who, like 'the Other Self', may all be figments of his imagination, but because in a context where capacity to feel is the only virtue he is the one character (apart from perhaps the minor figure of 'the Girl') who has any feelings. The result is that the social representatives, who should also represent the audience if the final scene is to be effective in changing their attitudes, are no more than cardboard caricatures. It was too easy for the audience to see Beckmann as a symbol of conscience and, because they identified with him while the Colonel, the Producer, Beckmann's wife and the stranger living in his dead parent's house all shut him out, to take their sympathy as a self-justifying substitute for action – which may have been one reason for the play's popularity in spite of the pessimism that caused Borchert to label it 'a play which no theatre will want to perform and no public want to see'. As one reviewer commented in 1948, any social point to the play was buried beneath 'the non-committal, secret delight in a monstrous personal sorrow'.[26]

The caricature of unsympathetic figures and this type of vicarious empathy is typical of expressionism, but there are signs that Borchert chose this approach consciously because of these qualities. The parallels to the classic '*Heimkehr*' ('returning soldier', lit. 'homecoming') play of the first world war, Toller's *The Limping Man* (*Hinkemann*, 1924), seem deliberate rather than derivative. There is the repeated emphasis on Beckmann's limp and its extension in his *alter ego*, the girl's one-legged husband who represents Beckmann's guilt. There is the grotesque cabaret performance, which is close to the parody of Hinkemann's reintegration in society – as a fairground strong-man who bites the heads off mice for a sensation-loving public – and the returning soldier in each play commits suicide (cut in Toller's second version) because a complacent society destroys his will to live. There is the same hopeless questioning of the purpose and possibility of living at the end of Toller's play, and both plays share the same, typically expressionist structure of seven sections, drawing on the mystical connotations of the number seven but representing the 'stations' of the Cross.[27] The significance of these parallels lies in their differences. Where Toller expresses outrage at the destruction of 'natural life' by the war and the consequent depravity of society (Hinkemann's wound castrated him, and with heavy irony he is advertised in the fair as the German 'bear man' incarnating virility), Borchert is concerned with indifference and the emotional deadening of guilt.

The parallels to another well-known play, Brecht's *Drums in the Night* (*Trommeln in der Nacht*, 1922), are even more detailed. Like Beckmann, Brecht's hero Kragler is referred to as a ghost and both are said to have returned from the dead. Both are grotesque in appearance, physical symbols of the mutilating effects of war; have even been imprisoned for the same length of time, 1,000 days; express a similar disillusion with idealism and the warlike enthusiasm of those who stayed behind; and each has a like reaction to the materialistic inhumanity of society. Where Beckmann jumps in the river, Kragler takes to the bottle, and the same adjectives are repeatedly applied to both: 'drinking', 'drowned', 'drunken'. But again the parallels have been chosen to emphasise an essential difference. Brecht's characters are all egotistic, predators by nature; men are presented as animalistic, as apes and swine; and Kragler cynically adopts the negative, 'realistic' standards of the corrupt, 'Darwinian' society to survive. Brecht's play, while still expressionist in style, is an attack on the emotionalism and subjectivity of the other expressionist romanticisations of the returning-hero theme, his basic point being that hypocritical

33

sentimentality and self-serving idealism were responsible for the war. The play associates the clichés of romance and nationalism, linking ammunition boxes and baby-carriages, love songs and anthems, and Kragler rejects the heroics of the Spartacist revolution as 'cheap theatricals'. For Borchert the betrayal of enthusiasm is secondary to the way those responsible ignore their guilt, and Kragler's cynical egotism is rejected in the figure of the optimistic, affirming Other. The Other is generally taken at his own valuation as the immortal life force in everyman, a symbol of courage in adversity, or as representing 'nature and the beauty of the world'.[28] In fact the Other is at most the cunning instinct for survival. His advice to Beckmann is to transfer his guilt feelings, to forget, to believe in the goodness and 'heart' of the figures who have murdered him by their selfishness and indifference. In this inverted world where Death is God, the Other is Mephistopheles to Beckmann's Faust. The 'eternal denyer' has been transformed into a 'yea-sayer' by the 1945 situation in which the present (Faust's 'passing moment') can only be affirmed by denying the past. He offers Beckmann the Girl in the same way that Gretchen is used to tempt Faust and, like Mephistopheles, ridicules the weakness of human will in the face of sexual attraction when his ruse is successful. He is only banished when Beckmann, promising not to forget the one-legged man, accepts that he is not only 'murdered' but a 'murderer'. For Borchert it is precisely Kragler's mask of hard-boiled insensitivity which characterised the general refusal to face complicity and responsibility for the decade of fascism – a theme which was still as relevant a generation later when Walser took it up in *The Black Swan* (*Der Schwarze Schwan*, 1964).

On the surface *The Man Outside* appears nihilistic. But it is hardly Borchert's aim to preach suicide, and as he said in a manifesto of 1939:

> We are denyers. But we do not say no out of despair. Our no is a protest. And we find no peace in kissing, we nihilists. For we have to build a yes again in our nothingness. We must build houses in the free air of our no...Indeed, indeed: in this farcically mad world we want to love once more and ever more.[29]

The denial here, of course, is a rejection of fascism, while the play is concerned with the easy affirmation of a cover-up. But the principle is the same. Self-deception, a sign of which is the absence of human feeling, negates the possibility of a positive answer, and

Borchert's solution is to force his audience into an emotional commitment to the real situation. The final questions to the public – 'Why are you all silent? Why? Will no one give an answer? Is there no answer???' (p. 54) – though similar in some ways to the ending of another Brecht play, *The Good Person of Setzuan*, are not really intended to provoke the audience into finding solutions but to bring home their guilt by association since conventional behaviour (as well as the way the questions are framed) prevents them from answering. Their silence implies their consent, both to Beckmann's accusation and to his despair, but as Borchert stated in a note to the original radio play:

> An injection of nihilism
> Often provokes
> People out of sheer fear
> To take the courage to live again.

Borchert's use of expressionist techniques gains a precision that other post-war plays in the same style lack from his overt reference to familiar works by Brecht and Toller. But these literary contrasts that define his intentions also undermine them. The literary borrowing removes the play from reality, since the '*Heimkehr*' theme did not have the same relevance in 1945 as in 1919. After the second world war there was no intact bourgeois society to shut the returning soldier out, and the general absence of food and work – Borchert's subject in short stories such as *Bread (Das Brot,* 1946) – was far more significant than the ex-soldier's isolation and rejection. The way the play presents the world in terms of caricature or allegory is indicative of this retreat, which leaves the sentimental and introverted expressionist 'I' as the only concrete element and demonstrates the basic stylistic problem in using the expressionist approach to deal with the experience of fascism and its aftermath. As with naturalism, although in completely different terms, the issues are reduced to the personal level or heightened into abstraction; and Borchert's dream-image of the general playing on a xylophone of bones is no more appropriate than Zuckmayer's daemonism as a way of coming to terms with the past or preventing its recurrence.

Now They've Started Singing Again also contains expressionist elements – the shape of seven scenes or 'stations'; the structural repetitions which form an emotional progression in the place of plot; the mingling of different levels of reality, in this case the dead and the living; typified social figures rather than individualised characters. But the basis of the play is philosophic not emotional, and pathos is replaced by a lyrical tone. Where a naturalistic play creates empathy through illusion and expressionism relies on emotional transference and identification, Frisch is concerned with establishing distance. His stage directions emphasise that the scenery 'should in no case give the illusion of reality. The impression of a play should be preserved throughout, so that nothing is compared with actual events, which would be monstrous',[30] and his *Diary* (*Tagebuch*) *1946–49* noted that the only justification for commenting on the war when one had not been involved was 'the freedom to judge fairly...It is the only way of retaining dignity in the midst of suffering nations'.[31]

This objectivity is most obvious in the equal treatment of both sides. Frisch gives the same propaganda phrases to the German high-school teacher and the Allied radio operator, who each refer to the enemy as 'devils' to be 'destroyed', and emphasises that there is no moral distinction between the bombing of civilians and the shooting of hostages. But this conscious avoidance of condemnation is also an evasion of commitment, a retreat into abstraction which results in the extremely general nature of the issues raised and the self-critical questioning of the function of art. The scenes are little more than a frame for ethical reflection. Each centres on a death but only one killing is shown, the execution of the Teacher which thus forms the climax of the play – and even this is presented in stylised, carefully undramatic tableau. The firing squad is off-stage, the shots are represented by 'a silence' and the Teacher 'stands unchanged', so that the weight is not on the act but the philosophical statements that precede it. Death is treated as a state, not an event, and horrors are projected through the response of the characters. Even argument is avoided. The accusation that the Teacher had betrayed the cultural ideals he taught, levelled at him by his executioner, Herbert his 'best pupil', meets no opposition since his 'treason' (stating Frisch's theme that 'our side does the same' as the enemy) came from his recognition that compromising with the fascists to keep his position indeed discredited his principles. The final scene is representative of the way conflict is excluded. The dead, whose views are the complete reverse of the living, stand side by side with the survivors but cannot communicate. Each scene in fact is a statement made at the point where the characters, distanced from the events by time or their own deaths, or numbed by shock, transform their emotional response into lyricism or moral questioning: justice against deserts, the relativity of innocence and responsibility, duty versus principles, all of which are linked to the ideals and aspirations symbolised in art.

Art is presented as spiritual expression. The Byzantine mosaic in the monastery, 'figures...standing in front of a gold ground, which means they stand in the unconditional sphere of the spirit' (pp. 89–90), signifies the dissociation of ideals from life which Frisch sees as the root cause of modern barbarism:

One of the decisive discoveries which our generation, born in this century but brought up still in the spirit of the previous one, made during the second world war, is that those filled with that culture, connoisseurs who could discuss Bach, Handel, Mozart, Beethoven, Bruckner with spirit and ardour, could equally play the part of slaughterers: the same individual. What distinguishes this type of man may be called an *aesthetic culture*.[32]

Similarly, Bach's choral *Matthäuspassion* stands for the illusory nature of artistic beauty which can even be called on to justify barbarity – 'millennia have sung, suffered, murdered for this kingdom that never comes...and yet is the whole of human history! Nothing on earth is more real than this illusion' (p. 102) – and Herbert, the mass murderer and sensitive cellist, modelled on Heydrich, is motivated by his 'disillusion' at finding that 'the spirit gave way, we knocked on it, and it was hollow' (p. 142). Yet the only answers to this cultural schizophrenia that Frisch has to offer are the same artistic forms that he condemns. The tone of the play is structured by the artistic references and their echoes. The lyrical association of love, hope, and the desire for a better world with nature and springtime, which forms a motif for all of the younger characters, is an extension of the poem by Mörike quoted by Karl and Herbert immediately after killing the hostages. The song of the dead, which acts as a counterpoint to atrocities, is keyed to the *Matthäuspassion*; and the hostages themselves are presented explicitly in terms of a mosaic which depicts the Crucifixion and Resurrection.

As the objectivity and philosophical focus indicate, Frisch's intentions in *Now They've Started Singing Again* are basically didactic. Themes are developed by linking the figures without regard to plausibility. Thus even the Allied radio operator is personally acquainted with Herbert, and it is suggested that in metaphysical terms Karl's mother, killed by the bomber-crew, was one of the hostages – 'there is a woman who you shot; she says she is your mother...All mothers are one, Karl' (p. 135). Other characters, typified and universalised (The Priest and The Teacher, The Woman, The Other, Someone), are allegorical representatives of ideas. Even the named characters are without psychological development and embody viewpoints which are clearly patterned and contrasted. Eduard, for instance, stands at the beginning for freedom, justice and peace for all, irrespective of nationality, while the radio operator states the case for revenge. In the final scene their positions are simply reversed. The play demonstrates an example to be avoided, and there is little subtlety in the ending where the living ignore the lessons the dead have learnt:

JENNY: All the pride, all the honour which your father strove for in his life –
CAPTAIN: It was all wrong, Jenny, the greatest mistake!
JENNY: You, his son, you will carry it on! (p. 146.)

Frisch puts his audience in an olympian position where they are assumed to be more aware than the living on stage who cannot see the dead and ignore their message – an effective technique for accomplishing his declared aim of 'posing a question in such a way that the spectators could not live from that hour on without an answer, their own answer which they could only give in their lives'.[33] But the formulation of this question is confused by Frisch's emotional involvement in the subject. At another point he admitted that the play developed 'out of the need to free myself from personal distress',[34] and although this 'Attempt at a Requiem' reverses the traditional prayer for the dead to rest in peace – the overt aim being that the dead should disturb the peace of mind of the living – the elegaic tone lends itself to sentimental vagueness. The positive elements on which an audience might base its answer are Rousseauesque: 'our real life is...in the blowing of a wind that brushes through the trees, in the play of endless water that runs over strange stones' in contrast to 'the world of events' and 'the money, the big business' of society (pp. 129–30). This life of idealised nature (shearing one's own sheep, baking one's own bread) is set in a frame of over-obvious religious symbols. The final tableau of the hostages is the Last Supper. Seated round a table breaking bread, the dead are assumed to take part in an unending communion, and the final speech offers an abstract solution replete with vaguely biblical associations:

THE PRIEST: Love is beautiful, Benjamin, love above everything. It alone knows that it is in vain and it alone does not despair. *He passes the wine to the next one, the song grows louder.* (p. 148)

The didactic intentions are undermined by lyricism – a retreat from reality into what has been neatly summed up as 'an esperanto of the heart'[35] – and the obverse of it is the daemonism that characterises Herbert, the epitome of fascism. Frisch in effect transforms Nazi atrocities into the expression of a moral rage, with the same motivation of metaphysical challenge that Hochhuth later picked up in the diabolic doctor of *The Representative*: 'We resorted to power, to the ultimate force, so that the spirit would face us; but the blasphemer was right, there is no true spirit...I see no limits to our power – that is the despair'. (p. 91)

The common failing in each of these plays is a lack of distance, expressed in sentimentality and their way of substituting symbols for analysis. But this problem of perspective was compounded by using dramatic conventions that had been outdated by historical developments – the moral and material bankruptcy of 'total' war and an unprecedented level of communal guilt. Zuckmayer's naturalism, a style already sucessfully dismissed by Brecht as incapable of dealing with the mass nature of modern society and the abstraction of economic relationships, falsified the issues; similarly the expressionism of *The Man Outside*, in presenting the issues on a subjective level, offered the public a vicarious form of empathy that substituted passive emotion for action. Both, in intention at least, are politically engaged but stylistically anachronistic, and Zuckmayer admitted as much when he withdrew *The Devil's General* in 1963 because the evidence at Eichmann's trial 'threw a false light on the play', while Borchert had recognised the inappropriateness of traditional art forms in his early manifesto – 'who will write a new harmonics for us? We no longer need the well-tempered klavier. We ourselves are too full of dissonance.'[36] Even Frisch, questioning the function of art as one of his major themes, uses a conventional form (the requiem) which makes his play ineffective, although he did develop a new approach. Instead of the full articulation of traditional art, the structure and theatrical surface of *Now They've Started Singing Again* is deliberately unfinished in an attempt to find a correlative for contemporary experience:

The sketch has a direction, but no ending; the sketch as the expression of a world picture which is no longer or not yet in harmony; as an aversion to a formal whole that exceeds the spiritual and so can only be borrowed; as a mistrust of the facility which prevents our age from achieving completeness in its own terms.[37]

The final result is too personal to provide a model, but various elements recur in later work: the oratorio-frame in Weiss' *The Investigation* (*Die Ermittlung*, 1965) or the anti-illusionistic theatricality in Dürrenmatt.

All three plays were immensely popular in the first decade after the war but provided no solution to dramaturgical problems. As Brecht noted in his journal for 1947, 'we must begin again right from the beginning'; and in 1964 the director Peter Palitzsch could still claim that although German dramatists were deeply concerned with contemporary issues and the immediate past 'yet the themes stay hanging in the air because of all the problems of style and formulation'.[38]

3. *Developments*

The empty space of German theatre was an open space; not simply a void but a *tabula rasa* that stimulated experimentation. Traditional dramatic models, despite the popularity of Zuckmayer and Borchert, had demonstrated their inadequacy as formulations for serious contemporary concerns. A new Shakespeare (as Kipphardt put it in his play, *Shakespeare dringend gesucht*, 1952) was urgently wanted, and up until the mid sixties practically every major play was greeted by critical articles headed 'Hope for the German Drama?' In England and America drama of social significance remained basically naturalistic – Terence Rattigan and Osborne, Miller and Tennessee Williams – but German playwrights returned to first principles, and the 1950s and 1960s were characterised by loud arguments about the philosophy of theatre. While these sometimes descended to personal attacks and were frequently statements of position rather than discussions, they provided a unique atmosphere of critical questioning which provoked stylistic initiatives.

The scope of the discussion was set by Friedrich Dürrenmatt. From the religious propaganda plays of the Counter-Reformation on, the Germans have traditionally looked on the stage as a 'moral tribunal' dealing with social problems, and Brecht's definition of entertainment as the pleasure of learning, as a technique of persuasion not an end in itself, is representative rather than atypical, so that (as Dürrenmatt remarked at the opening of his lecture on 'Problems of the Theatre' in 1954) theories of drama were commonplace. But in offering his own contribution, the comedy of grotesque paradoxes, he raised a fundamental issue: whether it was possible for the contemporary world to be represented on the stage at all. His questions covered the purpose and possibilities of theatre, its thematic and stylistic limitations, and the relationship between form and function, concepts and content, style and significance. Working on a McLuhanesque premise that the medium determines the meaning, he drew a distinction between the concrete, particularising nature of the stage and the anonymous, amorphous conceptual state of the modern world. Drama, as a rhetorical art which depends on a 'special condition' of tension between dialogue and situation, has to present society

41

in terms of human relationships. Certain ideas (Kafka's are an example given) are on a level of abstraction that is unsuitable for theatrical treatment. Others have become the study of such sciences as history or sociology, and the contrast between any dramatic and scientific treatment of the same material discredits drama, which simplifies because it must compress and abbreviate, but cannot abstract. Most significant for Dürrenmatt, the sphere of politics, which has figureheads, but no power figures, is automatically falsified by the indispensable actor. To have symbolic validity the type and status of the dramatic hero must correspond to the preconceptions of the age, and in contemporary conditions power cannot be credibly embodied by individuals: 'The state has lost its human contours, and just as physics can only interpret the world in terms of mathematical formulae, so the state can now only be expressed in statistics.'[1] The problem is one of scale, and theatrical conventions are the wrong yardstick for measuring modern politics. This basic point is the same as Frisch's criticism of art in *Now They've Started Singing Again* almost ten years earlier:

> HERBERT: Let me make the position clear: Your death. No one will know about it, no one paint it on canvas or admire it in an art gallery, you are not dying according to aesthetic principles...Your death is completely unnoticeable on the picture of reality...we are not shooting you alone but...your view of the world, which, as you see, was a lie.[2]

As solutions Dürrenmatt suggests parody, which asserts creative freedom and imposes objectivity by distorting, or 'unartistic' art forms, which are so light on the scales of literary criticism that they escape outdated standards.

But this surface frivolity is simply a way of slipping serious commentary in under an audience's preconceptions. Dürrenmatt assumes that theatre is inseparable from politics. Its primary function is therefore to expose and moralise, or at the least to 'demonstrate freedom', and this together with his perception that new material demands fresh modes of presentation aligns him with Brecht. Already in the 1920s Brecht had noted (as a starting point for his own development of 'epic' structures) that the five-act form was inappropriate to the internal combustion engine and the stock exchange so that 'the dramatic technique of Hebbel and Ibsen is totally insufficient to dramatise even a simple press notice'.[3] Dürrenmatt substitutes Schiller for Hebbel but uses exactly the same terms; his argument that 'heroes in the old sense' are 'no more than incidental, superficial and easily replaceable expressions' of complex powers echoes Brecht's analysis of 'cyclical crises in which the "heroes" change with each phase, are replaceable'.[4] Brecht developed his dramaturgy out of this analysis, and since Dürrenmatt quite correctly sees Brecht's 'epic' principles as based on a Marxist view of society one major thrust in his lecture is an attack on epic theatre: 'Brecht's thesis, developed in his *Street Scene*, that the world is an accident and what should be shown is how this accident came about, can yield – as Brecht himself proved – magnificent theatre, but does so by concealing the evidence.'[5]

There are inconsistencies in Dürrenmatt's arguments; for instance that the objective attitude of comedy is the equivalent to the double perspective of Brecht's 'alienation' devices, or that modern historical analyses discredit imaginative treatments of the same material since factuality is now the only criterion for truth – in contrast to the Greek audience's acceptance of history as myth which made the achievements of classical tragedy possible (a distinction derived from the peculiarly contemporary conviction that religion is a matter of imagination rather than belief). There are also inadequacies in his proposed solutions, which turn out to be either personal or too general to be useful – like his suggestion that the appropriate form for dealing with contemporary issues and conditions is 'the experiment' (no advance on Frisch's 'sketch'). But his questions focussed on concerns that were to become central, as in the fact/fiction dichotomy of documentary drama; and his demand that playwrights ask themselves 'how the mirrors that catch and reflect this world should be ground and set'[6] created a degree of awareness which no German dramatist could escape.

Not surprisingly, the first response came from Brecht. While granting that contemporary conditions were increasingly difficult to represent on the stage, he restated the basic concept from his 'Short Organon' (1931):

I cannot say that those dramaturgies, which I have particular reasons for defining as non-Aristotelian, and the epic acting-methods which belong to them present *the* solution. However, one thing is clear: The contemporary world is only describable for contemporary man if it is described as an alterable world.[7]

This concept of an alterable world was predicated on Brecht's typically optimistic belief in scientific progress. Steel withstood earthquakes, biophysics was capable of changing the natural environment. With increasing knowledge man could no longer be seen as the victim of incomprehensible laws, and in deliberate contrast to the adjectives used by Dürrenmatt to describe the world – 'anonymous', 'amorphous', 'formless', 'questionable' – Brecht referred to the humanising principles of communism. 'The question whether the world is representable is a social question', and instead of passively mirroring conditions from the outside an artist must present them from a 'critically involved' perpective.[8]

This in effect was a claim that Dürrenmatt's questions could be answered by political commitment, a position later taken up by such playwrights as Hacks and Kroetz, and it provoked a series of responses from Frisch. These emphasised the linguistic and imaginative elements of theatre, and show Frisch working out the theoretical basis for a play like *Biography : A Game* (*Biographie: Ein Spiel*, 1969). The alterability of the world is accepted, but conceived in far more radical terms since Frisch raises the whole question of theatre as an image-generator, defining 'reality' as an image imposed by ideologies. From this standpoint what we see as reality is not factually verifiable, being merely a view of the world, and as such is determined by general perspectives which substitute a shorthand of simplified concepts for the complexities of existence. These images are indispensable but become continually more unreal until they harden into ideologies, so literature's constructive function is subversive: 'to make ideology insecure by continually trying to bring the altering reality into focus' which 'then shows the discrepancy between the vocabulary of ideology and reality'.[9] Frisch developed this idea by disputing the way Dürrenmatt and Brecht had defined the problem of modern drama (in 1964, ten years after Dürrenmatt's lecture, an indication of the pervasive influence of his questions). Summarising theatrical history in terms of stylistic developments from Sophocles to Strindberg, he queried Dürrenmatt's implication that the stage had been successful in representing the world up to the modern age. From the 'mythological sketch' of Greek tragedy or Aristophanes'

invented world, reflected in the grotesque...the nearer we come to the present, the more we know about the word, the clearer it becomes how unrepresentable the complex reality is...However theatre defines itself, it is art: play as a response to the inability to copy the world...Even Brecht does not show the existent world...but models of the Brechtian-Marxist thesis, the desirability of another and non-existent world:

poetry...One has to alter in order to represent, and what is representable is always utopia.[10]

From such a viewpoint drama could only be a symbolic distillation of life, any changes were in the sphere of imagination, not reality, and the moral or political value of the theatre was dubious.

However, as soon as the concept of alteration is introduced the nature of a play's effect on the audience becomes the primary question, and it is at this point that Frisch reintroduces the criterion of relevance. In presenting an alternative vision, the theatre can change the audience's relationship to the world by putting accepted attitudes in question. It becomes a 'touchstone' of social values. Any immediate transformation of behaviour or thought-patterns is unlikely, but by testing experience against imagination 'there is a long range effect, an alteration of awareness', although coming from literature this change occurs on a linguistic rather than a political level.[11]

The general interest in this discussion and the influence of the Dürrenmatt/Brecht formulation of the issues is underlined by a questionnaire distributed to the leading dramatists of the time (1963) by the journal *Theater Heute*, asking 'Should the theatre be attempting to represent today's world?' and is it 'even representable on the stage?' Frisch's standpoint became the middle ground adopted by Dürrenmatt, Martin Walser and Günter Grass. Dürrenmatt, contrasting 'representing *the* world' with 'setting up *a* world', defined the aim of a play to be 'not reality, but the playing with reality, its transformation into theatre...reality is never recognisable in itself, only in its metamorphoses';[12] while Walser emphasised style as a form of perception, not a mode of presentation, and developed this into a theory of *Bewusstseinstheater* ('Theatre of Consciousness'). Grass went a step further with the proposition that all literature raises subliminal expectations, but denied any direct correlation between intention and result, using nineteenth-century cookbooks as an off-beat example of the indirect social effect of literature. (Designed for bourgeois budgets these changed the dietary expectations of the working classes, drove them into debt and ultimately contributed to the radicalisation of society.)[13] In its oblique and interminable indefiniteness this points to Dorst's assertion that since his plays are 'not linked to any one of the great materialistic or metaphysical blueprints of the world' they consciously avoid any attempt to 'improve' the audience. This in turn is not far from the absurdist denial of any political frame of reference, and parallels Hildesheimer's definition of 'the absurd dramatist' as a man aware 'that the theatre has as yet purified no one and improved no situation, and his work draws...bitter or comic consequences from this fact'.[14]

The opposite extreme is epitomised by Friedrich Wolf's ideal drawn from an incident in the Peasant Revolt:

The *avant garde* of revolutionary peasants had formed themselves into armed acting-groups. The moment to strike was set as the performance of the Shrovetide play, a carnival where the whole aristocracy of the country would be present. In the middle of the play of 'The Honourable Fool's Justice' in the year of grace 1514 the peasants drew the swords hidden in their clowns' costumes and struck down the watching knights...the play was transformed into bloody earnest.[15]

The assumptions in this model are typical, even if physical violence is replaced by shock-effects (Heiner Müller) or intellectual assault (Peter Weiss). The audience addressed is the opposition, the aim a radical change in consciousness. Significantly, the more immediate the intended effect, the less the stage relies on invented material or illusionistic presentation. Plays become 'facts', speeches quotations, scenery photographs. But the documentary writer's primary focus being the reaction of the audience rather than the representation of his subject, even the apparent absence of 'style' is itself a rhetorical technique. Extended to its logical conclusion this breaks the connection between form and content. A style is not selected as the appropriate formulation for a particular material but as a challenge to the audience's state of awareness. According to Günter Wallraff, for example, literature should have the same effect on the conceptual level 'as dynamite'. If it is successful in exploding habits of thought then society will be in continual upheaval, perceptions will change overnight, and with each shift 'new forms must be found'.[16] In practice, however, such rhetorical dynamite turns out to be very similar to Frisch's 'sharpening a particular awareness' – giving the public 'a more critical view of their environment' which, depending on the social class of the audience, either 'leads to new political attitudes, to joining a trades union' (Wallraff), or 'challenges' them 'to acknowledge their true colour', one that the play demonstrates is indefensible, so that the aim of a performance is to 'provoke the most intense opposition' (Weiss).[17] And changes of consciousness hardly measure up to ideals of direct political action. Friedrich Wolf commented that even the most committed of contemporary plays remained 'substitutes for political reality', while Brecht admitted that 'the effects of my intention [to alter the world], as I myself slowly had to recognise, were, small or large, no more than alterations in theatrical performance'.[18] In reaction various dramatists progressed from questioning the political effectiveness of theatre to a radical rejection of art. One of the clearest instances was Enzensberger's attack on Peter Weiss, condemning literature as a form of self-deception which substituted rhetorical postures for political strategy so that any author's commitment 'stays on a verbal level, it is exhausted in agitation' – a position Weiss himself approached in his commemorative speech for Che Guevara declaring that revolutionary practice had to supersede verbal protest.[19]

In response theatre was forced either into abstraction or onto the streets, a choice that Peter Handke set out in his essay on 'Street theatre and Theatre theatre'. Politics is assumed to be the sphere of action, definitive and committed; the opposite of theatre which, as a make-believe game, automatically transposes its subject and actors into symbols. For theatre to be politically effective every element of pretence must be eliminated. Only the minimal requirements are retained – an audience, who in the media-age need not even be present, and an action structured to reveal the underlying assumptions or disguised realities of society. This definition in practice turns out to be so general as to be meaningless since any event that creates public awareness counts as 'theatre' (although conversely it also, perhaps unintentionally, recognises the rhetorical nature of all contemporary radical activism in which a mass-march is a protest, the occupation of government or university offices is not a take-over of power but a passive gesture, even bombings are carried out as advertisements, and demonstration replaces political action):

Today's politically committed theatre does not take place in theatre-buildings...but in lecture halls when the microphone is taken away from a professor...When the commune theatricalises reality and successfully ridicules it by 'terrorising' it; and not only ridicules it, but in the viciousness of [society's] reactions reveals its insensibility, false nature and fake tranquillity.[20]

In the light of such a radical integration of art and life the only way for conventional theatre to retain its integrity is to limit its focus to language. On an introverted stage the question of how

47

contemporary reality should be represented becomes irrelevant. What remains is 'a playing space', linked not to society but to the individual's 'internal consciousness'. But as Handke implicitly admits this merely evades the issue. As a mode of perception language is socially determined, and even his most restricted definition of drama as 'a means of sensitising, stimulating, provoking reaction' reintroduces the category of social relevance since this is 'a means of touching the world'.[21]

This radical questioning of the nature of theatre, its functional relationship both to its source material and its audience – which was simultaneously a questioning of the nature of reality – provided the impetus for the wide range of stylistic developments in post-war German theatre. As a form of self-analysis it also had a strong thematic influence, and there are a striking number of plays that examine the role of the author. Unlike the traditional satiric self-defence (Aristophanes or Molière), these are dramatically treated, frequently tragic protagonists. They vary from such self-projections as Dürrenmatt's Schwitter or universalised representatives like Frisch's Intellectual, to historical and contemporary figures: Weiss' Hölderlin and Trotsky, Dorst's Toller, Grass' Brechtian Boss. But all reflect the problem of literary creativity and social responsibility in a critical light. Even the classics were adapted to illustrate these themes, as in Peter Stein's production of Goethe's *Tasso* (Bremen, 1969) or his more recent mammoth collage of *Shakespeare's Memory* (Berlin, 1977).

The first analysis of the post-war writer's dilemma was Frisch's *Great Wall of China* (*Die chinesische Mauer*, 1946). Even more obviously than his earlier 'Attempt at a Requiem', since it was a direct response to his journey through the ruins of Germany immediately after the war, this play uses every available means – Thornton Wilder's and Brecht's theatricality, shifts of time-frame and a farcical approach – to gain sufficient distance from the immediate situation for him to deal with the general question of man's destructive urge. As so often in Frisch's work the problem is of immediate relevance while the solution offered is escapist, a retreat into romanticism; self-fulfilment in selfless love which here is even admitted to be utopian by presenting it in anachronistic terms, the Modern Man and a Chinese princess from the distant past, the 'powerless' and the 'violated'. The play explores one of the themes of *Now They've Started Singing Again*, the power of illusions, which motivate men both to build cathedrals and to destroy them. The characters are divided into three groups, each of which exist on a different plane of reality. Modern (intellectual) Man, the audience's representative, is the catalyst for an imaginary historical action that demonstrates the psychological effect of power. This is interwoven with a masque of symbolic attitudes taken from literature; and the point at issue is the relationship of truth to art, reality to illusion in a world dominated by force. The stage is the intellectual scene, 'our consciousness', and in analysing the dangerous power of fantasies Frisch is hard put to it to distinguish the level of healthy mental activity (rational perception) from the damaging (illusion). Hence the heavy-handed parody of Shakespeare, anachronisms and speeches directly to the audience which break the action and present the characters as actors, as well as the tearing down of the scenery so that 'the stage appears as a stage'. Hence too the way Frisch carefully justifies his fundamental assumption that reality is dependent on perception by referring to modern physics – 'time is a function of space' – a link to the apocalyptic modern context of the atom bomb, always present in his Intellectual's mind as the inevitable end result of our political behaviour, that gives the rather static theme its dramatic urgency. (A scientific theatre for the scientific age.) On this conceptual stage ideas are paramount, and on the surface this puts the writer, who gives ideas their cultural expression, in an influential position. But literature is 'poetic imagination' which by definition 'misinterprets and distorts' reality, so that when this Modern Man attempts to write the truth even his most sincere denunciations of power, lust and oppression can still be turned into propaganda for the powerful, simply the production of art being presented as justification for preserving the status quo. So in Frisch's model if he is not forced into hypocritical compromise by fear, the artist is absorbed into the social hierarchy he attacks – as a court fool.

The problem is seen to be partly linguistic, since words (which embody ideas) contain different meanings, and the use of parody brings the nature of literature as a verbal artefact to the forefront of the play:

The figures which people our minds draw their existence ultimately from language. Hence the stylistic quotations: Brutus after Shakespeare, Philip of Spain after Schiller. Pilate we don't know from Roman history but from the Bible, hence the biblical quotations.[22]

There are also echoes of Nazi terms in the Emperor's speeches ('meine Getreuen', 'Männer die Geschichte machen' – 'my followers', 'men who make history' – and of course 'Heil!') and a demonstration of the propaganda-use of words: 'the people, the true people, are always content with their rulers'. Simply by definition, therefore, protesters are 'terrorists, subversive elements, agitators. Very useful words, Majesty; they nip truth in the bud'.[23] In terms of the play perception and action are both conditioned by language. The only way of learning about the world outside the limitations of personal experience is through words – and Brutus is misled by newspapers into believing the industrialists to be 'lovers of justice and the common good' (p. 67) – while without the words of the intellectual the people have no 'voice' and their revolution replaces one tyrant with another. Autocrats are 'the mental disease' of their era, 'the lie personified' which destroys the ability to think, while journalists are 'eunuchs' because they are integrated in the system, and the classics have only created 'ghosts' whose example is disastrous because (almost by definition) they are 'deaf to every development in human consciousness' (p. 21). Thus those cultural values embodied by figures like Romeo or Brutus, which are usually taken to be a defence against the intellectual brutalisation of dictatorship, are revealed to be delusions, empty forms. Their graceful polonaise is presented as a mechanical 'dance of death' (p. 49).

Frisch defines the writer's task in literary terms: to destroy poetic 'masks'. Direct political action is pointless since as long as the concepts remain, the same 'types' stay in power. Literature is ineffective, either illusory or misappropriated, and silence is suggested as the only logical response. A mute, Frisch's symbol for the suffering people, may provoke the self-styled 'Son of Heaven who is always in the right' to reveal his true nature as a murderer, but in spite of a comparison with Christ's refusal to speak in his own defence, for a writer silence can be nothing more than a self-defeating contradiction since if reality is defined by words only words can change the situation. Thus Frisch argues himself into an impasse, reflected in the circular structure of the play, and the unsatisfactory nature of the conclusion is perhaps responsible for the artificiality of the play as a whole. The meaning is emphasised at the expense of the dramatic events, the theatricality is obtrusive, and the farce discredits principles as well as false ideals:

MODERN MAN: First freedom of thought –
WAITER: With gin or without? (p. 20)

His theme can be stated very simply – 'every situation forces a choice: to be a witness for the mute or to be mute'[24] – but he had obvious difficulty in finding a theatrical correlative for it.

Similar difficulties recur in Dürrenmatt's *Der Meteor* (1966) which touches on some of the same problems, although this black comedy is more successful since the farce is rooted in the concept itself, rather than being an applied technique as in Frisch. Schwitter, the 'meteor' of the title whose fall from the heavens spreads arbitrary destruction on those nearest the point of impact, is Lazarus – but in reverse as befits the inverted morality of the contemporary world, an unloved man who cannot die. There is no sign of divine grace in his repeated resurrection, in spite of the naive affirmation of the Salvation Army. It is more an example of what Dürrenmatt sees as the monstrous egoism of the writer, for whom every aspect of existence is no more than grist for his own imaginative projection of himself in his literature, and it causes the deaths of all who relate to him because he has imposed his artistic vision on life (as in his story of the death of 'an innocent' which is reflected in the suicide of his young wife when he rejects her).

Literature here is an alternative world, quite simply non-reality. And it is shown by Schwitter's case to be untenable where it's a serious matter of life and death: the reality of death effaces the inventions that Schwitter had set up protectively around himself.[25]

After Shaw's *Major Barbara*, which was based on the paradox of Nobel, the inventor of nitroglycerine and 'merchant of death' who founded his Prize as a challenge to solve the problems he had created, any reference to Nobel on the stage is likely to imply the corruption of the intellectual, whose efforts to change the world are rewarded and financed by profits from society's most destructive aspect. Schwitter, as a Nobel Prize winner for literature – the equivalent of the gold chain awarded to Frisch's intellectual by the tyrant – sold out to society, and his literature is a negation of reality. It is in this sense that 'what Schwitter achieves is not eternal life but eternal dying'.[26] Dürrenmatt defended art in a programme note as an 'answer, as defence' which enables man to deal with reality by giving order to 'the events, the monstrosities',[27] but the play itself denies this assertion. Schwitter's

51

writing empties existence of its meaning by proposing false values, so that life comes to be seen as the 'supremely malevolent trick of Nature...a malignant infection of the earth's skin, an incurable sore'.[28] Its effect is the death wish that Schwitter himself embodies, and the correspondence between his artistic views and Dürrenmatt's work is obvious. The fact that the critic's oration at Schwitter's death-bed is an ironic paraphrase of the criticism levelled against Dürrenmatt, gives it added point: 'it was his nihilism that made him a moralist...His work was not a reflection of reality but an expression of impotence: his theatre, not reality, is grotesque...' (p. 45). Like Frisch's intellectual who is too interested in Pilate's question about truth to react to human suffering, Schwitter is a prostitute who fabricates make-believe emotion while even a call-girl (his wife) has real feelings. Dürrenmatt has followed his principle that 'a story is thought through to its conclusion when it has taken its worst possible turn'[29] – and applied it to art.

Dürrenmatt and Frisch question the relationship of drama to reality at a general level. Grass and Dorst explore the reaction of the artist in specific political situations. For Grass the artist's intellectual nature is a form of paralysis which prevents action because it sees events only in aesthetic terms, and his play is based on the premise that if the artist had been able to involve himself the revolution would have been successful. For Dorst it is the artist's idealism that makes him a political leader, and his participation causes the revolution to fail. Both figures are dramatists and the basic issue in each play is the theatricalisation of political action.

Grass' original intentions in *The Plebeians Rehearse the Uprising* (*Die Plebejer proben den Aufstand*, 1965) were to focus on 'history and its interpretation. Spiritual property and its owners. The day of National Celebration and the Shakespeare-Year',[30] but his choice of Brecht's reworking of *Coriolanus* and the 17 June Uprising as dramatic examples transformed his theme into an analysis of art and commitment. At first glance using Brecht as the central figure seems appropriate, since the argument that his ideology conflicted with his art is well-known.[31] In practice the immediacy confused the issues and the universal relevance of the intellectual dilemma was ignored. The specific identification of Helene Weigel and Erich Engel with Volumnia and Erwin obscured the more general reflection of such writers as Becher and

Kuba (Kurt Barthes) in the 'people's poet' Kozanka. Grass' concern was with 'the problematic nature of the intellectual *per se*', his objectivity and rational detachment, his irony which makes even a declaration of solidarity ambiguous, his involuntary search for aesthetic patterns in action and his dependence on those in power. This substitution of observation for experience is presented as the quality that defines an intellectual. It is the dominant characteristic of 'the Boss', derived from Brecht's theories of alienation and the 'withdrawal into lyricism' that Grass sees in Brecht's *Buckower Elegies* – hence the use of lines from 'die Lösung' and 'Böser Morgen' ('The Solution', 'Angry Dawn') in the play – and Grass throws it into high relief by stressing 'the intellectual arrogance on one side, the privileged position, and the partly unconsidered, helpless arguments of the workers on the other'.[32] The intellectual in fact is defined not by the particular quality of his reaction to a situation but by a simplistic contrast between the self-cancelling complexity of his mind and the commitment of 'the people' who supposedly act without thought, are direct, emotionally involved, innocent, and dominated by physical instincts. This is hardly a new perception – Thomas Mann commented on it in *Apolitical Observations* (*Betrachtungen eines Unpolitischen*, 1922), 'irony and radicalism, these are opposites, an Either–Or' – and its oversimplification throws the main interest of the play onto Grass' use of theatricality.

Tankred Dorst's variation on the theme of theatre and revolution, *Toller* (1968), is based on the same principle; but reversed and without the one-sided moral weight on action. Again the artist is seen as impotent – in the words of an army officer, 'Gentlemen, have you ever been defeated by a poet? *Laughter*' – and the same distinction is made between the directness of commitment and the double-sided vision of the intellectual:

OLGA: Without the correct political attitude nothing sound can be written...Poetry – today that means purpose! Or it is only irrelevant chatter.

TOLLER: As an artist I also have to understand the opposite side.[33]

But these are the views of characters, not (as with Grass) of the author, and it is a parody tribunal wearing the masks of 'capital', 'clergy', 'justice', 'military' which states that there is an unbridgeable gulf separating 'a poetic soul' from responsible political action.

The different perspectives in the two plays are summed up in the choice of historical situation. Grass takes the 1953 east German protest against productivity norms, which like other riots in Szczecin or Gdansk was initiated by workers and concerned with living standards not ideological change. Dorst's example is the Bavarian Räterepublik (workers' Soviet) of 1919, in which he sees parallels to the student revolutions of the late 1960s, and his use of Ernst Toller, the expressionist who became a leader of the revolutionary government in Munich, as a central figure transfers the focus from intellectual aloofness to the effectiveness of the artist's involvement. Here it is Leviné, the professional revolutionary who is characterised by Brechtian rationalism and self-preservation, while it is Toller as the artist who epitomises enthusiasm, idealism and absolute moral values: 'a symbol for these new ideas...that have moved men...influenced them, changed them!' (p. 18.) But the vision that inspires the revolution is also what betrays it, and the inner contradictions of the artistic temperament are outlined in the figures of the other poets, Mühsam and Landauer, and their opening proclamation:

MÜHSAM: There I see the promised land!
REICHERT: A word's missing in the proclamation: 'class conflict'.
LANDAUER: ...Our revolution must be a revolution of love...it must sweep everything along with it and outgrow class divisions. If our revolution is only external, it will soon congeal in superficialities.
REICHERT: Landauer, come down to earth, man! (pp. 10–11).

The poets take words for action, their proclamation is the rhetoric of hope, and their intervention remains on the level of symbolic gesture. Thus Olga, the Marxist intellectual, proclaims her 'solidarity' with the proletariat by painting the word on an outsize banner; Toller personally leads a magnificently anachronistic charge in a battle which ends in defeat, and the contrast of his eloquence at his trial with the silence of workers going to execution in the final scene reveals his commitment as verbal. Dorst's point is that Toller 'only damaged the cause of socialism with his politically undefined love of humanity', that it is the writer's positive qualities – 'pacifist, committed dramatist, effective speaker, sensitive and self-aware' – which undermine his ideals by giving him 'only a sentimental relationship to power, or none at all'.[34]

1   Grass, *The Plebeians Rehearse the Uprising*, 1966. The stage on stage: boxes
of Brecht's Schiffbauerdammtheater as scenery in the Schiller Theater.

In both plays the consequence of the intellectual's participation in politics is the same, and the choice of dramatists as protagonists is more than self-questioning. Reality is transformed into theatre in *The Plebeians Rehearse the Uprising*. The regression of actions into acting is automatic since the world that the stage mirrors is a stage; and this was stressed by the first production (Schiller-Theater, 1966), where the set reproduced the stage of the Berliner Ensemble, with copies of the Schiffbauerdamm theatre's baroque balconies flanking an inner proscenium (see Illustration 1). In this context everything is reduced to performance. The revolution on the streets is reported as if it were a sequence from Eisenstein's classic, *Battleship Potemkin*, or acted out as an improvisation; when workers enter they are cast as the plebeians in Brecht's play, a real fight is turned into a rehearsal by being repeated under the Boss' direction, and the Boss himself becomes Coriolanus, saved by the parable of the belly from the bitter workers who see his inaction as betrayal and try to hang him; when the revolt is over it is preserved on tape, to be edited and replayed as mere sound effects. The tension in the play comes from the contrast between the Boss' assumption that drama can teach (which presupposes a qualitative distinction: 'nature or my theatre')[35] and Grass' deliberate presentation of reality as bad theatre. Not only Volumnia borrows quotations from Brecht, but 'every word's rehearsed' (p. 20). The two moments at which reality breaks through the theatrical surface – the attempt to hang the Boss and the hair-dresser's passionate appeal which finally sweeps the Boss into commitment – are both melodramatic by contrast to the rational tone of the rest, and the hairdresser not only speaks over the footlights and in iambic pentameters but sees herself as Kattrin from *Mother Courage*. As Erwin comments, 'She could have been written by you, Boss' (p. 91). In his ironic preface on 'the Prehistory-Posthistory of the Tragedy of *Coriolanus*...down to Brecht and Myself' Grass states the Boss' tragic flaw to be that 'everything turns to theatre in his hands; slogans, speaking choruses, whether to march in columns of ten or twelve, everything becomes for him an aesthetic question'. (p. xxxvi). But in terms of the play, since there is no spontaneity this perversion of reality is illusory.

BOSS: Even Liebknecht and Luxemburg were romantics...
ERWIN: But in the end you came around to the aesthetic principle.
BOSS: Marx himself stressed it.
ERWIN: And Lenin says revolution should be practised like an art (p. 13).

2 Dorst, *Toller*, 1968. Agitprop puppets, placards and simultaneous stages:
documentary parody.

Although a similar point is put forward by Landauer in the first scene of *Toller* – 'a revolution, gentlemen, is a creative act' (p. 8) – this seems at first sight to be contradicted by Dorst's choice of style. His use of documentary film as a contrast to the artificial revue structure of the scenes presupposes a qualitative difference between reality and the stage, so that theatricalisation is an undesired effect of the artist's intrusion into politics or a sign that those involved are blind to the realities of the situation. Thus Toller is the 'stage actor' he is accused of being because he sees himself and events in a conventionally dramatic light. In the inserted scene from Toller's *Masses and Man*, (*Masse-Mensch*, 1920) he plays the central figure, the woman who defends individualism against the demands of 'mass-man', just as his personal heroism is an expression of Landauer's artistic principle – 'For us human history does not consist of anonymous processes nor simply of the accumulation of many small mass events and mass omissions, for us the agents of history are INDIVIDUALS' (p. 31) – and this attitude distorts others' perceptions because of its emotional attraction. At the moment when the Generals and Colonel Epp are organising the final assault on the Räterepublik the workers are parading with 'banners and placards. Pictures: Toller as Field Marshal. "The Victor of Dachau." "Toller ..."' (p. 73), and even when Toller acknowledges 'that the laws and consequences of his battle are determined by other forces than his good intentions' (p. 105) his perception is still subjective and he stands 'in a cage as in *Masses and Man*' (p. 103). But this overt theatricalisation is actually implicit in Dorst's choice of material. The play is based on Toller's own interpretation of his actions, *Ein Jugend in Deutschland* (translated into English in 1934 as *I Was a German*), rather than on factual evidence, and the supporting documentation that Dorst published is all, except for one telegram from Lenin, composed of the personal comments of those involved in the Munich Räterepublik. Dorst's focus – 'the process of self-dramatisation by a man in a specifically political, not private situation... Toller, the actor' – comes from the theatrical elements that he found in Toller's memoirs, while the perspective that he defines as 'realistic' because 'not following Toller's dramatisations but denouncing them',[36] is just as subjective being equally based on the views of participants. It is basically that of Rosa Leviné, who blamed Toller for her husband's death: 'intoxicated by the belief that his task in world history was to play the Bavarian Lenin, he was incapable of acting consequentially'.[37] So even though an objective reality is implied, it is present only in the counter-revolutionary forces, Noske and the leaders of the White Guards, who are two-dimensional figures shown only in action, externally; or in the brutality on both sides that asserts the status quo. The play's viewpoint is that of the revolutionaries, not just because they are the only characters with motives, emotions, arguments, but because the scenes reflect events through their eyes as theatre at different removes from reality. Even the actions of Leviné, the realist, are calculated for effect as manipulations or deceptions; and at the other end of the scale (as in Grass, though overtly rather than in response to a Pirandellian stylistic premise) are plays within the play – satiric sketches, over-lifesize puppets, scenes from *Masses and Man*, Mühsam accompanying a poem on the piano. Although Toller may claim that everything he has 'said and done is political' so that every line he writes is 'a consequential act' (p. 104), Dorst presents all the scenes as cabaret turns in a revue. The form itself demonstrates that any attempt to change the world by imposing a visionary ideal (by definition the working method of a dramatist who restructures reality for the stage) leads to the same situation as Toller, 'who in wanting to make a revolution, only made literature'.[38]

Perhaps hardly surprisingly, it is the most committed of the contemporary playwrights, Peter Weiss, whose work features the greatest number of writer-figures. De Sade, Hölderlin and even Trotsky, pictured pen in hand, his revolutionary past as memory-scenes, are all presented as authors destroyed by the dialectics of action, the gap between ideas and practice. Each represents individualism against the impersonal mathematics of revolution. In *The Marat/Sade* (1964) Weiss analyses the contradictions of his own position in philosophical terms, and the impotence of the final assault on the audience by the actor-inmates of Charenton, implied to be all the disengaged dramatist can achieve, points to his subsequent adoption of Marxism. *Trotsky in Exile* (*Trotzki im Exil*, 1970) and *Hölderlin* (1971) define the role of the revolutionary artist in response to Party criticism of his work.

Significantly, although *Trotsky* is presented as a documentary collage of historical events and speeches, the key scenes are imaginary. Neither Lenin nor Trotsky met the dadaists, whom they approved only as symptoms of capitalist decadence; and there

59

was no contact between Trotsky and the surrealists at the time in question, although as Maurice Nadeau has pointed out '"the struggle for artistic truth" in the sense of "the artist's unshakable loyalty to his inner self" was the only valid watchword, Trotsky believed. Breton, in recent years, said nothing different.'[39] The Zürich/dada scene is in essence a discussion on the relationship of political and artistic revolution: the function of art as knowledge or as imaginative liberation, the question of judging its effectiveness by political criteria, the demands of the proletariat as the new public. Behind the debate on realism – 'harmonious arches...idealistic steeples' in 'great works' versus 'groans, death-rattles, farts, belches, howls. That is our language. Music?...Who listens to music with a knife in his ribs' – lies the issue of individual freedom. But 'Art must belong to nobody but itself' is set against 'Art must take sides'[40] to show that both extreme attitudes are negative, being equally destructive in so far as they are mutually exclusive. Dada has been chosen as the extreme of irrational subjectivity in art to prevent any automatic alignment with individualism, but the scientific rationalism that defines responsible art as 'mass art, communal art' is discredited by the show trials of the 1930s. As an example of the suppression of the idealism and independent thinking which are the essence of a revolutionary approach, these mockeries of justice are directly linked by Weiss to the Leninist principle of utilitarian and impersonal art. The play's argument is that the one-sidedness of the Russian Revolution negated its principles – 'You have fundamentally changed the whole concept of ownership. But you have not succeeded in spreading the revolution in the hearts of men' (p. 93) – and the point is presented in similar terms to the dilemma of *The Marat/Sade*. Revolution must be centralised and authoritarian to succeed politically, but this by definition prevents 'the liberation of human consciousness' which gives it value. Here art is proposed as the force that frees Sade's 'cells of the inner self', and a positive synthesis is suggested: 'We must unite. We, the unpredictable, emotional artists and you, the planners, the designers. Undivided. Or our revolution will trickle away into the sand' (p. 48).

Hölderlin extends this theme. The solution merely hinted at in *Trotsky* is made flesh 'in the multi-level character of Hölderlin...The poles of Sade and Marat, the poetic visionary and the active politician are here presented in a *single* figure',[41] and Weiss brings on Marx to sanctify the poet's role as the conscience of the revolution. Again, though the basis for the play is documentary and even the perspective on Hölderlin is taken from an academic study (Pierre Bertaux' *Hölderlin et la Révolution Française*, 1969), this key scene is imaginary. The play ends with a tableau of Hölderlin's apotheosis, but this affirmation of the artist's function by Marx and of his art by posterity has little more force than wish-fulfillment in the context of the action as a whole, where the artist can only keep his integrity by a retreat into madness because 'however he dreams up a healthy world it is always defaced by circumstances'.[42] The play, like *Trotsky*, is an exploration of exile but on an inner, subjective level, with Hölderlin retreating from reality, while society, measured against his ideals, is portrayed as progressively more grotesque the more clearly its proclaimed principles are revealed as empty rhetoric. In Perten's Rostock production, for which Weiss' wife designed the costumes and setting, a series of caricature elements were introduced which culminated in the Gontard scene to epitomise the corruption of capitalism. Huge hats and towering wigs distorted the figures who moved with the artificiality of ballet dancers, and a green light, which shone through transparent green parasols carried by the women, created the claustrophobic underwater effect of an aquarium. Clearly we are meant to perceive the scenes through Hölderlin's eyes, with a progressive distortion reflecting the development of the double action as the revolution collapses into repression and Hölderlin withdraws into madness. The result, portraying society as insane, paradoxically emphasises Hölderlin's rationality: by contrast 'normal' writers and thinkers, Goethe and Schiller, Fichte and Hegel, are caricatured as corrupted impostors who have sold out their artistic principles to the grotesque establishment.

The problem with this approach is a lack of dramatic conflict. Hölderlin is set in simple contrast to society in general, and there can be no dialectical opposition since his antagonists are reduced to a single static dimension – Hegel the apologist for industrial imperialism, Fichte the proto-fascist, Goethe and Schiller as substituting forms for content in the reactionary detachment of a fake Parnassus. Such a simplification is intended to symbolise the difference between the illusory harmonies of traditional culture and Hölderlin's artistic aim 'to combine the contradictory' (p. 60) – and this of course refers back to Weiss' own artistic method which in *Hölderlin*, as in *The Marat/Sade*, is deliberately eclectic, linking Brechtian songs and commentary, Artaudian scenes of eroticism and violence, a Pirandellian play within the play and the hallucination of psychodrama, so that simply the combination of such different theatrical effects becomes a self-justifying sign of the approved political attitude. Hölderlin defines the aim of a revolutionary writer as

> not a return
> to the world of the Greeks
> ...but the necessity of finding
> images
> of our time (p. 56)

and the parallels that Weiss draws between the play's historical setting and the present day lend themselves to interpretations like Claus Peymann's production (Hamburg, 1971). Here the inserted scene from Hölderlin's drama, *Empedokles*, became an agitprop performance with the hero in the mask of Che Guevara and a banner – '1966 Che goes to Bolivia' – behind the actors. In Weiss' own estimate, as outlined by Marx, art is less direct:

> Two ways are practical
> as preparation
> for basic changes.
> The one way is
> the analysis of the concrete
> historical situation.
> The other way is
> the visionary shaping
> of deepest personal experience. (p. 174)

Hölderlin, as an artist, cannot free himself from words and is therefore incapable of action – something graphically demonstrated by his response to Marx. 'At last then we can/achieve something' Hölderlin cries, but the stage direction reads: 'He springs forward with an armful of manuscript pages, some papers fall to the floor. He stands for a moment confused, turns slowly around, goes to the sofa, sinks down on it' (p. 181). The function of poetry is seen as keeping the utopian idea of change alive when the revolution congeals in politics, so that Hölderlin's poetry is a 'mythology of hope' which acts as 'a paradigm' for 'those who come after' (pp. 57, 135).

As major characters, poets and particularly dramatists tend to be self-portraits reflecting their author's position. Even though the supposedly objective voice of theatre may be emphasised – Frisch's universalised Modern Man, Weiss' Hölderlin who analyses his psychological situation as an artist in the third person – the answers have mainly personal relevance. But, at bottom, introspective questions about the perception of reality and the artist's social role are stylistic questions: the treatment of subject material and the extent to which an audience can be manipulated. Technical experimentation may be individual, although normally, as in Dürrenmatt's borrowings from Wedekind or Frisch's use of Wilder, it is related to prior examples, and even non-conformist experiments like Vostell's 'Happenings' can be traced to the influence of American 'Guerilla Theatre'. The development of a style is something communal, and the history of postwar German theatre is largely that of the different artistic groupings.

As in England, where Joan Littlewood and the Royal Court Theatre influenced the tone of English theatre as a whole by encouraging particular groups of playwrights, certain directors were responsible for establishing new trends as they emerged in Germany – Peter Zadek's pop art in Bremen, Erwin Piscator's documentary theatre in Berlin, Claus Peymann's promotion of Handke and Thomas Bernhard, Hans Hollman's revival of Horváth which provided a model for the modern *Volksstück* (folk play). However the initiative for stylistic developments came from informal but influential associations of writers, Group 47, Group 61, Work-Circle 70, and to a lesser extent the Frankfurt Forum for Literature and the Vienna Group. These supplied feedback and a critical frame which was specifically intended to encourage new approaches and determined the direction they took. Unlike the literary movements of the twenties, they were not defined by exclusive theories and issued no manifestoes. The only English or American equivalent was Arnold Wesker's short-lived Centre 42, but that had the primarily tactical aim of providing direct contact between socialist playwrights and their intended working-class public. The focus of the groupings in the German literary scene was stylistic, and they show the contours of the period.

The most significant was Group 47, which set the standard and format, and could fairly claim to represent all major German authors up to 1966. Founded by Hans Werner Richter as a follow up to *The Call* (*Der Ruf* published from August 1946 to April

1947, when it was prohibited by the occupying powers), Group 47 was a forum for 'authors from all zones, all classes, all trends' to read their work and exchange views. Its line was taken from an article in *The Call*, 'German calligraphy or: Glory and Misery of Modern Literature' (November 1946) which called for a new linguistic approach to replace the rhetorical and semantic perversions of fascism, and the discussion of the relationship between subject, language and ideology remained a central concern. 'It was agreed that this new age must live and experience differently and therefore write differently; that there must be a revaluation in order to be accurate';[43] and as the issues changed with the rebuilding of German society and the tensions of the 1960s, there was a continual search for new forms. There was also one constant quality, a self-conscious and reflexive element, aiming at authenticity but in effect tending to substitute a concentration on style for socially relevant statement, which culminated in the linguistic abstraction of Handke.

Group 47, with its constantly changing participants, can be seen as a graph of literary activity. Almost all the post-war novelists and most of the major dramatists read at its meetings, Grass attributed his artistic development up to the mid 1960s to its influence and Frisch, even though he never participated personally, acknowledged that it 'had a formative function stylistically; not like a "school" at all, but setting criteria'.[44] The first style to emerge in the readings was deliberately bare, anti-illusionistic and unsentimental, and became known as *Kahlschlag* ('root and branch' or 'stripped down') prose. The major exponent was Richter himself, whose novels used ruthlessly simplified, colourless dialogue and the techniques of news reportage to create a photographic realism comparable to that of Truman Capote's *In Cold Blood*. The equivalent in theatre terms was the 'grey period' of the Berliner Ensemble, epitomised by Brecht's 1949 production of *Mother Courage*. This stressed the cynical perversion of ideals in religious war, and the bare stage, the cold intellectuality of the acting was explicitly intended to be 'a withdrawal course for the drug addicts' from the rhetorical emotionalism and stage heroics that had characterised the 'narcotic' drama of the Third Reich.[45] In the early 1950s this denotative plainness was superseded by the rediscovered surrealists (at the 1951 meeting one participant was reported to have exclaimed 'one more mention of Kafka and I shall scream!') and the readings included Hildesheimer's grotesque symbolism, Walser's early interior monologues and Ilse Aichinger's subjective, visionary poetry. This shift from the factual to the psychological or poetic was initially a reaction to the new materialism in German society, and the literary forms were partly derivative (Kafka and Borchert) or imported (James Joyce and the French existentialists), but it created receptive conditions for absurd drama, explaining its immediate adoption in the mid 1950s. It is the context for Grass' *Flood* (*Hochwasser*) and *Onkel, Onkel*, read at the Group's meetings in 1956 and 1957; and the imagistic expressionism of Weiss' early work also shows its influence. An alternative response to the growing economic complacency was satiric, represented by Böll's work or Peter Hirche's war play, *Triumph in a Thousand Years* (*Triumph in Tausend Jahren*, 1955) which looks forward to Walser's *Rabbit Race* (*Eiche und Angora*, 1962); and Grass combined both approaches in the grotesque parody of his novel *The Tin Drum* (*Die Blechtrommel*, 1958). The next major stylistic shift can be traced to the double impact of the Berlin Wall and the Eichman trial in 1961. Immediacy and authenticity became the criteria, stories were discarded for sociological collages, and already by the 1962 meeting the material presented was summed up as 'depiction and description...bureaucratic reports and military bulletins'.[46] Barely a year later these qualities of apparently direct presentation had spread from the reading circle to the stage as documentary drama. Discussion of the political function of literature in Group 47 at this point was a major factor in Weiss' change in technique and approach from *Marat/Sade* to *The Investigation*, as well as perhaps being partly responsible for the sudden switch in Grass' style represented by *The Plebeians*. Weiss read passages from *Marat/Sade* in 1963, stressing the rhythmic structures by beats on a hand drum; Grass read the first two acts of *The Plebeians* in 1964. Both revised their work after comments and suggestions from the Group, and *The Investigation* can be seen as a direct response to one of the critics in the Group, Marcel Reich-Raniki, who publicly challenged German authors to use the Auschwitz trial as literary material.

The final stylistic innovation from within Group 47 was signalled by Handke's attack on literary principles in general and detailed, descriptive 'pseudo-realism' in particular at the Princeton meeting in 1966 – both the high-water mark of the Group's prestige and the point at which it ceased to be a literary force, turning into a publishers' market which discouraged genuine experimentation. Peter Handke, normally taken to be a unique innovator, is a good example of the way influences spread through such groups as 47. Even his 'anti-literature' stance follows a consistent concern of the Group. His initial reduction of drama to linguistic analysis is a variation on the original *Kahlschlag* prose, while during the late 1950s and early 1960s there were a series of writers who discarded story-line and continuity and experimented with work structured on linguistic elements alone. In 1964, Hildesheimer had presented a radio-play, *Monologue*, a speech collage in the Handke manner, exploring language as a psychological determinant and exposing its moral effects. In 1967, the Group prize went to Jürgen Becker for *Margins* (*Ränder*), a novel based on philosophical premises very similar to Handke's: objects being only defined by changes (the 'margins' of the title), reality is the medium of consciousness itself, and consciousness is defined by language. This development which led to and surrounded Handke's early work can also be traced back to the Vienna Group of 'concrete poets' in the 1950s, whose use of language was based on constructivism and Wittgenstein, and who experimented with a theatre of 'facts', public acts of destruction intended as exercises in awareness.

The most significant trend after Group 47 was spearheaded by writers who broke away in the early 1960s in response to the social problems caused by increasing automation and the running down of industrial expansion in Germany. The aim of Group 61 was to represent the problems and interests of the working classes, to which attention had been drawn by a wave of strikes that began in 1960; but with the absence of any significant communist influence, the Party then being illegal in west Germany, this Group was centred on 'coming to artistic terms with the industrial working world', rather than an ideological position. The conventional depiction of workers in literature was rejected as a bourgeois perspective based on alien, distorting values, 'exotic', or at best sentimentalising the issues. The key was seen as finding a suitable style for dealing with the social effects of advanced technology, and the major problems were defined as 'participation in management, automation, cybernetics and the 40-hour week' – not the class war – and 'for this the workers' poetry of the twenties and thirties cannot serve as an example, nor the attempts of "Writing Workers" in the DDR'.[47]

Three interrelated approaches were used to develop a new style. Shopfloor workers were encouraged to write autobiographically about their jobs; but this initially resulted in traditional, poetic expression which clearly showed the undigested influence of German high school education. Even the most successful, Max von der Grun's novels, were based on nineteenth-century naturalism and used narrator-heroes as a focus for empathy which limited the scope of social commentary. Alternatively, writers took industrial jobs as investigative reporters, but as Günter Wallraff found, this created a problem of perspective. 'As a critic pointed out with justice, I could never be in the situation of those who have to work their whole lives in these circumstances and are completely at their mercy...For the social truth of my reports, that is a minus'.[48] The third variation was to print unedited interviews with workers, but this had the disadvantage that the subjects lacked any wider view: 'they betray themselves by accepting that the conditions in which they have to work are alright as they are, or cannot be changed'.[49] One way out of the dilemma was to establish seminars, with Trades Union support, to develop literary guide-lines through political education. Grass, Walser, and Wallraff all became involved with these seminars in the seventies, and Work-Circle 70 was established. The gains were an extension of literature into the forms of 'the bulletin, and short agitatory verses which almost had the characteristics of leaflets'.[50] Other experimental solutions were to extend the reportage, so that it revealed the structure of 'the system' by concentrating on the subterfuges necessary for the writer to get his material and the reactions of the management to his findings, or so that it focussed not on the comments in an interview but on the language. This was achieved most effectively by Erika Runge who set the phraseology and assumptions of the supposedly classless, affluent society in question by highlighting the workers' deprived vocabulary and stunted capacity for expression.

Although there are surface similarities to the 'Bitterfeld line' in east German literature, Group 61 developed its formal solutions from documentary literature; and work like Wallraff's or Runge's shows the influence of contemporary media technology. Questions of perspective and authenticity were raised in a way that set new standards for documentary drama. Their rejection of 'pseudo-objective or aesthetic impartiality'[51] is reflected in the way dramatists like Weiss switched from the balanced presentation of apparently open questions to overt commitment at the end of the 1960s; while the factual integrity of every detail (which became a requirement for Group 61, not just a stylistic principle, after repeated legal actions) led to plays such as Enzensberger's *Havana Hearing* (*Das Verhör von Habana*, 1970) where dialogue was taken directly from court transcripts, without even the compression and heightening of *The Investigation*. Group 61 also gave rise to the Recklinghausen theatre festival of 'discussion plays' and social documentaries, ranging from *The Havana Hearing* to *Employers* (*Arbeitgeber*), a simple demonstration of the letter of the law on workers' election of management representatives, which improvised on comments from the audience to show how their preconceptions differed from the statutes. Group 61 dominated German literature in the early 1970s and the development of a popularising dramatist and director like Fassbinder from linguistic surrealism to TV documentaries on working conditions is a good indication of its general influence. Erika Runge's approach also provides the background for the minimal dialogue and stark presentation of the way the exploited accept the brutality of their existence in plays like those of Kroetz – some of which have also been filmed by Fassbinder.

Another aspect of Group 61 work, creating 'awareness of the technological nature of modern society' by helping the workers themselves to express their perceptions and 'so contribute to changing social conditions in favour of the worker',[52] was echoed in the 'happening'. This became an accepted aspect of stage work in the 1960s through Claus Bremer's productions in Ulm. As a theatrical phenomenon it developed independently, a mixture of futurist theories and American examples, Marinetti and Rauschenberg; but its aims paralleled those of Group 61 – to 'make people aware of the time they live in' through participation which 'alters their attitude to themselves and things around them'.[53] German 'happenings' were rather more structured than their American equivalents, and their qualities can be illustrated by one of the Ulm productions. The audience, split into random groups, were taken from the theatre through the town in buses fitted with loudspeakers, over which a tape of verbal *objets trouvés* from news reports and advertising commercials was broadcast. The airport, a car-wash and a slaughterhouse were on the itinerary, as was the town square, equipped with television screens showing distorted pictures. The audience's reactions, picked up on hidden microphones, were amplified in the form of broken speech fragments, and each 'scene' was given a title. For instance a graveyard was labelled 'The chronic aspect of consumerism'. Another location, a dark field announced as 'A place in the sun', showed the intended effect of juxtaposition and contrast: the ground was heaped with bones illuminated by dim blue 'death lights' and the audience were directed to 'run around and tell someone your life story', while being offered praline chocolates to eat. In practice this type of participatory drama was frequently merely be-wildering, but in theory it was intended to be highly political. It challenged the audience to reconsider their preconceptions (not unlike Handke) by putting the banal in a grotesque perspective, and attempted to persuade them 'not to accept everything that [Society] expects...to support their opinion against other opinions, to protest against injustice...to show civil courage'.[54]

The significance of stylistic experimentation, the attempt to extend the subject matter of drama, can also be seen in the Experimenta festivals organised by the Academy of Theatre Arts in Frankfurt. In theory the aim of the Experimenta was to explore the range of theatrical expression and the possible variations in actor/audience relationship. In practice, as in *What a Theatre!* (*So ein Theater*, Christoph Derschaus, 1971), a parody of round table discussion on the function of theatre and its social effectiveness, it tended to become a denunciation of theatre as such on the grounds that the commercial system trivialised even radical experiments, turning new vision into novelty value. However, the Experimenta did succeed in providing a platform for some of the most significant new developments – Handke's *Offending the Audience* (*Publikumsbeschimpfung*, 1966); Weiss' departure from his established style in *Song of the Lusitanian Bogey* (*Gesang vom Lusitanischen Popanz*, 1967); Bazon Brock's attempt to transfer pop art to the theatre; Peter Stein's production of *Tasso* (1969) which attacked 'the classics' by using an artificial acting style to undercut Goethe's characterisation, and direct address from the actors to question the relevance of their roles; as well as two of Kroetz' first plays in 1971. Apart from testing new initiatives, the Experimenta also gave exposure to experimental theatre from outside Germany, notably Beckett's short plays (1966), Ann Jellicoe and Arrabal (1967) and the New York Bread and Puppet Theatre (1969). To some extent any undertaking of this kind is self-defeating since it tends to fossilise experiment by institutionalising it – but the constant questioning of criteria has been demonstrably effective in forming new styles, and the works staged have included most of the more interesting theatrical developments in west Germany since 1966.

In contrast to the productive questioning of dramatic principles in the west, the DDR gives an impression of monolithic coherence. The area of discussion has been carefully defined by political criteria, while theoretical debates are 'official' (being usually initiated by academics and spokesmen at Party conferences) and therefore prescriptive. The basic issues may be similar (one leading journal is *Sinn und Form – Meaning and Style*), but the area of experimentation is limited by firm guide-lines. Theatre is seen as a Schillerian 'moral institution', and artistic considerations are subordinated to a concept of social relevance that requires subjects to be 'representative' and effects 'positive'. Within this frame the most significant arguments have been about the relative value of epic techniques versus socialist realism, and the function of classics in the modern context. This is consensus theatre – 'our socialist art is not the result of any formal innovations; its new quality is shown distinctively in its socialist content'[55] – and only Brecht was able to establish any independence.

On the plus side east German authors are assured of the social significance of their work; what western Prime Minister can one imagine making official speeches about theatre? But this flattering attention also has the disadvantage that nothing which is not politically approved can be performed, no matter what its artistic merits.

The major guidelines were established in 1951 when the Congress of the SED Central Committee proclaimed a 'struggle against formalism in art and literature' and set up a State Commission for the Arts to control the theatre. Brecht's *The Trial of Lucullus* (*Vehör des Lukullus*) had to be revised and *Days of the Commune* (*Die Tage der Kommune*) was banned, only reaching the stage in 1961 when 'the example of the Paris Commune which was destroyed by false humanity' could be interpreted as a defence of 'the correct use of power by the new class, the proletariat' in 'securing the national frontiers' (i.e., building the Berlin wall)![56] The type of drama approved was the 'factory play' (*Betriebstück*) – melodramatic treatments of socialist triumph over western industrial spies and saboteurs, or the conversion of recalcitrant individualists to communal work – which Kipphardt's drama-turge, Amadeus Färbel, summed up in *Wanted Urgently: Shakespeare* as

kitchen-living-room, political meeting, sabotage, socialist brigade... These plays are like the pap in a cow's stomach, except that instead of grass it's thoughts and old sheets of newspaper that are regurgitated.[57]

In 1959 after an attack on 'dialectical teaching theatre' for 'sectarian tendencies' by no less than Walter Ulbricht himself, the SED called for a 'writing worker's movement'. Known as the 'Bitterfeld line', this led to the formation of 'workers and peasants theatre groups'. Factory workers were also enlisted by professional theatre companies, particularly in Halle and Mag-deburg, to advise on play selection; critical discussions following performances were organised with working class audiences; and workers with literary talent were encouraged to use their own experience as subjects for drama. By comparison with Group 61, the results were conventional, and the qualities are well illustrated by Horst Salamon's *Yellow Mica* (*Katzengold*, 1964). Salamon, an inspector in the mine rescue service, bases his plot on a pit disaster; but the realistic details are relegated to background for a sentimentalised black and white depiction of the evils of egoism and the virtues of socialism. The first version ended in the self-sacrifice of a misunderstood hero, whose reputation had been blackened by his jealous superior. Revision (with professional advice) turned the tragic action into suspense and removed 'negative' elements. The 'villain' became inexperienced instead of viciously self-centred and was reformed by remorse for the death of the hero, who is then found to be still alive after all.

This is a fair example of the approved social realist style. No Marxist would object to the principle laid down by the editor of the influential *New German Literature* (*Neue deutsche Literatur*) that all work 'should be written from a clear political standpoint, so being partisan',[58] but the artistic limitations of associating objectivity with a particular political analysis become obvious as soon as one descends from the general to specifics. Thematic demands have stylistic implications, and a statement by the Chairman of the Department of Aesthetics at Leipzig University is worth quoting at length because the rhetoric is indicative of what was expected from the theatre. Literary works are to be judged by 'whether they embody an artistic truth', which sounds unexceptional, but

given this premise, it is essential to note the distinction between truth and honesty...we must energetically reject any attempt to apply an abstract concept of honesty. Such as: the honest writer or philosopher is one who says and writes what he thinks...we must not allow ourselves to be fobbed off with an abstractly formulated 'honesty', but must ask what the poet believes and feels, what his commitment is and for what his artistry fights. Most intensely we salute the honesty of a Maxim Gorki...of a Pablo Neruda...and a Bruno Apitz, who make it a point of honour to perceive the great truth of our epoch, the historical mission of the working class and the natural justice of the socialist structure, to preach it artistically and to show how the working class carefully takes into their hands, classifies and develops everything great and valuable that mankind has created up to now in its cultural development.[59]

Integrity becomes synonymous with uncritical affirmation, the function of art is to present ideals for the public to follow, and standards are to be taken from the cultural heritage. This causes thematic problems for drama. The establishment of a socialist state is assumed by definition to have resolved any basic contradiction between the interests of the individual and society, and at the same time characters are to be 'socially anchored' figures in situations 'characteristic of our time' with specific 'class' (i.e., proletarian) not 'universally human' qualities.[60] This limits serious dramatic opposition in practice to conflicts between the younger generation and anachronistic survivors from the pre-socialist past, of which Helmut Baierl's *Frau Flinz* (1961) is a good example. In the 1960s, plays that contained other forms of conflict were banned. Peter Hacks' *Anxieties and Power* (*Die Sorgen und die Macht*, 1960 – revised version, 1962) and *Moritz Tassow* (1964) were taken off after only a few performances; rehearsals for Heiner Müller's *The Building-Site* (*Der Bau*, 1965) under Benno Besson were broken off, and his *Change of Residence...* (*Die Umsiedlerin oder das Leben auf dem Land*, 1961), forbidden after a single student performance, only reached the professional stage (as *Die Bauern – Peasants*) in 1976.

After the events of 1956 in Hungary and Poland the official line hardened, and it became clear that good intentions were not enough. What defines a subject as acceptable is not simply the author's commitment, but a play's effect on an audience. In 1959,

Kipphardt was dismissed from the Deutsches Theater for refusing a (dramatically inept) propagandist play by Gustav von Wangenheim, while a speaker at the Congress of the Free German Federation of Trades Unions asked

Where are the sources of art? There where the impression of our red flags in the sunlight on May 1st at our great class demonstration incites a worker to paint a picture of waving flags, of marching masses...Art begins there where the delegates to this congress, stirred by communal experience, joyful over the solidarity with our Soviet colleagues, rise up and sing the International together.[61]

Art, from its inception to its effect, is conceived as emotive and inspirational; and this theatre of enthusiasm explains the attack on Brecht as 'in the camp of the bourgeois left-wing radical'.[62] The 'abstract intellectuality' of epic theatre and its dialectical structure, which presented subjects from opposing viewpoints, was liable to misinterpretation. 'Open ended' plays, dramatising problems without suggesting solutions, were seen as lacking in 'commitment'; and 'the theory and practice of the so-called dialectical theatre' (that of Brecht's followers, particularly Hacks and Kipphardt) was attacked because its artistic methods 'do not correspond to the methods of socialist realism, and therefore have a bourgeois and petty-bourgeois, not a proletarian class-content'.[63] As a result, paradoxically, Brecht's influence has been greater in the west, where for example there were forty-two productions of his plays in the 1974/5 season as against five in the DDR, and the limitations on the dramatist can be indicated by the production history of Hacks' *Anxieties and Power*. Complying with the requirement that plays present 'everyday stories' about industrial workers based on actual not invented material, Hacks followed up a letter by three steelworkers published in *Neues Deutschland*, and researched material for his play at a factory in Bitterfeld where the Party's exhortation to exceed production norms had resulted in such a drop in quality that the briquettes manufactured were useless. After extensive rewriting suggested by a committee of director, dramaturge and critics, through which the emphasis was transferred from the original, politically embarrassing industrial problem to the workers' search for (approved) solutions to the situation – which did not include letters to the newspapers – the play was tried out in Senftenburg in 1960. Further thematic revision was required before it could be accepted by the Deutsches

Theater (where Hacks was the resident playwright) in 1962 – when it was attacked in a key note address to the March SED congress. The play was promptly withdrawn even though after two script changes it followed the clichés of socialist realism so closely as to be almost a parody. In the final version the drop in productivity from restoring quality causes impotence in the protagonist, who joins the communist party and solves his sexual problems by introducing technical improvements in the factory as a result of his new ideological clarity. This unintentional comedy was not the reason for the official censure, but the lack of 'objectivity' inherent in dialectical drama. 'Hacks...obviously believes that we create new mistakes in overcoming mistakes...The Marxist dialectic doesn't simply stress the battle of opposites, but seeks their unity and reciprocal penetration.'[64]

It is fashionable for DDR theorists to acknowledge that developments in socialist realism 'depend on its positive relationship to science'.[65] But in practice the question of stylistic relevance to contemporary conditions is reduced to 'typical characters in typical situations', and the ideal formal requirements' of drama have been summarised in highly traditional terms:

concrete plots, fates that can be followed through, verifiable attitudes and actions, recommendations to the audience which arise out of the play, figures whose exemplary development has the goal of qualitative alteration.[66]

Socialism seen through a socialist perspective requires empathy instead of critical distance, and although the demand for characters 'who bear the qualities of the new men, whose actions are fine and exemplary', has more recently been modified to the requirement that a play show 'the development of the socialist personality in the collective' (reflecting the insight that individualised heroes are inappropriate to the mass-realities of industrial society), the intended effect is still 'that the spectator identifies himself with the figures who embody the Party and the working class'.[67]

After Czechoslovakia in 1968, prominence was given to two other didactic forms. The 'Lenin Celebration' was accompanied by an emphasis on historical drama which drew parallels between the October Revolution and contemporary problems, while the Halle theatre initiated a mix of documentary and 1920s agitprop techniques in *Teaching and Learning Stimulus* (*Anregung für*

Lehrende und Lernende, 1970). This was a two-part cabaret of sketches, songs and reportage in the style of TV current-affairs programmes, broken by discussion with the audience.

Apart from overt didacticism, justifiably attacked by Baierl for 'flattening' character by making every speech, even 'in bed or in the hay', refer to a play's 'problem', the main direction in DDR drama since the mid 1960s has been the development of what is called 'the great form'.[68] In the search for 'new classics' the two leading playwrights, Hacks and Müller, have turned to poetic history and mythical romance (Hacks' *Margarete in Aix*, 1969 and *Adam und Eva*, 1973) or to adaptations of Aristophanes, Plautus and Sophocles – via Kleist and Hölderlin – and Shakespeare: Hacks' *The Peace* (*Der Frieden*, 1962), and *Amphitryon* (1967); Müller's *Oedipus Tyrann* (1967), *As You Like It* (*Wie es Euch gefällt*, 1968) and *Macbeth* (1972). The general west-German response rejects this trend as an 'emigration' from reality to a formal illusion of harmony. But even farce and operetta can have considerable acerbity and critical point as Walter Felsenstein showed in his brilliant productions for the Komische Oper, which revealed Offenbach as biting social commentary. And in spite of critical disapproval Hacks, who defines the 'proper theme of contemporary art' as 'the relationship of utopia to reality',[69] achieved a technical brilliance and a stylistic virtuosity in his poetry which has made *Amphitryon* the second most frequently produced contemporary play in west Germany since 1964. For Hacks, what illuminates reality is precisely the gulf between the utopian vision on his stage and our everyday experience, and in a play like *Amphitryon* the classical harmony of his later comedy is heightened to contrast with the modern world. Müller, on the other hand, gives his adaptations direct relevance. His *Macbeth*, a fatalistic analysis of the impersonal violence of power comparable to Edward Bond's *Lear*, shows the emotional immediacy that even a verse treatment of traditional material can have by the vehement response it provoked – mainly on the lines of 'nothing is more alien to the spirit of socialism than a pessimistic interpretation of world history'.[70] The models for both Hacks and Müller are Brecht's adaptations, which formed the basis of his post-war work and established the principle of *Aneignung* ('appropriating' classics to make them part of our modern awareness); and conversely the success of Brecht's *Coriolanus* in Wekwerth's production (1964) was partly due to the reciprocal influence of the 'new classicism'. The Shakespearian concept of passionate tragedy was grafted on to Brecht's 'scientific' analysis of a social example to such an extent that commenting on Ekkehard Schall's performance as Coriolanus, whose 'fall' he found 'too cold-blooded... In short, I miss the tragedy at this point', Wekwerth stated the actor's aim should be 'to involve the audience so deeply that they are intensely disturbed at the moment of his fall and feel pity for his inability to learn'.[71]

Although the 'new classicism' has produced some good theatre, it is more a refuge from the politics which prevented Hacks' and Müllers' *Zeitstücke* from being performed than a viable method for presenting contemporary issues on the stage. Most critics seem to believe that the situation eased after the eighth SED congress in 1971 which approved critical disagreement within 'collective guidelines', and Ulrich Plenzdorf's *The New Sorrows of Young W* (*Die neuen Leiden des jungen W*, 1972) is often seen as a sign of this. A variation on Goethe's story, Plenzdorf's Werther does not commit suicide for love. He is destroyed by the conflict between his non-conformist individualism and the collective values of society. But plays in an unconventional style still go unproduced; and (like Wolf Biermann, the first gifted political poet since Brecht) one of the DDR's promising young playwrights, Thomas Brasch – whose *Paper Tiger* (*Der Papiertiger*) was performed in Austin, Texas in 1977 – has been forced to follow Kipphardt and Hartmut Lange into west Germany. Critics, too, betray dissatisfaction with the general quality of the work that does reach the stage. A frequent complaint is 'provincialism', and summaries of theatre seasons in *Sonntag* (1962/3), *Theater der Zeit* (1975) and *Neue Deutsche Literatur* (1976) indicate why. In 1962/3 out of a total of twenty-six new works by east German authors, nine were subtitled *Lustspiel* (light comedy), five *Schwank* (farce) one *Komödie*, and four of the remainder were detective-thrillers or children's plays; while from 1972 to 1976 although 160 new plays reached the fifty stages in the DDR, only fourteen were produced more than five times.

One problem has been the isolation of the DDR theatre. If western plays had been available as catalysts or comparisons the 'new classicism' would probably never have been established; but only a very limited range of foreign plays (except for work from 'socialist brother countries') has been produced. Günther Weisenborn in the 1960s and, more recently, Weiss are the only west Germans, Sean O'Casey the only contemporary English-speaking playwright to be performed with any regularity. The stylistic advances in the west are rejected as the products of a capitalist 'culture industry' which substitutes the 'superficial invention and development of methods' for 'the presentation of experience';[72] and the criteria for accepting western plays for production are symptomatic of the insularity of the DDR.

1. Has the author...in a searching observation of his environment, the society, the state in which he has to live, recognised what degrades the lives of [his fellow] men? In his search for answers has he attempted to base himself on the first scientific world view?...

The second criterion is that the play should present a society which is clearly distinguishable from the 'so very different conditions' in the DDR without being so alien as to appear incomprehensible – in other words that the subject must not only be the evils of capitalism, but correspond to the DDR Party line – while the final criterion in effect implies that only the unsuccessful are eligible:

3. Will the theatrical presentation of the play in question, or a project of the author's, help him to overcome isolation in his homeland?[73]

4. *Images*

Just as the German postwar experience of bombed-out cities and military occupation, the 'economic miracle' of industrial regeneration, student revolution and urban guerillas, the cold war division of the country and the Berlin wall is qualitatively different to the social history of America and the rest of Europe, so German drama developed in different patterns. Its main trends, being direct responses to specifically national situations and political pressures, do not correspond to the wider European and American theatre movements. As a result, even though foreign plays, in particular Thornton Wilder at the end of the 1940s and more recently Edward Bond, have acted as models, while conversely the major German dramatists have achieved considerable success on the world stage, it is sometimes difficult to see their place in the international context. The attempt to re-establish poetic drama by Eliot, Fry and Maxwell Anderson, the neo-naturalism of O'Neill's last plays, Williams and Wesker, or the Artaudian experiments of Genet and the Living Theatre had comparatively little impact on German playwrights. The only exception is the theatre of the absurd.

The importance of the absurdist movement in the German theatrical scene tends to be underestimated because its leading German exponents, Hildesheimer and Michelsen, have produced only minor work, while its philosophy seems out of tune with the overwhelmingly political concern that distinguishes German drama. However, the uncomfortable and uncompromising vision of the French absurdists, with its roots in the destruction of war, the humiliation of France's defeat and the spectacle of her leaders collaborating with the enemy, was in many ways appropriate to the German situation. Its anti-materialistic, poetic principles were also attractive as a counterweight to the philistine prosperity of the late 1950s and early 1960s, and its influence can be widely traced. Not only did Grass and Dorst develop their styles out of the absurdist approach, but Weiss' early plays are similar, aspects of both Dürrenmatt's and Handke's work are comparable, and Thomas Bernhard demonstrates its continuing significance. Beckett and Ionesco first emerged from experimental studio and student stages to the professional theatre through German productions;

78

since 1958 almost all the premières of Ionesco's plays have been in Germany; and both Ionesco and Beckett have directed major productions of their own work (*Endgame* in Berlin, 1967, and *Waiting for Godot*, 1975; *Victims of Duty*, Zürich, 1968) – an indication of the serious interest in the ideas of absurdist theatre, which as a result were better understood than anywhere else outside Paris. However, German dramatists adapted the absurdist approach rather than imitating it, and the way in which they deviated highlights some of the unique qualities of German drama. At the same time it means that standards cannot be directly transferred from Beckett and Ionesco to even Hildesheimer, who explicitly labelled himself an absurdist.

The premises for the theatre of the absurd, outlined by Camus in his essay 'The Myth of Sisyphus', were that technological progress had accentuated the gap between human aspirations and achievements, revealing the meaninglessness of existence, that therefore any 'higher aim or meaning' in life was illusory and religious or ideological beliefs were at best forms of self-deception.[1] Metaphors and prayers having been 'crushed' by mechanised warfare, ethical restraints or motivating hopes are seen as equally invalid in a context of 'cruel mathematics' (pp. 63, 12). 'Absurdity' is defined as a perception of the disproportion between reason and the 'primitive hostility of the world', between man's 'intentions and the reality' (pp. 11, 22). The emphasis is on confrontation, divorce, in the light of which consciously living without illusions is the only possible affirmation. Thus for Camus lucidity has a moral value and the function of literature is to transmit existential awareness. But since any separable meaning is automatically counterfeit, being yet another deceptive rationalisation, this awareness could only be expressed through the form, 'the concrete signifies nothing more than itself' (p. 72). The medium, in a way that McLuhan was later to popularise, was the message because for the absurdist 'it is not a matter of explaining and solving, but of experiencing and describing' (p. 70).

Camus' essay struck a nerve in a wide range of postwar authors who are not normally thought of as absurdists, and Frisch's *Don Juan or The Love of Geometry* (*Don Juan oder die Liebe der Geometrie*, 1953) is almost a gloss on one of Camus' examples of the absurd man: a Don Juan whose acts express the logic of 'intelligence that knows its frontiers' and in whom 'sensual pleasure winds up in asceticism' (pp. 52, 56). Even within the

79

Parisian school of absurdists, however, Camus' ideas were formulated in different ways. At one end of the scale plays like *The Bald
Prima Donna* (1950) satirised bourgeois society, attacking
conventions of behaviour and assumptions of order. But
characteristic absurd drama either aspired to an ideal of 'pure
theatre' in which 'a play is a whole performance, the subject is
only a pretext, and the text is only a score'[2] – hence Ionesco's
emphasis that *The Bald Prima Donna* was 'a parody of a play, a
comedy of comedies'[3] – or presented a vision of the absurdity of
existence in dream-imagery. It is perhaps typical of the logical
quality in German theatrical experimentation that these two
directions were given their fullest expression on German stages.
Beckett's Berlin production of *Endgame* epitomised the self-
reflexive line, which he summed up elsewhere with typical ambiguity as 'just play'.[4] Ionesco's *Victims of Duty* in Zürich provided
an example of 'drama that is not symbolist but symbolic; not
allegorical, but mythical; that springs from our everlasting
anguish; drama where the invisible becomes visible, whose
ideas are translated into concrete images, into reality'.[5]

Beckett's staging concentrated on bringing out the thematic
implications of the form in his play. He arrived in Berlin having
already worked out every detail with a mathematic precision which
reflected the carefully structured symmetry in the text, the exactly
balanced numbers of entries, the description of Clov's kitchen as
a perfect cube; and his primary concern in directing the play was
to create patterns out of exact repetitions or geometrical visual
shapes. Hamm's chair had to be dead centre on stage, and his
posture at the end was to be identical with the opening. In the
prayer sequence the three pairs of hands and bowed heads were
organised into exact equilateral triangles, and whenever Nagg and
Nell appeared their hands were equidistant on the rims of the two
ashcans. Each time verbal patterns recurred the actors were
instructed to use the same tone of voice, and as Beckett pointed
out 'there are no accidents in *Endgame*, everything is built up of
analogies and repetitions'.[6] This patterning, which Beckett
specifically called 'pythagorean', is a direct illustration of Camus'
concept of absurdist art as the expression of 'lucid thought' which
'repudiates itself' in the act of thinking (p. 72). Applied to a
disintegrating universe, rational ideals of harmony and proportion
are bitterly ironic. This effect of negative artifice, echoed in the
complete separation of questions and replies, word and gesture,

as well as in the colourless staccato of the delivery (Beckett's constant directive was 'More monotony!'), also relates to the positive aspect of the play's statement. From the title on in *Endgame*, the element of play is stressed – Hamm's first words are 'Me to play'; his penultimate sentence is 'since that's the way we're playing it...let's play it that way'[7] – and Beckett's production underlined the chess image. Clov was made to move in zig zags, the knight's two squares forward and one to the side, and Hamm's role was explained to the actor as 'the king in this chess game that was lost from the beginning. He knows from the start that he has made nothing but senseless moves.'[8] The stage has literally become the board to which Pozzo had (rhetorically) compared it in *Waiting for Godot*, so that this form/content unity where a game becomes its own justification, a refusal of 'significance' being the only significant statement possible in a meaningless world, is extended to include the theatre through the double meaning of the word 'play'. Throughout rehearsals Beckett referred to *Endgame* as 'simply a basis for acting' in which the meaning was 'purely dramatic' and could only be understood in (and as) performance, and in an unusually frank moment he commented:

the link between the individual and things no longer exists...There are so many things. The eye is as unable to grasp them as the intelligence to understand them. Therefore one creates one's own world, *un univers à part*, in order to withdraw...to escape from chaos into an ever simpler world...I have progressively simplified situations and people, *toujours plus simples*...The value of the theatre lies for me in this. One can set up a small world with its own rules, order the game as if on a chess-board – Indeed, even the game of chess is too complicated.[9]

By contrast Ionesco emphasised the subconscious, instinctive level in his play. Like Beckett, he came to rehearsals with all the details of his production pre-set, but instead of being elaborated intellectually the actors' portrayal of their roles had to correspond to a primary image, and his directives were repeatedly prefaced with 'In my original vision...' *Victims of Duty* is in some ways a puzzle-play and has attracted a multiplicity of interepretations, but Ionesco gave it a coherent, straightforward meaning. He outlined his motive for writing it as 'spontaneous research' into 'the unconscious', stated that the scenes (in particular the sequence where the central figure, entangled in a wood, sinks down beneath the mud, reappears as a child and climbs up a ladder to fly in a strong blue light) were transcriptions of his own dreams, noted that according to a psychologist these were dreams which Jung had catalogued, thus linking the subjective with archetypes, and commented that

the main theme. . .is the revolt against the *super-ego* and the defeat of this super-ego. The policeman – that is censorship, the conscience of society, which is also the father, that is the incarnation of society – is killed by the anarchist. . .Like all new, revolutionary tyrannies this tyranny too sets Choubert back in the social order and imposes on him the behaviour of a child, that is of a repressed person. . .a super-ego with the beard of an anarchist.[10]

From this perspective Choubert becomes the ego, 'the inner I', Madeleine the id, and the stage was transformed into a mindscape, with Madeleine and the Policeman acting as twining creeper and tree in the forest scene. Hence the figures were not presented in psychological terms as individuals; their changes in age, relationship, attitude were sudden switches that reproduced the arbitrary transformations and startling contrasts of dreams, and the actors were instructed not to search for personal motivations. At the same time the different scenes were acted with as much physical realism as possible. The descent was illusionistic with Choubert, lit with a green light from beneath, gradually sinking through a trap downstage centre. For the flight a ladder was lowered from the flies and the actor's climb was real, not mimed. This followed Ionesco's principle that 'authentic realism only exists in concrete symbols',[11] and the effect was to make the stage an image rather than an impression of a dream.

Beneath the obvious differences between these two productions there are certain shared elements. As various critics have pointed out the stage in *Endgame* can be taken to represent the inside of a head, with the two windows as eyes, an interpretation which brings Beckett's play close to *Victims of Duty*. Conversely in *Victims of Duty* the self-reflexive theatricality which characterised Beckett's production of *Endgame* is also present, as in one scene where Ionesco had Choubert parodying a series of outdated acting styles while the Policeman and Madeleine took the role of a viciously insensitive and shallow-minded pair in the audience. And the qualities of these two productions can be clearly seen running through one direction in German drama. There is, of course, no question of influence since these performances postdate much of the more absurdist work of Hildesheimer, Grass or Dorst.

Their interest here lies in the way they bring out intrinsic qualities which recur in the German absurdists' use of the stage – the irrelevance of conventional political or social definitions of 'problems', the artificial structuring of scenes to parody rational assumptions or to introduce an element of game playing, the use of graphically presented images, the emphasis on theatre as theatre and the quality of theatrical or psychological introversion.

Some of the ways in which German absurdist theatre varied these patterns are indicated by Wolfgang Hildesheimer's Erlangen Speech (1960). He quoted Camus and followed his line that the logic of causal relationships had no place in drama, that a play's structure should embody the reality of an arbitrary existence; yet the theatrical form he proposed differed significantly from the school to which he was claiming he belonged. Where Beckett or Ionesco had rejected naturalistic social analysis outright as being based on and therefore only capable of expressing an illusory concept of existence, Hildesheimer criticised it simply as too limiting, and although he denied any possibility of theatre improving political situations or individual spectators, his stated aim is to radicalise his audience. He extended Camus' concept of the existential confrontation between hoping, purposeful man and an irrational universe into theatrical and social terms, so that his definition of absurd drama becomes a confrontation with the public who automatically resist its perception because 'it brings their own absurdity before their eyes...they therefore regard the theatrical action as absurd. So a stimulating reciprocal relationship is established. Theatre and public appear equally absurd to one another.'[12] Indeed, though in Hildesheimer's view Ionesco's *Rhinoceros* (1959) is disqualified, being as 'obvious as a fairy-tale, as interpretable as an allegory' (p. 8), his interpretation of absurd drama is didactic: 'every absurd play is a parable' (p. 4). This is qualified by drawing a dubious distinction between the biblical type of parable as a purposeful analogy, which presents a moral indirectly, and a symbolic reflection which is 'a parable of life precisely through the deliberate lack of any statement. For life doesn't state anything either' (p. 5). This definition is very close to Frisch's position in *The Firebugs* (*Biedermann und die Brandstifter*, 1958), 'a teaching play without a lesson', and the influence of Brecht is obvious in Hildesheimer's comment that 'absurd theatre is a parable about the alienness of men in the world. Its action therefore serves to alienate. It is its final and most radical consequence' (p. 13). Hildesheimer is not alone in interpreting absurdist ideas through a Brechtian perspective, and the direction he outlines is characteristic of the way German playwrights combined Brecht and Beckett, presenting social critiques, but as images which rule out ideological interpretations.

If Brecht's influence was one major factor that modified absurd theatre in Germany, another was Kafka whom Ionesco refers to as the prototype of an absurdist, in revolt against the dehumanising and estranging identification of individuals with their social function, whose vision of man 'astray in...the labyrinths of the world' showed how 'when man is cut off from his religious or metaphysical roots' by his integration into society 'he is lost, all his struggles become senseless, futile and oppressive'.[13] Kafka's work, burnt by the Nazis, was unavailable until the publishing houses were re-established in 1949–50. Consequently his surreal metamorphoses and bureaucratically anonymous monstrosities came as a revelation to the younger German writers and conditioned their interpretation of the absurdists, whom they discovered at the same time. The Gide–Barrault version of *The Trial* (*Der Prozess*), which appeared in Berlin in 1951, and the Brod adaptation of *The Castle* (*Das Schloss*) staged in 1953, were applauded as tragedies of a 'modern Job' which 'gave articulation to today's atmosphere', and when *Waiting for Godot* was staged in Berlin (also in 1953) the tramps were seen as Kafka-figures who have given up the struggle that destroys K, the protagonist of *The Trial* and *The Castle*: 'it is that which makes this superficially confused and bewildering play so clear, so convincing, so full of meaning by the end'.[14] In the deliberate ambiguity of his images and the homelessness of his outcast characters defined only by their unfulfilled desires, Kafka is very close to Beckett; and the violent dream atmosphere of Weiss' early plays, Hildesheimer and Michelsen's exaggeration of mechanical clichés into hallucinatory poetry, or the prison symbolism of Dorst's *Freedom for Clemens* (*Freiheit für Clemens*, 1961), all of which are taken from Kafka, dovetail into techniques from the French absurd theatre without any incongruity.

The short plays of Grass and Dorst are the most interesting examples of German absurd drama and its development. Each presents an image of existence as a situation – not a conflict, which would imply a resolution. Unlike the French cult of inarticulacy, their characters can express themselves and communicate (even if, as in *Freedom for Clemens*, speech is reduced to words tapped out on prison walls), but surreal farce is always substituted for argument. Grass began his career by writing ballets for his wife, a professional dancer, and in *Flood* (1957) it is the patterns of movement that contain the meaning – 'Future. It's like a flight of stairs. There's always a floor above you and then another floor and then comes the roof, and then back down, one flight, two flights to the cellars. You call that a future?'[15] – while *The Wicked Cooks* (*Die bösen Köche*, 1961) was originally performed as a ballet (1959). *Flood* is a plotless play, structured simply by the rhythms imposed on Noah and his family by the rising and ebbing water, which can be variously interpreted as moral turpitude, material possessions, or time, while *The Wicked Cooks* is conceived as a paper-chase in which the act of running is its own justification. Similarly in *Freedom for Clemens* Dorst stresses that 'the movements of the figures should be pointed, rapid, stylised, almost dance-like'; and since the rhythms, which are underlined by 'rapid finger-exercises on the piano', regulate the speeches the actors are required to be 'jugglers and acrobats capable of using dialogue the way a tightrope-walker would use a pole to keep his balance on a swaying rope'.[16]

This is in line with Ionesco's concept of a play as a score for performance and, as in Ionesco, it is united with grotesque clowning. Grass introduces a music-hall pair wearing 'large, grotesquely distorted rat masks' in *Flood*, brings on his characters out of packing-cases and grandfather-clocks (*à la* Ubu) in *The Wicked Cooks* or conjures them up in circus routines out of eggs, a heap of salt, a trumpet; while one play, *Rocking Back and Forth* (*Beritten hin und zurück*, 1960) has a clown as its central figure. Dorst, whose early plays were scripts for a Schwäbing marionette-theatre, draws his figures from *commedia dell'arte* or *grand guignol*, and his intentions are clearly outlined in the opening stage direction to his first full-length play, *Autumn Party* (*Gesellschaft im Herbst*, 1958):

The stage should not be too large. Its proportions could be scaled to the stage opening of a puppet theatre: broad and fairly low...The characters, with the exception of the countess are deliberate clichés – in the same way that the old *commedia dell'arte* brought the characteristic cliché-figures of its time into play.

This artificiality goes together with overt and self-reflexive theatricality. There are no other prisoners in *Freedom for Clemens*, and the tapping on the wall is made by a stage-hand. Grass' Noah and the cooks, like Beckett's tramps, comment on the audience, while the action of *Rocking Back and Forth* is an attempt by a director, an actor and a playwright to build a stage action around the clown, who is explicitly referred to as the symbolic epitome of absurd drama.

Beneath this theatricality which parodies itself, however, these plays have specific social reference and a political point. Clemens' prison is both a refuge from the violence and impersonality of urban life and a symbol for the way society indocrinates and regiments the individual, removing even the concept of freedom. The farce of Grass' *Only Ten minutes to Buffalo* (*Noch zehn Minuten bis Buffalo*, 1959) reveals the emptiness of bombastic idealism – the title is taken from a poem by Theodor Fontane, learnt by every German schoolboy, which is equivalent to 'The boy stood on the burning deck'. In *Flood* the whole of human experience and history is contained in photographs (mainly mislabelled), an idea Grass returns to in his novel *The Tin Drum* (*Die Blechtrommel*, 1959) where the comparison is explicit in Oskar's question, 'is there anything in the world, any novel which has the epic breadth of a photograph album?'[17] The image of each play is a theatrical snapshot and, as the photographic metaphor indicates, the relationship to life is rather different from Beckett or Ionesco. Unlike the novel form which allows a multiplicity of images, Grass' short playlets oversimplify, but a play like *Onkel, Onkel* (1958) is designed 'to represent the reality of an entire epoch, with its contradictions, absurdities...and criminality'.[18] The perspective is similar to *The Tin Drum*, where society is presented as caricature through the eyes of Oskar, the dwarf who literally sees the world from beneath. Here the key figures are two monstrous slum-children, who remain the same age throughout while the protagonist Bollin ages, and like Oskar they symbolise 'the madness of our century' in the egoistic inhumanity and amorality of the child. Their only reaction to watching a man being buried alive is curiosity, they steal Bollin's watch and pen, cajole his revolver away from him, shoot him to see if it is a real gun and run off, indifferent, to play the game of their time:

SPRAT: ...You take it and threaten me.
SLICK: And then?

SPRAT: Then I beg for mercy and undo my braids.
SLICK: What for?
SPRAT: You gotta when you beg somebody for mercy.
SLICK: Hm. And then?
SPRAT: Then you gotta rape me.
SLICK: Are you nuts?
SPRAT: Sure, I read it in the paper. Conductor rapes minor.[19]

The Tin Drum is narrated restrospectively from an insane asylum. In *Onkel, Onkel* the same ironic distance is created by the grotesque distortion of stereotypes. Bollin is presented as an efficient executive, whose guiding principle is 'the law of series' (p. 94), 'the man who finally carried statistics to their logical conclusion' (p. 83) – but his profession is murder. This reversal of a cliché is itself reversed, since in each scene the acceptance of criminal violence as natural by his intended victims makes him incapable of acting. A fifteen year-old girl and her mother ignore his threats, and instead of a rape and double killing he finds himself reading a fairy story and holding the mother's wool. A prima donna is so eager to immortalise herself by death at his hands that the presence of a photographer is required to record her last moments, and Bollin runs away in panic to 'remain normal' when she tries to seduce her would-be murderer. The stage is filled with surrogate images of violence – stabbing and shooting a doll, chopping down a Christmas tree – but the only killing is his own. The absurd situations and the brutalised language graphically represent the effects of decadence, its vicious sentimentalities and moral corruption, in a series of overlapping images, and Joachim Kaiser's comment on hearing Grass' reading of the play at the 1957 meeting of Group 47 is apt: 'in the surreal Berlin-world of Grass the "Belief in Mankind" is brilliantly destroyed. Brecht and Ionesco are godfathers.'[20] However, as Martin Esslin noted,[21] Grass' plays are extensions of his poems. As such, although they have considerable power, the point is often ambiguous. The general relevance of *The Wicked Cooks*, for example, was immediately obvious to its audience from the way the action illustrates every conceivable variety of intimidation and coercion – begging, betrayal, blackmail, bribery, threats, violence and moral superiority – but the symbol of the secret recipe, which is both the salvation 'of all gastronomy, not to mention...Humankind' (p. 257) and at the same time nothing but 'an excuse for running,...a hypothetical goal' (pp. 288–9), is uninterpretable. Critics, believing that the fake count who owns the recipe had been make up in 'a mask' of Grass' features because the actor (completely fortuitously) had a similar moustache to Grass, saw the play as an allegory of the artist's relationship to society. Grass himself, however, while refusing to limit the play's meaning by giving any specific keys to the symbols, explained during rehearsals – to the actors' bewilderment – that this was his 'labour movement play' and the cooks were trades unionists.[22]

All symbolist writing of course is liable to misinterpretation since images can only comment obliquely and their impact is subjective, but the German absurdists intensified the problem. The imagery of playwrights like Grass or Hildesheimer gives an impression of being allegorical, but is actually (and deliberately) without the coherent system of equivalents which makes allegory meaningful. Its apparent social reference encourages us to draw parallels and search for relevance, while the absurdist approach denies the validity of any such reductive rationalism. Unlike Godot and his letter, Grass' count and recipe cry out for interpretation. But absurdist techniques, devised to present the permanent and universal aspects of existence in terms of unanswerable questions, inevitably blur any intended social statement – so it was hardly surprising that although every critic found a different meaning for *The Wicked Cooks*, the actual political reference went unnoticed. A poetic image convinces us by emotional immediacy. It is a felt truth. By contrast metaphors can only be grasped at an intellectual distance. Grass uses the distortions of a deliberately naive vision to simultaneously involve and gain detachment, and his ironic perspective in which the monstrous is accepted as normal or cows turn into sailing ships, ships into steam engines (as in *Only Ten Minutes to Buffalo*), too often recedes into grotesque fantasy.

Dorst's solution was to frame his images in a semi-epic ambience, so that the audience's attitude is conditioned by apparently Brechtian connotations, as in *Great Denunciation by the City Wall* (*Grosse Schmährede an der Stadtmauer*, 1961). The setting is clearly chinoiserie *à la* Brecht, and as in *The Measures Taken* (*Die Massnahme*, 1930) or *The Good Person of Setzuan* the characters act out events and comment directly on their intentions and the situation:

3   Grass, *The Wicked Cooks*, 1961. Absurd multiplication, regressive images.

THE WOMAN: ...I must speak cleverly with him, so that he doesn't make mistakes in answering. Because he wants to come to me I pluck up the courage to risk the dangerous game that these officers command. The emperor has taken a man from me, he must give me a man.[23]

But the play-acting is open pretence – the Soldier and the Woman are both aware that her real husband is dead, so are the two officers who have set up the trial to pass the time for their amusement – and it is not politics (as in Brecht) but the nature of sexual relationships that determines the outcome. The woman's need for love is overpowering, and her possessiveness turns their make-believe hut into a prison for the soldier who, like her husband, escapes into the army with its 'inflexible, impersonal, unfeeling' armour (p. 38). Like Brecht's characters the soldiers wear masks, but here instead of distinguishing their social position the 'armour and mask-like helmets, in which they appear horrifyingly huge' (p. 13), transform them into faceless puppets who 'all move in exactly the same way' (p. 10). The focus is on the situation of the individual in an inhuman world, not on the inhumanity of an alterable social situation, and as such typically absurdist. The Brechtian elements are only 'the simplest, most easily comprehensible' techniques for controlling the transformation of an 'invented reality...into play and to reveal it as truth'.[24]

Dorst's aim is to create 'self-contained' plays in which the stage is an 'absolute space' and action is 'true to itself' in that it 'moves effortlessly according to its own laws...on the knife-edge between stylisation and reality'. Any ideology, 'the great materialistic or metaphysical world pictures', or any attempt to deal directly with contemporary issues is rejected as oversimplifying reality. Instead Dorst proposes 'a dramaturgy of negation...of absolute appearance, of simulated postures instead of metaphysical positions'. Since his drama contains no 'fixed system of values' any judgement, even the Woman's denunciation of the blank wall of laws and morality, only has validity in its particular dramatic context. The only positive quality is the act of artistic creation itself, which not only forms the theme of one play, *The Negress* (*Die Mohrin*, 1963), but is reflected in several of his protagonists: the poet Toller, or the Countess in *Autumn Party* and the Woman in *Great Denunciation* who both 'attempt to overcome the anonymous, merely functioning automaton-world through a pure act of imagination'. Hence Dorst's choice of stage conventions which are highly stylised, 'where theatre...has triumphed over the idea or the message'.[25] His characters are modern updatings of *commedia dell'arte*, or disguised clowns and puppets, his situations are drawn from pantomime or the Chinese shadow theatre, and his dramatic effects are based on consciously traditional techniques: substitution, reversal, the play-within-a-play. This overt artifice automatically transforms reality, even when it is overlaid with a documentary or apparently naturalistic surface, as in his later work, and it is precisely this distancing through formal structure that he sees as making his play-theatre relevant to the modern audience: 'through the theatrical events on stage ...reality itself is put to the test. It must measure itself against this world of total appearance and deception, recognise itself in it, set itself in question and – perhaps – alter a little.'[26]

The complex relationship of Dorst's self-contained theatrical images to reality was distorted in the case of the *Great Denunciation* by the fact that the Berlin wall was erected four months after the play was completed, so that the Woman's curse – 'I'll beat against you with my head until you cave in! *You* I hate most! Why this wall that keeps me apart from the man?' (p. 38) – gained an unintended political immediacy. *The Bend* (*Die Kurve*, 1960), is a better illustration. The two protagonists are clown-figures, interpreted in the manner of *Waiting for Godot*, but their dress as shabby undertakers with top hats is only at first glance incongrous to the nature setting. Unlike Vladimir and Estragon, this complementary pair of brothers are epitomes of old-fashioned social virtues, sober, hard-working, modest, content. And they have an apparent social function – burying drivers killed on a dangerous bend, repairing their cars and reselling them. The latest victim is (literally and figuratively) the fall-guy, full of self-importance whose well-meaning responses have the opposite effect to what he intends, and the action is based on the classic structure of discovery and reversal. The victim is the Permanent Secretary to the Minister of Transport, who is carrying in his briefcase the letters that the brothers have written to salve their consciences after each of the twenty-four accidents. Against all expectations he survives and the brothers, who have saved his life, murder him because he promises to do what their letters request and rebuild the road – which would remove their livelihood. This grotesque, contradictory action, the underlying artificiality and a pattern of repetitions transform the topical issues of road-safety and the accident-rate to universal questions of death, 'the point on which everything turns' (p. 106), and the role of chance. The road is presented as a metaphor for life, for which there are 'no specific road-regulations. Unfortunately' (p. 89), while traffic (using the double-meaning of *Verkehr*) is 'the intercourse...between man and man' (p. 96). But this metaphysical interpretation itself is undermined by the way it is imposed – through a funeral sermon which, being *kitsch*, rehearsed as a set piece and delivered as a recitation for its subject's approval, is revealed as empty rhetoric:

in a preaching tone: When disaster strikes, anywhere in the world, and it ambushes us in our everyday routine by all its shocking senselessness: then we feel ourselves given notice, then suddenly the curtain is torn away from an abyss. With comfortable words and with a pleasant, easily-lived-by morality we disguised it. Now disaster has struck once again (p. 85).

The absurd vision has no more validity than the assumptions of order and social purpose that it shows to be illusory. We are left with a theatrical image; but one which faces us with the false sentimentality, hypocritical transfer of guilt and spiritual emptiness of modern society because, as Dorst points out, 'the precise logic of the unfolding action...stands in grotesque disproportion to the moral free-wheeling of the dialogue'.[27]

German absurdists never had the philosophical consistency of the French school. Man remained for them the Aristotelian 'political animal' rather than the existential mortal and, as Walser noted, their adoption of absurd principles was really a reaction to the apparently insoluble problem of finding literary perspectives to express contemporary conditions: 'one despairs at the unrepresentability of real inhabited surroundings'.[28] And during the 1960s a series of political events reinforced the stress on social relevance in their images. First the Eichmann and Auschwitz trials gave politics an inherently theatrical form, and provided a model for dealing directly with the past and communal guilt. (It is no accident that courtrooms outnumber even artist-figures on the German stage; indeed documentary drama is hardly conceivable without the trial-format.) Secondly, the Vietnam protests acted as a focus for literary engagement, and the student revolt involved authors in the political process. Grass, for instance, was already campaigning for the SPD when he wrote *Onkel, Onkel*, and his address to the 1966 meeting of Group 47, 'On the Lack of Self-Confidence in Court-Jester-Authors Considering the Non-

Existent Court', was a parodistic attack on the absurdist position. Then on the literary level there was the impact of Brecht, whose work had been a casualty of the cold war and only began to be produced in west Germany with Palitzsch's emigration from the DDR in the early 1960s, even if instead of following Brecht's example Grass and Dorst deliberately used his technique against itself – as in *The Plebeians Rehearse the Uprising*. The result was an increasing directness and technical sophistication in their work without any change in their intentions. In 1974 Grass still rejected 'politically committed literature' as 'a will o' the wisp' (*einen 'weissen Schimmel'*) commenting that works based on foregone conclusions 'clash with reality'.[29] Similarly in *Toller* Dorst effectively denies the possibility of meaningful political action by deliberately choosing a situation where all aspirations for a better world are demonstrably delusive: 'Objectively these revolution-aries had no chance. That turned all their actions, hopes, quarrels into bloody farce.'[30] In their later plays, then, Grass and Dorst present recognisable social realities and political positions, but life is still compressed into theatrical images which reduce significant acts and a sense of purpose to role-playing and pretence. The ironic distance is the same as in their more obviously absurdist plays, and the closer the contact to actual events the more radical their questioning of reality.

In sharp contrast to their authors' earlier work, *The Plebeians* and *Toller* are based on documentary fact. Grass incorporated details of the uprising word-for-word from Arnulf Baring's *Der 17. Juni 1953* and Joachim Leithäuser's *Der Aufstand im Juni*, and even took his interpretation of its significance from Baring's commentary. Similarly Dorst worked together with a historian, Helmut Neubauer, and supported his play with a volume of documentation which was over half as long again. Yet significantly the major criticism against both plays was that they distorted facts. Erich Engel (the Erwin of Grass' play) attacked Grass for maliciously perverting the truth –

I have never come across anything dirtier, baser than this play...a scurrilous attempt to piss on the boots of a colleague behind his back when one isn't equal to him in any other way...Herr Grass sticks his head out of the CDU arse and makes recommendations on 'a correct political attitude' to Brecht the poet.[31]

– while Toller's widow protested that Dorst's play contained gross factual inaccuracies, and students distributed pamphlets to the audience claiming that it was an unhistorical misrepresentation designed to support bourgeois propaganda about revolution as a 'pathological phenomenon'. The reaction of both authors was similar. Grass denied that *The Plebeians* could in any sense be 'categorised as documentary theatre'.[32] Dorst pointed out that since theatre was by definition 'arranged fiction', quotations and documents had the same status as the music hall turns, dream sequences and symbols; 'not, as in a documentary play, as evidence for historical truth, but like all these scenes and dialogues as particles of reality'.[33]

Leaving aside the vulgarity of an attack like Engel's (and his tone was typical of DDR commentary on *The Plebeians*), the violence of the criticisms indicates the distance of these plays from conventional political drama. Instead of taking a recognised position which can be attacked or defended in conventional terms, they discredit the principles on which all political positions are based, and the howl of abuse (from both extremes of the political spectrum) is logical as a response to the way they transform factual material into images of the irrationality of politics. In these plays it is precisely the awareness and moral idealism, without which no situation can be changed, that make any action impossible. As a consequence the 'particles of reality' are revealed as theatre. In Grass' play, where the German workers merge with the imaginary plebeians of ancient Rome in Brecht's Shakespearian mirror, neither the uprising on the streets nor the performance of *Coriolanus* get past Act I, scene I. The Boss diverts a real insurrection into a rehearsal which never goes beyond the discussion of revolutionary first principles. Instead of acting, the workers become actors, and the uprising is shown to be tokenism, summed up in its only achievement – tearing down the flag from the Brandenburg arch, which symbolises success at the moment of failure. Even the possibility of effective radical action is seen as a myth since 'conscious revolutionaries' can only be found in a form of art which, like Brecht's drama, deliberately falsifies human nature for ideological reasons and presents us with paragons when 'not only the original [Shakespeare], but even the historical sources and the reality outside his own windows, refused to provide them'.[34] Politics are reduced to rhetoric, and this is echoed in the play's construction where variations in the verse rhythms are used as a substitute for dramatic action. It is also responsible for one of the play's major flaws since the dialogue is largely built up of slogans (the verbal equivalents to acts), and the effect is that commented on by the Boss: 'I can hear whole platoons of orators sucking the word "freedom" empty' (p. 108). There is also a contradiction between Grass' demands on the audience and his treatment of material. The subtitle, *ein deutsches Trauerspiel*, not only relates to the theme with its ambiguity – 'German tragedy'/'a tragic game played by Germans' – but signifies Grass' intentions. *Trauerspiel* is a specific critical category, unique to German drama, which Grass explicitly adopts because 'What was decisive for me was that I didn't want to present just the fall of the Boss – that would have been a tragedy – but the failure of all involved, the workers as well as the intellectuals, the eastern as well as the western system'. Grass distinguishes between tragedy, based on myth and dominated by the sufferings of a symbolic individual; and the *Trauerspiel*, which is based on history, presents an epoch through political forces and social relationships, and deals with 'the guilty and entangled behaviour of various groups not single people. That is already in the title of "the Plebeians", in the plural.'[35] Hence the Boss' final accusation which transfers his guilt to the audience of 'innocents'. Responsibility however implies the possibility of alternative action, and this is ruled out by the use Grass makes of Brecht's 'dialectical' dramaturgy which, like Brecht's acting technique, 'allows the other possibilities to be inferred and only represents one out of the possible variants...Whatever [the actor] doesn't do must be contained and conserved in what he does.'[36] Instead of presenting alternatives that create a frame for independent decision or suggest feasible actions, Grass' contrasts are contradictions, and the multiplicity of shifting viewpoints in *The Plebeians* cancel out in the double mirror of a stage within a stage. Life as theatre in which 'even chaos has to be rehearsed' becomes 'theatre in itself' – what happens turns the claim that drama has a social function into a mere label ('we call it the "theatre for others"')[37] – and the final image when the props and stage-hands have been cleared away is a dark theatre, an empty world. The same effect can be seen in Grass' next play *Beforehand* (*Davor*, 1969), 'an attempt to present a social attitude of a particular time from five positions, full of contradictions', each of which is 'relativised' by the others.[38] As in his poetry,

> ...my big yes
> Forms sentences with a small no.

Toller expresses a similar negative vision. The hero as actor, revolution as literature, idealism as illusion in light of the grotesqueness of a reality epitomised by the forces of repression. The action – the proclamation of an independent participatory democracy, the internal struggles between communists and idealists, military assault from the outside, defeat and trial – is presented ironically through a counterpoint of shifting viewpoints, multiple impressions, breaks and contrasts. Factual presentation is inflated into pathos and undercut by comedy. Documentary sequences are juxtaposed with naturalistic private scenes exploring personal relationships, set against caricature or naive folk-play representations of events, and extended into on-stage theatre – agitprop, cabaret, scenes from *Masses and Man*. These multiple impressions culminate in the last scene. On an upper stage level the trial of Toller proceeds. Documentary testimonials to his character are read out, but the speakers in his defence wear 'masks which distort their features slightly towards the expressionistic' while the listeners who judge him are laughing caricatures of the capitalist Establishment, and Toller's well-known reply affirming his commitment to revolution is not only spoken 'in a cage as in *Masses and Man*', transforming that corner into a mental stage on which we see the poet-politician's self-projection as the hero of his most famous political drama, but also continually interrupted 'from above' with catcalls and cries of 'Bad literature, alibi for bad deeds!' and 'Actor!' Simultaneously on the lower stage a *Freikorps* officer reads out a list and at each name a worker with his hands on his head is led across the stage between lines of soldiers, exiting behind a tiled wall with 'Munich Slaughterhouse' painted on it. The effect is to contrast Toller's compulsive volubility with a silence so full of significance that the passion of his speech itself reveals his words as empty. While Toller's sentence (5 years imprisonment) is proclaimed 'a victory for humanitarian sentiments', the executions are carried out – but even this level of reality is reversed into art, with each shot of the firing squad stylised as the flash of a photographer's bulb. At the same time two further perspectives are provided for this counterpointed action. Downstage a married couple, seated in bourgeois comfort on an antimacassar-covered sofa, congratulate themselves (and the audience) on the return to peace and normality.[39] On projection screens above short extracts from René Clair's *Entr'acte* of a ballerina filmed from beneath, followed by

an upper-class funeral procession in slow motion, present death
– and art – as absurd. Reality becomes subjective, relative; and
since Dorst's criticism of political action as self-dramatisation is
expressed in overtly theatrical terms it refers back to the play,
which thus undercuts itself. The theme of history as 'bloody
farce' is itself seen as farcical. We are left with theatre. As in *The
Plebeians*, though here paradoxically because it is overfull, the
stage is empty.

In Palitzsch's production *Toller* became a parody of the documentary play. Specifically it was a take-off on the man who had
made the label 'political theatre' his own, Erwin Piscator, and its
three-storey open playing area, multiple projection screens,
mechanised stage with central revolve and podiums that slid
forward on each side were clearly reminiscent of Piscator's classic
treatment of Toller's *Hoppla, we're alive!*, (*Hoppla, wir leben!*,
1927).[40] Quite apart from its appropriateness as an object of
parody, this application of Piscator's techniques also highlit the
play's implications. The mechanised complexity of the setting
mirrored the puppet-like nature of characters trapped by their
roles, while as a media event it gave the incidents of 1919 a very
contemporary tone. Dorst's negative images – the anarchist
whose protest is limited to forcing a well-mannered proletarian to
tread caviar into a 'bourgeois' carpet, the nightmare dance of
anti-semitic students wearing Jewish clown-noses, and above all
the bleakly ironic glimpses of Toller between the battle lines
helplessly trying to stop the fighting, or desperately carrying away
the bodies of hostages, whom he had been unable to save, in an
unsuccessful attempt to avert a massacre of revenge – are in fact
intended to have an immediate political point. For Dorst the
Munich *Räterepublik* was 'a moment at which European history
could go one way or the other. The lines can be drawn from this
point', and he sees this idealistic attempt to establish socialism as
leading directly to Hitler taking power.[41] This follows Toller's
own perception that the *Räterepublik* was unviable and its defeat
'gave the counter-revolutionary forces the strength and élan to
organise themselves'.[42] Dorst's farcical treatment, which undermines both the revolution and Toller's acceptance of the guilt for
his failure, is thus a perspective on history; and the play
deliberately oversimplifies by introducing fascist tendencies into
the actions of 'the people'. 1919 merges with 1933, and Palitzsch's
production underlined the parallels to the 1968 student revolt by

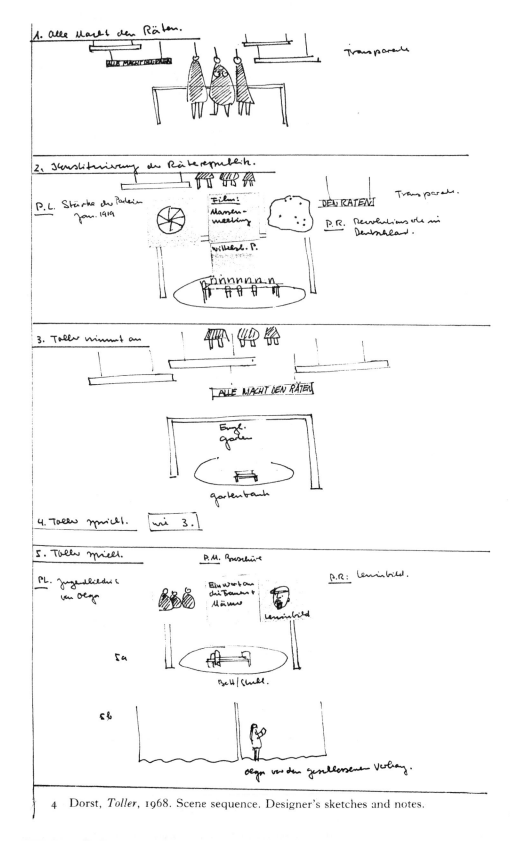

4 Dorst, *Toller*, 1968. Scene sequence. Designer's sketches and notes.

DESIGNER'S NOTES

1. Workers demonstration against parliamentarianism ['All form worker's councils']
Centre-stage: Puppets 'Parliament' 'The Bourgeoisie' 'The General'
  Demonstrators (Agitator, young man, 2nd young man).
Side Stages L and R: Workers' choruses [*Sprechchöre*]
Bridge: Demonstrators (placards)
Film: Workers' demonstration (1919)
Texts L and R: 'Down with the Bourgeoisie' 'All form workers' councils'
Sound: Rhythmic chorales

1/2 Puppets flown (hangman's noose)
  Workers move off singing.

2. Proclamation and Establishment of Workers' Republic [Räterepublik]
Centre-stage: 2 Tables, various chairs. Mühsam, Lipp, Landauer, Paukulum,
  Gandorfer, Reichert, Men, 2 Trades-unionists, Delegates
  To them: Toller.
Photo-Projection Centre: Wittelsbach Palace [texts (sc. 1) stay]
Screen: Bedroom Picture/Mass meeting-Film
Photo L and R: Royal Bavarian Crest, above text: 'Tomorrow the Workers'
  Republic'/Diagrams: Comparative strengths of political parties, 1919:
  Distribution of revolutionary centres in Germany (map).

3. Toller accepts
Centre-screen: Photo-Englischer Garden.
  Bench. Toller, Landauer
  To them: Lipp [texts (sc. 1) stay].
Sound: Bird Song.

3/4 Centre-screen: Rear projection, shadows of workers [superimposed
  on Garden] Projection-screen up.

4. Toller speaks to the masses
Centre-stage: Toller, Landauer, Red Guards, Workers, Students, Civilians
Side-stages L and R: Workers' chorus dissolves to workers/old actor and old
  woman.
Bridge: Demonstrators
Film: Toller – magnified in close-up
  (Toller's speech becomes taken over by the film: Toller, quick change)
Sound: 'The Internationale'.

4/5 Centre screen: Brochures, leaflets.

5a Bedroom conversation Toller, Olga
Centre-stage: Bed. Toller, Olga.
Photo L: Theatre Placard 'Masses and Man', then Lenin portrait
Photo R: Theatre Placard 'Revenue', then family picture Olga as child.
5b Olga reads before closed curtain.

DESIGNER'S NOTES

19. The last session of the republican regime
Centre-stage: Table, chairs (downstage: sandbags, mattresses). Gandorfer, Paulukum, Reichert, Olga, Leviné
To them: Maenner. To them: Toller.
Centre Screen: Wittelsbach Palace
Photo-projection L and R: Government decrees
Sound: Distant artillery-fire.

20. Leviné abolishes the republican government
Centre-stage: Dais, Benches. Leviné, Reichert, Workers (interrupters)
Side-stages L and R: Workers/Toller (in disguise).
Photo L: Lenin, then 'Red Hand'
Photo R: Liebknect, then 'Red Hand'
Banners: '8 More Days of This Government and Bloodhound Noske will be in Bavaria', plus other key phrases from speeches
Blackboard L: Löwenbraü, crossed-out price, new price beneath
Blackboard R: Potato-salad, crossed-out price, new price beneath

20/21. Toller goes to the front
Side-stage L: Cell wall, barred window, stool, bucket. Toller, Leviné, 2 Guards.
Sound: Distant noise of previous scene.

19/20/21 Shadows of workers moving behind the photo-projections.

22/23. The arming of the workers
Side-stage R: Desk with red flag, chair. Citizens.
Centre-screen: Quotations from Landauer about passive resistance
Placard: 'Take up arms!'
Bridge: Workers with rifles and flags
Sound: Song, 'Under the waving red banner'.

24. Suicide of a Poet
Centre-stage: Period furniture. Toller (20 years older).
Film: American ladies listen to Toller's lecture with coffee and cakes
Blackboard R: 16.5.1939 Ernst Toller reads from *I was a German*
Placard: 'Bloodhound Noske fires on Bavaria'
Sound: Applause.

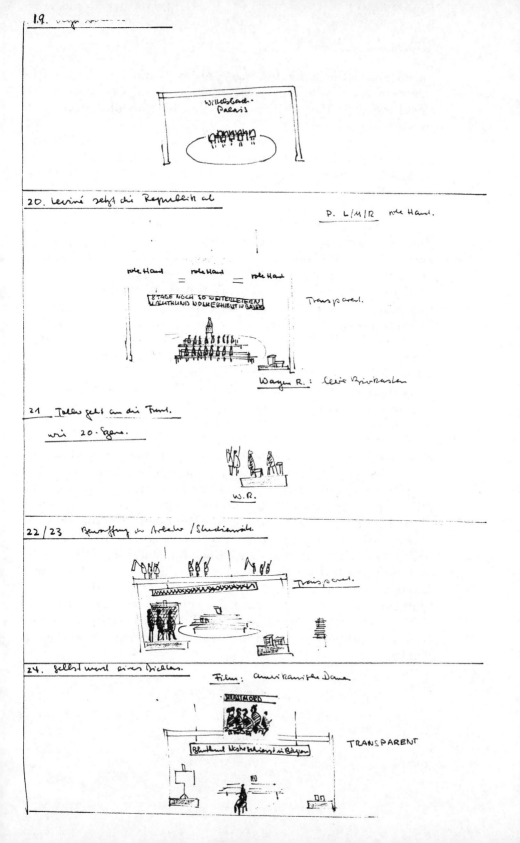

visual associations. Leviné made up as Lenin became a cliché image of the revolutionary *per se*, film of the *Freikorps* troops marching into Munich was paralleled by film of Soviet tanks moving into Prague.

Students in the audience took the point. There were protests at some performances, discussions with the actors after others, and leaflets were distributed to the audience criticising the 'reactionary' viewpoint of the play – 'Palitzsch quite deliberately degrades the role of the people to a supernumerary appendage which moves around the stage singing leftist litanies and waving red banners'.[43] Such reactions indicate the effectiveness of applying the absurd approach to politically charged material, and Dorst's aim of undercutting all preconceived political opinions was made even more explicit in the TV version of the play, which emphasised the provocative elements of the stage production. The title, *Red Murder* (*Rotmord*), was taken from Nazi propaganda vocabulary, and the material was presented from an overtly fascist perspective to force a radical confrontation with socially acceptable attitudes, while distorting camera techniques were ironically designed 'to be appropriate to such an emotion-laden "great" subject'.[44]

The freedom to mix different techniques and standards of representation that comes from taking the stage itself as the basic level of imaginative reality gives the self-reflexive form considerable vitality. It also allows material to be presented from multiple viewpoints, while the way in which this type of drama establishes a reciprocal relationship between art and life, each illuminating the other, opens up new possibilities for the sophisticated treatment of intellectually subtle themes. Ambiguities are underlined by the 'dialectical' structuring of associative images, and the result is highly theatrical. At the same time the cancelling effect of its extreme complexity means that the style developed by Grass and Dorst is only appropriate for a negative (or at best anarchist) political vision, and it is hardly a coincidence that Dorst also published a cartoon version of *Toller*. There is a logical progression from Kafkaesque images through Grass' snapshots to comic-strip theatre.

5. *Models*

If German variations on the absurd can be traced back indirectly to Brecht, the form of two of the more significant contemporary theatre movements springs straight from his work. One, which has come to be known as 'dialectical drama', follows his work at the Berliner Ensemble in the 1950s. The other, 'parable theatre', has had more time to become established since its initial impetus came from the Zürich productions of his major plays, *Mother Courage* (1941), *The Good Person of Setzuan* (1943) and in particular Brecht's own productions of *Puntila* and *Antigone* in 1948. Consequently it was Swiss playwrights like Friedrich Dürrenmatt and Max Frisch who were first to follow Brecht's lead, and they picked up on his earlier work, adapting his parable approach.

The term 'parable' is often loosely applied to contemporary German drama and needs definition. It has obvious links to the biblical mode of teaching in which spiritual values are expressed in everyday images; but instead of giving the universal a human scale, the Brechtian approach seeks to reveal general laws by removing them from the familiar, and instead of remaining on the level of simile where faith is *like* a grain of mustard seed, the Brechtian method uses direct transposition, setting accepted behaviour in a context where it becomes abnormal or where, with the customary surface removed, we can see the workings of a process. The way a parable relates to reality can vary. At one extreme it verges on allegory, a metamorphosis of reality into ideal or mock-heroic one-to-one terms. This may simply be a matter of disguising the obvious to create the additional interest of a puzzle. It may also be used to channel emotion by choosing symbols that generate specific responses, so that when the allegoric equation becomes clear those responses are transferred sublimi-nally to the real object, as in Spenser's glorification of Elizabeth I or Pope's denigration of Grub Street. Alternatively it may be a way of giving abstract concepts a tangible imaginative shape, as in the medieval *Romance of the Rose*; and both these traditional aspects form part of the parable technique. But on stage such symbolic comparisons take on a physical shape which is necessarily specific, literal, and therefore limiting, instead of remaining on an imaginative plane; and in a play like *Arturo Ui* the identification of the grotesque gangsters with Hitler and Hindenburg must be immediate. The result is an apparent oversimplification. Hence the failure of *Arturo Ui* when first produced during the war and its later success when the historical figures had receded sufficiently so that Hitler and Goebbels could themselves be taken as metaphors. At the other extreme parables approach the conventional type of play which draws moral lessons from past events, and are distinguished from straight historical drama only by their focus, *Galileo* being treated as a paradigm for contemporary issues rather than exploring the intrinsic meaning of a historical situation.

The primary characteristic of Brecht's plays that has earned them the parable label is distance, not only in the way action is portrayed from an objective viewpoint, avoiding (at least in theory) emotional involvement in the characters' subjective experience, but in their settings where contemporary issues are treated in terms of the historically or geographically fantasised and far-away. The Weimar Republic and its dissolution into the Third Reich become transformed into an imaginary Chicago-gangsterdom, where the problem is not Hitler as a person but the social weaknesses that lead to fascism; the deforming pressures of competitive capitalism are illustrated in a Setzuan inhabited by gods, or in a romanticised, Kiplingesque India; the moral betrayal of the atomic bomb is demonstrated by an Italian renaissance example. This distancing is a way of generalising which avoids the associated danger of abstraction. The figures remain individuals, not expressionistic universal symbols, although at the same time deliberately fantastic elements in the setting make it unnecessary to explore personal motivation or provide character development. Consequently Brecht's figures, while convincing and frequently striking personalities, tend to be static – which can have a didactic point, the audience (supposedly) learning from Mother Courage's experience precisely because she does not. Alternatively, if a change in a protagonist's nature occurs, as with Galy Gay, Shen Te or Puntila, this is externally imposed through a change in the character's social situation. This may correspond to Brecht's concept of 'a materialistic presentation – to let the social being of the figures determine their awareness ',[1] and it certainly reinforces the concreteness of the drama. But perhaps because of the simplification of an imagined, as opposed to observed reality, such unmotivated changes are always so extreme that they give an impression of schizophrenia which is seldom convincing on an individual level, even though it succinctly expresses Brecht's view of the effect of an unjust society. The imaginary quality in the stage-picture, however, is a primary element of parable drama. Strangeness and artificiality have a positive value. They have the Wordsworthian effect of making new things familiar and familiar things new, by offering a context in which unquestioned ideas can be set in unusual relationships or apparently abnormal behaviour patterns will be accepted. For Brecht this had a political function, presenting the world as alterable, undermining the view that human circumstances were determined by Fate or Nature, and worked in the same way as his technique of alienating a character's words by linking speeches with contradictory actions – Mother Courage counting her profits while cursing war, or Brutus beating a slave during his monologue condemning Caesar's tyranny. In short, theatrical alienation (*Verfremdung*), Brecht's basic technique for creating parables, is a way of using overt artificiality to make the facts and figures transparent, ensuring that they are not to be taken seriously in themselves but 'seen though' as examples. The focus is, as it were, on the general issues in the gap between what a character says and does, and this type of dramaturgy 'works without psychology, without individuals' so that, in one of Brecht's typically scientific metaphors, 'the epic precipitate dissolves *circumstances* into *processes*'.[2]

Frisch has singled out two of his plays, *The Fireraisers* (1958) and *Andorra* (1961) as 'parables' on the grounds that 'reality is not imitated on the stage, but reaches our consciousness through the "sense" that the play confers on it', the subject being 'openly unhistorical, fabricated as an example...from synthetic material'. At the same time Frisch tried to shift the emphasis by substituting alternative definitions – preferring 'fable' or 'model' to the term 'parable' – since the parable approach provided a valuable non-illusionistic style which concentrated on significance rather than appearance, but its didactic implications automatically distorted his intentions. *Andorra*, for example, deals with the themes of self-realisation, role-playing, self-images and the 'graven image' of a person imposed by society, the same individualistic themes that Frisch explores in such novels as *Bin* and *Stiller*, while the form (and the political associations of using 'the Jew' as his example of an image) arouses expectations of a moral message on a different level. The result is an apparent non-statement, a cliché conclusion which has led to criticism that the play fails to provide any real analysis of anti-semitism. As Frisch put it, such a form 'tends toward *quod erat demonstrandum*. It's little help then to protect myself through subtitles: "Learning play without a lesson". The parable implies a lesson – even when I'm not concerned with teaching.'³ Hence his downplaying of the moral by stressing the 'model', an imaginary working out of possible systems, 'a dramaturgy of disbelief, a drama of permutations'.⁴

The Fireraisers is an excellent example of how real situations are transformed into theatrical models. Frisch's *Diary* gives the initial impetus – the 1948 communist take-over of Czechoslovakia, where President Beneš dug the grave of his own liberal ideals by appointing the communist leader as Prime Minister. However, the interest is not in actual events, but in their structure as a classic pattern of appeasement which mirrored the way Hitler had gained power under Hindenburg; and instead of attacking evil in the form of any specific ideology, the focus is on sins of omission, an accusation which is almost impossible for any individual to refute: 'precisely the lack of commitment, the silence about the evil one knows, is probably the commonest form of our complicity'. This abstraction of the political to a level on which it has personal relevance is illustrated by the first treatment of the material: 'One day a man comes, a stranger, and you cannot help but give him soup – and bread as well. For the injustice he suffered, according to his story, is undeniable, and you don't want it to be revenged on you...'⁵ Frisch then reworked this as a radio-play. The bare outline was elaborated by adding elements to guide the audience response which also fleshed out the anonymous 'you'. Now named Biedermann, with connotations of the *Biedermeier* furniture (the equivalent of Victorian) that stands for bourgeois moral values and *Jedermann* (Everyman), the protagonist becomes an object lesson in how not to use literature. He models his treatment of the arsonists, receiving them into his home and pretending not to know what they are doing, on a sentimental novel in which the innocence of a girl reforms two criminals, despite the lack of any correspondence, either moral or physical, between such a heroine and himself – and his pretentious self-satisfaction is graphically demonstrated when he falls asleep over the book while claiming to be deeply moved. A narrator, interposed between the situation and the audience, stresses that this figure is both invented and representative of qualities 'in ourselves'; and the perspective is established by the title, *Burleska – an unlikely story*. These elements recur in the play script in an overtly theatrical form, distancing the action by its artificiality. The narrator is now a whole chorus of firemen, parodying classical fate-tragedy, and the novel becomes a play-within-a-play, a burlesque of *Everyman*. At the same time the generalities of the original outline are given a concrete shape. Social guilt is shown as a specific crime, Biedermann's exploitation of Knechtling (literally a diminutive of 'serf'), the inventor of the hair-oil formula from which his wealth comes, who is driven to suicide by ingratitude. Similarly political power is turned into the box of matches that Biedermann hands over to the firebugs. The final development of the material was the addition of an 'Afterpiece' for German productions (1959), which both underlined the play's relevance to the German experience with a reference to the post-war economic miracle –

> Risen again from rubble and ashes
> Is our city...
> Tall, modern buildings,
> Gleaming with glass and chrome
> But at heart just the same as before[6]

– while removing any limited political interpretation by extending the action into eschatalogical farce. The form became that of an inverted morality play, with an epilogue in hell replacing the prologue in heaven of *Everyman* – an element picked up in the German première under Piscator, where the setting was reminiscent of the two-tier medieval stages but the 'Heavens' became the firebugs' attic filled with gasoline drums. Time and place were left undefined, the bare boards of the theatre, and in the opening chorus Biedermann and the firemen were spotlit as disembodied faces in a void; while the multiple associations of the action were spelt out by posters around the auditorium walls, which set Korea, Suez and the atomic bomb side by side with the Reichstag fire and the 1939–45 war (see Illustration 5).

For Frisch there is an inevitable gap between reality and its definition in art which is only bridgeable through a symbolic fiction, hence the anti-illusionary form: 'instead of pretending that [the action] is happening before our eyes a model is demonstrated, an experiment'. Objectification and open artificiality are the tools by which this transformation is achieved. Events become a cautionary tale, making theatre 'a terrifying distorting mirror ...for the most alien thing one can experience is to see oneself from the outside'. Frisch was trained as an architect, and his description

5 Frisch, *The Fireraisers*, 1959. Morality play setting: the model with placards and screens to illustrate the wider implications.

of how he contructs plays emphasises the functional nature and rational approach of this type of drama – 'a first ground-plan, scribbled on a cigarette packet, and then the enlarged working drawings with exact sizes and notes of material...'[7] – and the way the final version of *The Fireraisers* was reached follows this quite closely. The refining process of different adaptations made it for Frisch 'technically the most superior' of his plays, but this perfection itself highlights one of the intrinsic flaws of 'model drama'. As Frisch himself acknowledged, it made the final impression too mechanical.[8]

Dürrenmatt collaborated with Frisch on the stage-script of *The Fireraisers* (the Knechtling material was his suggestion, and he advised extending it to develop Biedermann's character and moral ambiguity),[9] and the pattern of *The Fireraisers* also offers an illuminating insight into how Dürrenmatt handles his dramatic material. The formation of a name like Claire Zachanassian, the old lady of *The Visit* (*Der Besuch der alten Dame*, 1956), out of Zacharoff, Onassis and Gulbenkian indicates a similar method of abstracting reality to create associative images, and the same reinterpretation of Brechtian principles forms the basis of Dürrenmatt's plays. He defines his writing as an 'experiment', 'a setting up of independent worlds' with building blocks drawn from the present: 'the take-off point of drama is the finding of a poetic fable. Drama then becomes an attempt to turn out continually new models of a world which continuously challenges new models'.[10] Dürrenmatt's theoretical essays are empirical rather than definitive, and his ideas relate to whatever play he is engaged with at the time, being mainly formulated as polemical counter-attacks in a running war with the critics. As such they are frequently contradictory, but taken as a whole certain clear outlines emerge, and it is in terms of this framework that his drama must be evaluated.

Each play is a 'fictitious model...of possible human relationships', an imaginary hypothesis of a 'mathematical' kind, defined as such to contrast with the Brechtian type of social analysis which, being 'scientific', is seen as following the Newtonian precept '*hypotheses non fingo*' and thus dependent on a fixed theory of reality. Dürrenmatt, like Frisch, finds the inner form of Brecht's parables dogmatic. To overcome this structural tendency he deliberately chooses subject-matter that contains a multiplicity of problems rather than illustrating an axiom – 'the value of a play lies in its problem-potential, not in its clarity of statement'.[11] Following this line, the basis of Dürrenmatt's dramaturgy becomes the conceit (*Einfall*) and randomness (*Zufall*).

Given the idea [*Einfall*], then comes the sketch-phase. The possibilities are played through. The ten or twenty plots which the idea allows for are projected. The further I progress, the more the picture alters and the more the laws that are inherent in the idea crystalise.[12]

Brecht's classic example of his own approach is *The Street Scene*, an accident involving a truck driver forced to work overtime, reported by a witness in such a way as to show the social causes of catastrophe and the action that would have prevented it. This assumption that altering a cause produces a determinable result on the effect presupposes a logical consistency in events. Dürrenmatt deliberately gives a parallel example. Two private cars travelling in opposite directions hit each other in avoiding a deer that happens to cross the road; different witnesses give conflicting versions of the facts, and there is no connection between the drivers that led them to drive away from their starting points at the only moment that could have caused the collision. Where Brecht's audience are given a conclusion about how to act (even if it is implied rather than explicit), Dürrenmatt's are left with questions about the logic and meaning of action itself. The aim is to force them 'to imagine how the world might be at its most rational', and this is achieved by presenting negative utopias, the most extreme examples of senseless disaster. Even in a play like *The Exception and the Rule* (*Die Ausnahme und die Regel*, 1930) Brecht's parables represent norms. Inhuman behaviour is typical of an unjust society and the abnormal is simply a natural response in a perverted context. By contrast Dürrenmatt's model-situations are always exceptions because he always chooses the most shocking or extreme set of developments, so that possibility replaces laws of probability. This means that the logic by which he selects a plot from the range of projected alternatives is intellectual, an abstract pattern, not the cause-and-effect logic of events, and therefore any impression of necessity is sleight of hand: 'A story is thought through to its end when it has taken its worst possible turn. The worst possible turn is not foreseeable. It comes about through chance...The more methodically men proceed, the more drastically chance affects them.' At the same time this arbitrary 'fate' is presented as openly artificial. The exaggeration is carried to deliberately absurd lengths in which the stage is piled with bodies, or a Lazarus with a death-wish is repeatedly resurrected, the identical method of murder is reduced to farce by repetition, or a sordid killing is glorified by inflated pathos. Death itself is 'only a theatrical trick...the best conceivable exit'.[13] Theatre is nothing more than theatre, and stage illusion is undermined by deliberate naivety.

This exaggeration linked with theatricality forms the basic structure of Dürrenmatt's work – the grotesque, which he has defined as both the natural expression of his perception and as a technique of representation:

Comedy alone is appropriate to us. Our world has led to the grotesque as it has to the atomic bomb, in the same way that the apocalyptic pictures of Hieronymus Bosch are grotesque. But the grotesque is only a tangible mode of perception, a physical expression of paradox, the form of the unformed, the face of a faceless world; and just as in our thinking we now seem unable to manage without the concept of the paradox, so also in art...[14]

It is customary to see Dürrenmatt as part of a grotesque school of contemporary writers which includes Ionesco and the absurdists, responding to an alienated world in a style developed by the expressionists and Pirandello.[15] But although there are certainly links between Dürrenmatt and Wedekind or Jarry, his use of the grotesque is more classical, as his references to Aristophanes and the folk comedy of Nestroy indicate. It is a means of achieving perspective, not the perspective itself; a way of gaining precision, objectivity and distance, of forcing the audience to take a moral stand while retaining the playful artificiality of a literary game. As a form of parody, the grotesque unites a high degree of imaginative freedom with specific physical detail, challenging the audience to recognise the essence of their society in a distorted stage-picture. For Dürrenmatt 'comedy is a mousetrap', trapping the spectators in inappropriate responses by juxtaposing the horrifying and the ridiculous, presenting tragic characters in a comic context which mixes farce and pathos, and using sudden reversals to show the unexpected relevance of an apparent fiction or the abnormality of a situation facilely accepted as ordinary.

Such an approach is intrinsically moral, but there is nothing programmatic about it. Dürrenmatt's claim that 'tyrants fear only one thing: a poet's mockery' is in effect an ironic denial of political purpose. Ideologies and manifestos are rejected; the decisive existential questions can only be solved 'by each individual, there is no communal solution', and his attitude is neatly summed up in 'I am a protestant and I protest'.[16] Where this is made the theme of a play, as in *Hercules and the Augean Stables* (*Herkules und der Stall des Augias*, 1963) Dürrenmatt shows his capacity for self-parody, and avoids any message or solution – which by definition would divert the spectator from developing his own standpoint, even if it was no more than an exhortation to do precisely that – by transforming it into a deliberate cliché: cultivate your own garden. It is Augias, the politician whose bureaucracy has defeated the heroic individualism of Hercules and so frustrated 'the unique possibility that comes and goes', who claims to be creating 'the right conditions, so that Grace – if it comes – will find a clear mirror for its light' by turning the 'fabulous dung' of politics, that buries his country, into a private garden; and Dürrenmatt's deeply felt attitude of being 'discontented, passing on your discontent, and so altering things with time' is presented ironically.[17] The only statement we are left with is self-negating, the deeper the excrement the taller the flowers – which follows Dürrenmatt's principle of the paradox:

It is my sometimes unfortunate passion to want to put the richness and variety of the world on the stage; so my theatre often becomes ambiguous and seems to confuse. . . when people desperately search in the chicken-coop of my plays for the egg of meaning which I stubbornly refuse to lay.[18]

Dürrenmatt works by indirection. Society is represented oblique-ly, any apparent message (and particularly one that reflects his own views) is undermined by irony because any personal solution must be individual. Thus each spectator is left free to 'pose himself the question as to how far the situation on the stage is also his situation'. On one level this approach merely acknowledges the commonplace that different audiences can respond signifi-cantly differently to a play and so completely change its meaning.[19] But it also points to the way Dürrenmatt attempts to provoke reactions by multiplying associations, rather than controlling his audience by limiting the imaginative connections they can make. That Dürrenmatt still expects a particular response, however, is indicated by the disillusion in some of his comments on freedom of interpretation: 'Theatre is only a moral institution insofar as the spectator makes it one. Consequently, the nihilism that many of today's spectators see in my plays is only a reflection of their own nihilism.'[20]

Dürrenmatt's early plays, *It Is Written* (*Es steht geschrieben*, 1947) and *The Blind Man* (*Der Blinde*, 1948), were resounding failures. They contain many of the same thematic concerns as the later plays – the question of justice, the problem of personal responsi-bility, the gap between what a man stands for and what he does, between appearances and reality – together with the recurring figures of the judge in a clown's mask and the executioner, but presented these in straight terms as serious historical drama. Success only came when he turned to comedy in *Romulus the Great* (*Romulus der Grosse*, 1949), where the theme of justice is treated as a paradox in which betrayal becomes the only virtue, where victims turn out to be their own hangmen, and where potential tragedy is turned into farce by mock-heroic parody, Romulus being reduced to a chicken-farmer whose hens are all the Roman Emperors. This was still basically a costume drama, and Dürren-matt only developed his characteristic 'model' distortions of contemporary society with *The Marriage of Mr Mississippi* (*Die Ehe des Herrn Mississippi*, 1952).

This play and *The Visit* are the clearest examples of Dürren-matt's variation on the 'model' technique, and the most marked change in his development is the use of open theatricality. Thus the major revision in the 1967 version of *It Is Written*, retitled *The Anabaptists* (*Die Wiedertäufer*), turned it into a play-within-a-play by adding a theatrical framework in which the Bishop becomes a theatre patron, and Bockelson, the revolutionary, is a strolling player. In *Mississippi* the action, introduced as stage play and beginning with the death scene that forms the final episode, is constantly broken by direct address to the audience, cuts and flashbacks. Characters are introduced by pictures that float down from the flies, events are illustrated on an immense comic strip, figures enter through a grandfather clock. In *The Visit*, the structure is simpler, but the artificiality is the same. Scene changes are open with façades soaring into the flies, different parts of the town are shown simultaneously, townspeople mime deer, trees, a woodpecker, and the ending is a parody of the final chorus from Sophocles' *Antigone*. On the one hand this extreme stylisation emphasises the artificiality of the stage image, as in the farcical patterning of poisoned coffee cups in *Mississippi* or Claire Zachanassian's nine identical husbands and twin blind eunuchs of *The Visit*. On the other hand the open theatricality liberates the imagination. Anything can happen, and Dürrenmatt's indulgence of his own fantasy is a challenge to the audience's. This intention is most obvious in *Mississippi*, where the doctors trooping onto the stage through the clock and the different scenes through the two windows, 'to the right the branches of an apple-tree, and behind it some northern city with a Gothic cathedral; to the left a cypress, the remains of a classical temple, a bay',[21] exactly parallels Alfred Jarry's setting for *Ubu Roi* (1896):

doors opening onto snow-covered plains under blue [summer] skies, mantlepieces with clocks on them swinging open to turn into doorways, and palm trees flourishing at the foot of beds so that little elephants perching on bookshelves can graze on them...A set which is supposed to represent Nowhere...and the action takes place in Poland, a country so legendary, so dismembered that it is well qualified to be this particular Nowhere, or, in terms of a putative Franco-Greek etymology, a distantly interrogative somewhere.[22]

The comparison with Jarry is worth going into in some detail since it illuminates unsuspected aspects of Dürrenmatt's work. Jarry's satire, as his friend Apollinaire commented, exceeds its object to such an extent that it creates an effect of hallucination.[23] Beneath his comedy of total warfare with its crudely insulting and childishly simplistic surface, is a sophisticated manipulation of vision. The grotesquely one-dimensional figures, exaggeration, parody, juxtaposing of the inflated and the prosaic undermine our everyday frame of reference. The scatological obscenity and gratuitous violence are shock techniques to cut out or short-circuit normal reactions. We try to apply socially approved feelings in the presence of death to a mass demolition of characters who are literally chopped to mincemeat, torn to pieces, impaled or exploded, only to find it funny because such extreme and wholesale slaughter discredits or deadens our conventional responses – particularly if there is no relation between cause and effect, as when a character is chopped in two and both halves continue to function as before, or a character's hair is set on fire and his only comment is 'what a night, I've got hair ache'.[24] Jarry's plays are based on his theory of 'pataphysics', a 'science of imaginary solutions' which 'will examine the laws governing exceptions and...will describe a universe which can be – and perhaps should be – envisaged in the place of the traditional one', working on the premise that the laws of physical science are no more than 'correlations' of 'accidental data which, reduced to the status of unexceptional exceptions, possess no longer even the virtue of originality'.[25] His aim is to impose this 'pataphysical' vision on his audience, freeing our imagination by making our normal concept of reality, and in particular of the social world, untenable. As the epigraph to the final play in the *Ubu* trilogy implies, traditional concepts are 'ruins' and the only way of effectively abolishing accepted views of life is to use the bricks to erect 'fine, well-designed buildings', in other words alternate visions (p. 106).

Not only Dürrenmatt's aim of forcing us to imagine a more rational world but his techniques, particularly in *Mississippi*, are strikingly similar. Murder is treated in the same way, as wildly extravagant multiple killings which have no perceptible effect on the victims who get up and go on as before. The setting, again echoing Jarry, 'expressed the indefiniteness of the locale (in order to give the play its spirit of wit, of comedy)',[26] while the same hallucinatory effect, achieved by a short-circuiting of habitual responses through overloading the audience's capacity to rationalise the picture presented to them in any normal terms with complex illogicalities and incongruities, was the hallmark of the original Munich and Zürich productions. Perspectives were expressionistically distorted, the furnishings dwarfed the actors, extraordinary shadows tricked the eye (see Illustration 6); while

6   Dürrenmatt, *The Marriage of Mr Mississippi*, 1952. Paradoxical perspectives: the actors dwarfed by the furniture.

the actors wore exaggerated make up and costuming – the Minister with a completely shaven head, monocle and elongated cigarette-holder in a gold-lamé coat and top-hat, Anastasia with grotesque eye make-up and immense earrings, the Maid wearing an outsize Alice-in-Wonderland bow on her head – and they moved like puppets in a demonic cabaret with stylised rhetorical gestures. At the same time the piling up and complex interweaving of events was explicitly 'so that anyone who begins to try to set them out in a logical relationship loses himself',[27] and one of the actors was reported as saying 'I'd feel happier if only I understood a fraction of what is going on here.'[28]

Beneath the deliberately confusing surface, which Dürrenmatt made simpler and less abstract in later versions, is a model of European civilisation, reduced to 'the story of a room'. Different cultural periods are represented by the furniture – a plaster Venus de Milo, Gothic clock, Louis Quinze and Empire pieces, *fin-de siècle* mirrors and the *Biedermeier* coffee table of the bourgeoisie – and the general relevance was made plain in the film version (1961) which was shot in all the main European capitals. The progressive demolition of this room forms the basic structure of the play, while the forces of disintegration are symbolised in the main characters. Mississippi and Saint Claude, social reformers who ran a brothel together until inspired respectively by the Old Testament and Marx, stand for opposite versions of absolute justice, Mosaic Law and Communism. Both destroy themselves by their refusal to compromise, paving the way to power for the Minister, the cynical pragmatist without principles. The other extreme of the idealistic spectrum is represented by Übelohe, a Don Quixote of selfless – and powerless – love, whose only achievement is his own physical and financial bankruptcy. All four circle around Anastasia (the name means literally 'one who will rise again' as indeed she does in the play), a figure representing the world itself as the object of their desire in the shape of a high-society whore. All this symbolism is rather over-explicit. Übelohe appears in a battered tin helmet with a bent lance under the circling shadow of a windmill, the Minister spells out Anastasia's significance: 'as you have betrayed your husband, so you will betray me, and so on. For you what is will always be stronger than what was, and what will be will always triumph over the present. No one can grasp you; whoever builds upon you will perish' (pp. 82–3) and embraces her at the end saying 'I...embrace the world' (p. 119).

Unlike *Mississippi* where the melodramatic bedroom-farce plot is only a scaffolding for intellectual acrobatics, *The Visit* is both simpler and subtler since theme and character are integrated in the action. Instead of reflecting the colourful diversity of the world in formal complexity, the structure embodies a terrifyingly direct logic. A millionairess, having bought up and deliberately bankrupted a small town which threw her out as a young girl when she became pregnant, pays a 'visit of mercy'. She proposes a bargain. Her seducer, who had bribed witnesses in her paternity suit in order to marry a wealthier village girl and is now (because of his childhood friendship with her) the town's most respected citizen, is to be killed in exchange for prosperity. The town rejects the offer, but their moral resolve is undermined by poverty, they begin buying on credit, finally persuade themselves that the punishment is moral, and execute him. The action is simultaneously a revelation of evil beneath an apparently normal surface, forcing us to condemn a society we had associated with our own, and an analysis of the power of money to distort moral principles. Like Anastasia's house, the town of Güllen is a model of civilisation in miniature: 'a city of Humanist traditions. Goethe spent a night here. Brahms composed a quartet here'.[29] By the end the cultural attitudes that forbade murder have been inverted and Alfred Ill's trial and execution take place under Schiller's banner, 'Life is serious, Art serene' (p. 89). On the surface this is a straightforward demonstration of the corruption of spiritual values by materialism as moral credentials are replaced by buying on credit. But on a deeper level this is not a perversion of culture but an expression of its intrinsic nature. Culture can only exist when there is a superfluity of wealth. It is thus the product of exploitation based on the very qualities its ideals condemn. The money that comes from (a prospective) murder not only provides fur coats and cars, but commissions the artist to paint portraits instead of signs, provides a new bell for the church, and allows Ill's daughter to learn French. Since art is a luxury, the Schoolmaster's substitution of poverty for money as the root of evil is more than mere irony. The point is the same as that argued explicitly by Mississippi:

Our families caused heads to roll haphazard, I demand death for the guilty. They were called heroes, I am called a hangman. If my professional success throws an unfavourable light on the best families in the country, it only means that I am showing them up in their true light (p. 68).

The typical inner structure for Dürrenmatt's plays is the trial. Mercy and justice are constants in his work, separated in the figures of Public Prosecutor, Mississippi, and Angel of the Prisons, Anastasia, or united in a figure like Claire Zachanassian, the avenging Fate who loves the man she kills and carries him off to the Isle of the Dead. But mercy and justice are divine prerogatives. Consequently they can only appear in human form as grotesque parodies, distorted and so comic, apparently undermining the morality themes. And on this level Dürrenmatt's plays are closely related to his detective stories, a genre normally read for light entertainment, in which serious questions can be raised precisely because no philosophy is expected. The surface of mystery, pursuit and danger, like the comedy of the plays, is designed to distract us, while the way the stories work out slips moral timebombs beneath our defences of set thought-patterns, and the conventions of crime and the whodunnit are used to focus on the process of justice itself. *The Puncture* (*Die Panne*, 1956) epitomises this technique. A travelling salesman is forced by a puncture to spend the night in a retired judge's house. In exchange for his lodgings, he agrees to take part in a mock trial for the after-dinner amusement of the other guests, an ex-prosecutor, ex-defence lawyer, and one-time hangman. The cross-questioning reveals a fact that he was unaware of himself, that it was his conduct which drove his former boss, whose job he now holds, to commit suicide. A mock death sentence is passed, but the salesman takes the game seriously and hangs himself. As he asked at the beginning:

> What crime am I supposed to have committed?
> PROSECUTOR: An unimportant point, my friend. There's always a crime to be found.[30]

Given this premise (which makes Dürrenmatt's argument deliberately circular), categories of good and evil no longer apply. In *The Visit* too all men are equally guilty, and here again the legal process is a sham. The trial of Ill by the townspeople is a cover for Dürrenmatt's trial of society, and they condemn themselves in sentencing him. The process is that of *Romulus*, where the audience are intended to believe, like the characters who see themselves as Roman patriots, that 'this emperor must be removed' as a traitor because his actions are designed to deliver civilisation into the hands of the Huns. We set ourselves up as his judges, only to discover that he is 'judging the world', that we are defending what he had recognised as a morally indefensible state of affairs, and that his apparent crime is the action of a just man carrying out a justified verdict.[31] The only difference in *The Visit* is that the ambiguities are set up at the beginning instead of being revealed by a sudden reversal. Claire is as much an embodiment of absolute Mosaic justice as Mississippi, but her rigidity is plain in her mechnical limbs, ivory instead of flesh, and this particular 'Last Judgement' (p. 19) is 'an ascent from the infernal regions' (p. 27). In these terms Ill is an inverted Christ-figure and his sacrifice brings a false salvation which damns his fellow townspeople. Similarly *Mississippi* discredits all political or religious attempts to change a world in which history is the 'utter ruin' of ideals (p. 97), progress a 'yearning for ever more distant paradises' (p. 119). It is this kind of judgement that has been mistaken for nihilism – even though the exaggerated extremism of Dürrenmatt's condemnation itself signals that it is not meant to be taken literally. The inverted model is intended as 'a testing of reality, of the correctness of beliefs', and the conclusions are undermined by presenting them as farce (the theatrical equivalent to the 'lightness' of the detective-story). 'Laughter manifests human freedom', and comedy comes from the perception of a situation as ridiculous. Dürrenmatt's form follows the same 'worst possible turn' principle that in his plots leads to death – but 'the worst possible turn that a [serious] story can take is the turn into comedy'.[32]

The reason why Dürrenmatt has so frequently been misunderstood comes partly from the way he overestimates the 'distance' of comedy and the value of irony as a 'philosophic' perspective. But the accusation of nihilism also stems from the length to which he goes in forcing the audience to formulate personal solutions (itself a rather overhopeful expectation). For example, where Brecht in the epilogue to *The Good Person of Setzuan* implies the correct solution by listing only all the false answers, Dürrenmatt refuses to lay any 'egg of meaning' and presents positive as well as destructive values in an equally parodied form. Romulus and Übelohe are 'men of courage; the lost world-order is restored in them', while Ill is 'a man who in recognising his guilt lives out justice and who, in death, achieves greatness'.[33] But Romulus is made a clown as well as a traitor to prevent any identification with him. Ill only accepts his guilt in transferring it onto the town, a reverse scapegoat whose original crime of bribery is the Zachanassian method in miniature. Übelohe is a diseased drunkard who is (literally) reduced to Mississippi's level on the floor when the firing starts – a comparison underlined in the first version of the play by a comment from Saint-Claude, 'so they crawled on their stomachs like animals . . . they who aspired to improve this world'. Although when taken to its extreme in a play like *Portrait of a Planet* (1970) this technique of parody tends to an olympian viewpoint from which all moral distinctions are lost, it has certainly been effective as provocation. Dürrenmatt has been accused of blasphemy on more than one occasion, while a gymnastic association in Mönchen-Gladbach demanded that *The Visit* should be banned as an 'obscene work' that defamed the ideals of sport – reactions which in an ironic way parallel his own reaction to society: 'The world (and with it the stage that signifies this world) is for me something monstrous, a riddle of calamity which must be accepted, but before which there must be no capitulation.'[34]

Dürrenmatt's avoidance of commitment, his claim that 'the stage is not a battlefield for theories, philosophies and manifestos, but rather an instrument whose possibilities I seek to know by playing with it',[35] is itself on one level an ironic provocation. It does not correspond to the facts. Purely stylistic exploration is an element common to all Dürrenmatt's work as his subtitles ('a fragmentary comedy', 'a requiem for the crime novel', 'a still possible story') show, but a play like *Mississippi* is literally a battle between ideologies. Even though there the action demonstrates no philosophy and didacticism is ruled out by imposing a multiplicity of contradictory viewpoints, this type of drama is highly intellectual. Conceptual models entail conceptual characterisation. In spite of the repeated stress that 'there is humanity to be discovered . . . behind each of my figures' or that 'I have described people not puppets, an action not an allegory',[36] the people in Dürrenmatt's drama are not psychologically developed individuals but embodiments of social forces or ideas. They are incomplete in the sense that they have no independence from the dramatic situation, and there is little variation in the speech patterns of different characters. Each is defined by contrast to the others as parts in the functional 'shape' of the play as a whole, the five principals in *Mississippi* for example being 'developed each out of the others' – a method that Dürrenmatt calls 'inductive' in an attempt to distinguish his approach from Brecht's, but which has exactly the same effect as the contrasted Brechtian 'deduction' of

characters from a premise. Their significance is primarily that of
symbols, and if Claire Zachanassian and all her retinue are rigid,
containing 'no further possibility of development' within themselves, the same is true of a character like Ill whose only development is to accept an imposed role, so achieving 'a monumental
quality'.[37] This is underlined by the recurrence of the same figures
in different plays, Claire being a variation on Anastasia, equally
indestructible and just as much a social-columnist's cliché or
fashion-plate personification of the Whore of Babylon, though
more grotesque with her false limbs and the contrast between her
age and marital activities. Claire's semi-mechanical body corresponds to Worringer's classic definition of the grotesque as the
perception of the animation of the inorganic, and this objectifying
comedy is even more obvious in the minor figures. The opening
stage directions in *Mississippi* propose the coffee table as 'really
the main character in the play' while listing the three executioners
together with vases and cups as 'further objects'. In *The Visit*
states of mind are presented, with great economy of detail, as
material possessions – a gold tooth, a typewriter, ubiquitous
yellow shoes – and the drama is not even that of symbolic individuals but of the mass, like *Frank V*, where 'the real hero is a
collective' who are 'marionettes' on the strings of 'the larger
system'.[38] The structure is that of a communal progression, each
section of the play ends with an action carried out by all the
townspeople as a unit, and their nature as automatons is indicated
by the final chorus where all speak as one.

Dürrenmatt's development has been towards simplicity of form
together with increasingly oblique statement. The complex interpenetration of simultaneous scenes and different time-frames in
Mississippi came to be seen as 'a dramaturgical dead-end'.[39] *The
Visit* is much more direct in exposition, but uses images in which
appearance contradicts reality. Where the progressive destruction
of Anastasia's room represents the history of western civilisation
allegorically, in Güllen the same moral regression is shown by
increasingly luxurious objects, and the true nature of the slums
is revealed by transforming them into neon-lit penthouses. This
inversion makes the model-situation more imaginatively effective,
as does the economy of imagery – the brilliant definition of
poverty by a negative, a station the train does *not* stop in; or
epitomising the first step up the social ladder to riches by new
shoes – and this development reaches its fullest expression in the

tightly-knit plot of *The Physicists* (*Die Physiker*, 1962) or the spare concision of *Play Strindberg* (1969).

The atomic bomb, perhaps the dominant post-war issue and one which Dürrenmatt repeatedly refers to as conditioning his view of the world, has provided a major theme for politically concerned German dramatists. It presents a natural focus for questions of personal responsibility, of the individual versus the state, of man's control over his own existence. It is also a graphic illustration of the legacy of war. The moral dilemma of the physicist has been explored by Brecht, Zuckmayer and Kipphardt as well as Dürrenmatt, and the contrasts in treatment are illuminating. *The Cold Light* (*Das kalte Licht*, 1955) and *In the Matter of J. Robert Oppenheimer* both present the human problems in individual terms by drawing on real figures, Fuchs and Oppenheimer. In Zuckmayer's naturalistic dramaturgy, however, any general significance is reduced to the melodrama of spies and sexual romance, while Kipphardt's documentary techniques only serve to underline the impotence of the single person: 'we, the physicists, find that we have never before been of such consequence, and that we have never before been so completely helpless'.[40] By contrast Brecht's treatment in *Galileo* brings out the issues in such a way as to imply a solution in the distancing perspective of history, but the representative nature of his parable-figure assumes that the modern physicist is free to act and that the solution lies with the individual – a 'heroic' answer which indeed contradicted Brecht's own political observations and principles, and which was modified in later versions by adding indications of a pre-revolutionary social situation. Dürrenmatt's fantasy 'model' brings the questions home to a public of non-scientists and allows for a positive response without simplifying the difficulties. It indicates the historical background (Newton and Einstein, but as popular images of the physicist *per se*, adopted masks not actual people), argues the issues as paradoxes, and even more obviously than in his other plays forms a mousetrap for the spectator's conscience.

The approach is laid out in the '21 Points' appended to *The Physicists*:

17. What affects everyone can only be solved by everyone.
18. Every attempt by an individual acting on his own to solve what affects everyone must fail....
21. Drama can outwit the spectator into exposing himself to reality.[41]

The figure of Möbius, named after the Möbius-strip, the mathematical model on which the front becomes the back and forward movement reverses itself, points to how this works in the play. Anything the audience accepts at face value as reality is immediately shown to be illusory by being transformed into its opposite. We are told that Beutler and Ernesti suffer from the delusion that they are Newton and Einstein, and Beutler enters dressed in eighteenth century costume. However this image undermines its own premise, being a 'proof' of Beutler's belief which in fact destroys its credibility because it implies that his madness is a conscious role since (as the programme notes to the première carefully pointed out) 'schizophrenics are known to need no costume to act out their *idée fixe*'.[42] He then confirms this by admitting his persona to be a pretence, only to base his claim to sanity on the proposition that he is the true Einstein, 'Newton' having been adopted only to avoid disturbing Ernesti's delusion. And we are then brought round full circle by the Doctor's 'it is I who decide who my patients think they are'[43] – which in turn throws doubt on her sanity. This first scene contains the pattern of the play as a whole. Behind their masks 'Newton' and 'Einstein' really are scientists, and behind the scientist is the spy with a rational reason for being in a madhouse. But this apparently sane behaviour is in the final analysis idiocy, being based on a premise – that power politics is rational – which is demonstrably false because the leaders of society, in the shape of the Doctor and her family portraits of the industrialist, the politician and the general, turn out to be mad. The fake Newton is stated to be 'the author of the theory of Equivalents' (p. 48), a neat key to Dürrenmatt's method, which forces the audience into a constant re-evaluation of their assumptions while at the same time disguising serious intentions as farce. Möbius is also Solomon, the symbol of wisdom, and on this level *The Physicists* is about the abuse of knowledge – not only the application of physical discoveries to destructive purposes, but the arrogance of the individual who attempts to solve the problems of the world by unilateral action, an insane presumption which leads only to the nihilistic despair of Möbius 'Song of Solomon to be sung to the cosmonauts' (p. 66). He is, in effect, the Icarus of the atomic age, raised by his intellect to a point where he makes himself responsible for mankind as a whole, only to find that this is an evasion of his responsibility. The true image for Möbius' withdrawal from society in order to avoid its misuse of his genius is his family's escapism into the sentimentality of Buxtehude's music or the South Seas, because 'What was once thought can never be unthought' (p. 50). The continual Pirandellian unmasking of apparent reality as questionable is intended to make the audience uncertain of received opinions, forcing us to search for personal answers; and this is reinforced by the way familiar arguments are presented by the three physicists: 'orders are orders...you haven't a monopoly of knowledge...the freedom of scientific knowledge... [physicists] must become power politicians...today it's the duty of a genius to remain unrecognised' (pp. 52–9). These arguments are not only deliberately given the form of Sunday Supplement clichés; in covering the whole range of possible general solutions they lose any real meaning, and are all overruled by the ending which follows the same pattern as Dürrenmatt's other plays. The simultaneous turn from apparently positive, but superficial argument into grotesque farce, and the extreme nihilism of 'Now the cities over which I ruled are dead, the Kingdom that was given into my keeping is deserted: only a blue, shimmering wilderness. And somewhere round a small yellow star there circles pointlessly, everlastingly, the radioactive earth' (p. 67) is both a shock and a challenge to each spectator not only to imagine a more rational solution but, unlike Möbius, to act on it.

The effectiveness of *The Physicists* comes from its form rather than any deep or original analysis of the issues. Discussing 'Problems of the Theatre' in 1954, Dürrenmatt had proposed Aristotle's unities as the ideal dramatic form, but one that was no longer usable since modern drama was forced to invent material and its stories were therefore unknown. But the subject here is assumed to be familiar enough for the ideas to need no serious exploration, so the unities, straightforwardness and stichomythy of Greek tragedy can be deployed. The results are an intensity and concentrated focus which, applied to comedy, gain a certain irony in themselves, quite apart from the deliberate incongruity between the rationality of the form and the madhouse context. However, the play's structure is not that of plot but thought-patterns, paradox being seen as the basic law of intellect, while instead of a logical, cause-and-effect progression the relationship between each scene is determined by the desired orchestration of audience response. The murder investigation is presented as a model for the rational processes of deductive discovery, and the detective, whose questioning opens each act, is an open clue for the spectator, whose task is equally to find a solution. Even murder itself, reduced to an almost incidental action by farcical repetition and by a parody of romantic novelettes ('she loved me and I loved her. It was a dilemma that could only be resolved by the use of a curtain cord', p. 14), is little more than a factor in conditioning the right critical attitude; its human significance is removed, and it becomes an image for the sacrifice of individuals to abstractions. Similarly the reversal/discovery of the final scene, where the scientists' refuge becomes their prison, while their self-sacrifice and good intentions are made meaningless by the empire-building insanity of the Doctor, who has copied all the notes Möbius destroys, is not a logical development from the preceding action but from the need to provoke a particular reaction. The unities too are not used, as in neo-classical drama, to structure a body of material but, brilliantly, as techniques to arouse and direct a specific set of responses in the minds of the audience.

An achievement on one level frequently means sacrificing other qualities, and this economy and focus is at the expense of character (which again is typical of parable or model drama). The figures are fixed, limited to their function, and any impression of life comes only from switching their masks. Clockwork has replaced characterisation, though the types are recognisably those of Dürrenmatt's other plays. Möbius is an extension of Übelohe and Ill, the 'courageous man', and his defeat is the same, while the monstrous Doctor Mathilde von Zahnd is a further embodiment of Anastasia and Claire Zachanassian, now reduced to an insane hunchback.

The Physicists and *The Meteor* (which only reached the stage in 1966) were begun at the same time and worked on together as 'companion-pieces', one conceived as a play of 'pure situation', the other as 'pure action'.[44] This separation of the different elements of drama is symptomatic of the way Dürrenmatt has refined his models into increasingly simple forms, a development which reaches its extreme in *Play Strindberg* (1969). This is drama stripped to its skeleton, and the basic level of the play is neither situation nor action but 'the unison of a trio playing together with complete precision developed from the work of the three actors. The art of acting'[45] – which is also a description of its theme. The misuse of English in the title is deliberate, a pointer to the ambiguity of an adaptation which makes its source the object of

its criticism, taking Strindberg's social commentary as an image
of the society it condemns, so that the play form itself epitomises
hyprocrisy and pretence, and Strindberg's autobiographical personal relationships turn into theatre. Thus 'critical theatre',
Dürrenmatt's own label for his work, gains a double meaning in
this transformation of *The Dance of Death* into a comedy about
bourgeois tragedy. The mutual laceration of unhappy people is
presented as an exercise in role-playing, giving the audience a
double perspective in which a tragic psychological state is simultaneously a rhetorical ploy, so that social criticism coexists with
a situation of farce. Strindberg's view of existence overlaps with
Dürrenmatt's typical concerns, life as a state of dying being the
central premise of *The Meteor*, the parody of bourgeois marriage
as a hypocritical lie based on the poisoned coffee-cups of social
convention going back to *Mississippi*. But with the self-reflexive
theatricality which equates social with dramatic conventions, these
themes are totally integrated in stage action, symbols or intellectualised statements can be avoided, and characters are grotesque
in what they do, not what they are.

'Plush X Infinity' was how Dürrenmatt summed up what
disturbed him about Strindberg, and his text makes the audience
(which he has always assumed to be an educated one and here
expects to be familiar with *The Dance of Death*) vividly aware of
these qualities by their extreme absence. The dialogue is cut to
isolated, single noun sentences. What is left still corresponds fairly
closely to Schering's 1926 German translation of the original, but
there is now hardly an adjective in the play, and spiritual
transcendence is reduced to 'staring into the infinite' (p. 30)
which turns out to be a form of catalepsy. This is as it were a
minimal model – 'In the great world...life goes on just as it does
here: It's only the dimensions that are different' (p. 75). The
intention is no different from Dürrenmatt's other plays – as he
outlined it in the ironic mouth of Übelohe, 'to investigate what
happens when certain ideas collide with people...whether or not
the material universe is susceptible of improvement'[46] – but here
the world is that of the stage, while ideas are represented indirectly
as social forms and empty moral principles, behaviour patterns
being the external expressions of ideology. The setting is without
scenery, a circular acting area lit from directly above like a boxing
ring by a battery of spotlights, and the scenes, announced as twelve
'rounds', each start off with a gong. The same formalisation is

applied to the occupations of the characters, which are presented as set pieces: 'Conversation Before Dinner', 'Philosophical Discussion', 'Photograph Album Scene'. Dürrenmatt's alterations of Strindberg's plot also emphasise artifice, introducing exactly balanced parallels into the structure and replacing personal attitudes by deliberately adopted masks which the characters can interchange in a manner comparable to *The Physicists*. Alice and Kurt are explicitly lovers, Edgar names Kurt's ex-wife as his future bride. The accusation of embezzlement becomes an invention by Alice to destroy Edgar, who turns it to his own advantage. Edgar pretends he has proof that Kurt is a master criminal to punish Alice for her infidelity, and Kurt goes along with the deception to test her love for him. Everything reduces to theatre.

Play Strindberg is the most frequently produced contemporary play in Germany since the war – a recognition of its theatrical effectiveness. Dürrenmatt's earlier stylistic confusion or the deliberate misleading of the audience has been replaced by clarity and concision. But the economy that gives it intensity also leads to abstraction, which is the major flaw of this type of drama. Even when didacticism is avoided, the model form still subtracts individuality from the characters, and it is this lack which has always made farce a minor genre. Dürrenmatt disguises this here by the identification of the figures as actors, but they are still at bottom cyphers.

Two of Martin Walser's plays, *Rabbit Race* (*Eiche und Angora*, 1962) and *The Black Swan* (*Der schwarze Schwan*, 1964), the first parts of an unfinished trilogy analysing the postwar German scene, indicate ways of avoiding the one-sided intellectuality and flat characterisation associated with the model form. Walser's attitude to Brecht is as ambivalent as Dürrenmatt's, and there is a similar sense of social commitment without ideological answers which has the same effect of transforming political issues into moral questions. He even refers to these plays in Dürrenmatt's terms, calling them purely theatrical 'examples' to distinguish them from 'illusory' imitations of reality, 'comedies with a tragic content', reflections of a 'grotesque' vision of society.[47] But Walser is no mere follower of Dürrenmatt, and the atmosphere of his plays is significantly different. Where Dürrenmatt draws on Wedekind, Walser is influenced by Kafka, who was the subject of his doctoral thesis, so that his central theme, which is also the basic focus of his novels and more domestic drama – Darwinian survival through adaptability and the conditioning of the present by the past, of individuals by institutions – is interpreted as a psychological problem.

Like Dürrenmatt, Walser took Brecht's parables as his starting point, but instead of analysing social structures in general terms to convince an audience of the need for political action (Brecht) or to challenge them to imagine a more rational world (Dürren-matt), his aim is to create a state of self-awareness through recognition. Reality is defined by perception, not by objective fact, and in his novels details of everyday life are presented through the protagonists' vision, existing only as components of a stream of consciousness. This worm's eye or key-hole perspective, accumulating minutae to portray the mentality of a representative figure – ironically named Kristlein, petty Christ, in *Half Time* (*Halbzeit*) and *The Unicorn* (*Das Einhorn*) – is not possible on the stage, and in his plays Walser replaces it with an openly symbolic world. In *Rabbit Race* this is deliberately crude. The oak around which the action takes place stands for typically Prussian virtues. Inhabited by crows and a solitary nightingale (the castrasted Alois), Germany is a Choral Society. The ground defended in 1945 is an area of historic graves. These are all clichés from the popular imagination, and the extreme naturalism of the setting parodies the fake idyllicism of German *Gemütlichkeit* – real trees and bushes on a hillock, which in the original Berlin production was built on a revolve and turned to show different vistas as the characters moved through the wood in obvious imitation of Reinhardt's classic *trompe l'œil* staging of *A Midsummer Night's Dream* (see Illustration 7). Every time the word 'nature' was mentioned the twittering of birds was heard, and the whole play was presented as a folk-song, culminating in set-pieces like the artificial sweetness in a castrato rendition of 'Über allen Gipfeln ist Ruh'. These popular images are contrasted throughout with the characters' actions to reveal their emptiness. Instead of imitating the symbolic qualities of the oak in the confusion of the final stages of the war, the Nazi officials allow Alois, whom they have just condemned to death for treason, to tie them up around it so that they can save themselves by claiming to be prisoners of the Allies if the SS arrive, or of the SS if the Allies win. The German *Götterdämmerung* is reduced to a shabby farce; the German audience's imaginary world is discredited.

7 Walser, *Rabbit Race*, 1962. *Trompe l'œil* scenery and farce.

Walser's approach is summed up in his treatment of Alois, who stands for the German 'folk'. Superficially he resembles Schwejk, the literary ideal of robust realism, whose exaggerated subservience is a disguised form of social opposition which exposes the ruling classes' assumptions of superiority as unjustified. But his true nature is nearer to Woyzeck, the archetypal victim who epitomises the inhumanity of the system which exploits him. The 'folk', in the shape of Hašek's or Brecht's Schwejk-figures, can be seen as guaranteeing the basic integrity of the German people whatever their apparent actions, a last self-justifying excuse for the public, saving them from acknowledging their complicity in Nazi war crimes. Walser removes this defence by reversing the image. Where Brecht's Schwejk is an example of passive resistance, Alois is an enthusiastic cooperator: 'historically...our people always participate. Meek and tractable; easily led therefore into evil', and his castration is intended to symbolise both this pliability and (something that hardly comes across in the play) the true status of the Germans, 'disbarred from all rights by this terrible political adventure'.[48] Alois is not only the subject of a perverted medical experiment, like Büchner's Woyzeck. His acquiescence as a victim is what makes the system possible, and imprisoned in a concentration camp under the Nazis, committed to a lunatic asylum by the revanchist Germany of the 1960s, he also mirrors the behaviour of his torturers on a symbolic level, breeding rabbits with Jewish names which he slaughters for their skins. This ambivalence is the key to Walser's treatment of the post-war experience. As a man always out of step Alois is a clown figure, but in essence he is no different from the self-serving characters who keep their positions by (literally) changing their coats. The only distinction is that he adapts less skillfully, still singing communist songs under the Nazis, still commemorating the Führer's birthday in the 1950s. Comedy is manipulated to embarrass the audience – as in the way a Jew, distractedly wandering the woods calling for his sons who have been killed in a concentration camp, is presented as a figure of fun and not with (acceptable) pathos. The bad taste is deliberate, but it is also a reason for the play's lack of success.

In *The Black Swan* Walser's techniques are less open to misunderstanding. Instead of the structural contrasts of *Rabbit Race*, where the attitudes of the 1960s are juxtaposed with those of 1945 and 1950, the same characters being shown reversing their principles twice – a double negative implying that the German present is no different to the fascism which officially no longer exists – in this play the past is seen indirectly by its distorting effect on personalities. Again the setting is metaphoric, but here the symbolism is an expression of the characters' neuroses, and the atmosphere evoked by descriptions of the oppressive air like wet clothes, spiders' webs or soot, is a psychological one. Its subjective nature is underlined by the contrast to the bare stage, clinically lit, which in Palitzsch's original production was backed by stark black and white projections (tree branches, a wall, the barred windows of the institution) with the scenes being played out as demonstrations on a low front-stage platform. The protagonist, a youth who bears the same name as his father, Rudi Goothein, once a doctor in a concentration camp, is obsessed by guilt feelings for his father's crimes. In a reverse transference he claims responsibility for these atrocities, committed before he was born, is taken for treatment to one of his father's former colleagues, Liberé, who now runs a psychiatric clinic, and finally commits suicide under a tree pruned in the seven-branched shape of a Jewish candelabra. The play is based on *Hamlet*, and it is never clear whether Rudi is actually deluded or simulating madness to force the older generation to assume responsibility for their past, which is the psychiatrist's diagnosis: 'Perhaps he's only acting. Tortures himself in front of us. Till we can't stand it any more. A purposeful and fully conscious pretence.'[49] In the first version of the play Rudi's suicide causes Liberé to give himself up to justice. This was changed, both because it offers a scapegoat for the audience and because the police are irrelevant, Walser's principle being 'each his own judge'; and in the final script even his death is ignored by the other characters, who continue to deaden their consciences with empty social rituals, in this case a farewell party.

On the surface *The Black Swan* appears a psychological case-history; but there is no exploration of personal motives, Rudi's identification with his father is left unexplained, and the actions of the characters are determined by symbolic relationships rather than being expressions of their personalities. Walser intends his figures to be representative as well as individualised – hence their ironic names, Goothein being literally 'good death', while Liberé, a false name for a false freedom, is really called Leibnitz, which is intended to indicate that fascism had its roots in acceptable philosophers and must thus be seen as part of the mainstream of German development, not an abberation.

Similarly while the plot concerns an individual's suicide, the structure is a paradigm of all the possible reactions to guilt. Rudi takes on himself the guilt that his father refuses to face. Liberé acknowledges his responsibility to himself but leads a life of pretence to avoid the consequences of his past, while his daughter Irm, the Ophelia-figure to Rudi's Hamlet, demonstrates the extreme psychological effects of adaptability. She has persuaded herself to believe the lie that they were in India during the war, only to find that her escapism still contains the elements of concentration camps. Her imagination has simply transposed the chimneys of Auschwitz into Indian burning ghats, and her fascination with these self-imposed 'memories' of Suttee symbolises her retreat from reality. At times the two levels fail to merge, as in the suggestion that Irm's state results from being raped by her teacher as a child. Quite apart from being too obvious a political reference, this lacks conviction, having apparently left no discernible traces in her personality or attitude to sex. But the intention of this double vision is clearly to challenge the audience's self-awareness, a game of truth which is perhaps too overtly spelt out: the present can only be meaningful if the past is acknowledged and if one is conscious of one's own potentialities, hence Liberé's question to the younger generation – 'Have you ever thought what you might have done if it had been up to you then, if you had been old enough...you, the boastful moral hero' (p. 51). There are repeated references to the Eumenides, but no suggestion of how atonement may be achieved. Rudi's

> Let us from time to time remember
> That we are forever guilty (p. 72)

(spoken ceremonially by the madmen in his Hamlet-like play-within-a-play) is no solution. As with Dürrenmatt, the spectator is forced to reach a personal answer, and the unrelieved gloom was intended to have a positive value in portraying 'the negative conditioning-factors' in society 'as negative', the one-sided suicide and hypocrisy containing its opposite 'as a white shadow'.[50]

Walser developed his theory of a new form of theatrical realism while writing these plays, and it is indicative that he chose to write a psychological 'fable' in 1964, the year of the Auschwitz trial.

Rejecting 'newspaper realism' and 'discussion theatre' as superficial, he defined theatre as 'the place where society's consciousness is presented for analysis, noting and testing its developments'.[51] In Walser's special use of the term, realism ('*Realismus X*') is an internal revelation of something unperceived.
Anything accepted has already become a cliché, a substitute
for perception which disguises the true relationship of people to
their social environment. Established intellectual viewpoints and
the stylistic forms that express them being automatically 'idealistic,' falsifying experience, drama must be anti-ideological, continually dealing with new concepts of reality. In a sense this is close
to Heisenberg's indeterminacy principle – the act of perception
itself alters what is perceived, so that consciousness is a condition
of perpetual change – and it is hardly accidental that one of the
major images in Walser's first play, *The Detour* (*Der Abstecher*,
1961), is the Heraclitean river. Walser's focus, then, is on the
spectator's state of awareness rather than external events, and the
structure of his drama is intended to affect this state, not to reflect
preconceived notions about 'reality'.

The practical implications of this can be seen in *Rabbit Race* and
The Black Swan. Both are deliberately artificial in style, 'imaginary
fables' designed to express contemporary consciousness by
contrasting the present with memory or the immediate past, an
exaggeratedly unpleasant picture that the spectator 'gradually
recognises...as far more relevant to him than he had suspected.
A topical spark has detonated.'[52] This immediacy is also present
in the details of the fable. Since the subject of these plays is modes
of vision, their conditioning and manipulation, any distancing in
the form of a Brechtian emigration to a fantasy world would only
confuse. Being subjective, perspectives that alter with the personal
experience of different spectators, the material of this type of
drama cannot be represented directly in the fate of a conventional
protagonist, and the model form that Walser has developed is in
many ways an adequate stylistic solution. It both provides a
structure, unrelated to plot or naturalistic considerations, which
catches states of consciousness at the only point they become
visible, in transition, and allows the use of symbolic characters,
which show these states of consciousness in all their major
variations. At the same time the necessity for the audience to
identify with the symbols limits the relevance of this type of
drama. Dürrenmatt's Güllen stands for all the western world,

Walser's oak has a specifically German reference. His approach, when he outlines it in general terms, seems to have a wide validity – 'The fable generated by realistic perception is not fooled by reality, rather it demonstrates to reality what reality is. It plays with reality until it admits: that's me'[53] – but as examples of this approach his plays are narrow in scope, and the themes are non-transferable, while a technique that actually succeeds in discomposing its spectators (by comparison Handke's apparently more overt abuse of the audience is positively flattering since it attacks social roles, not subconscious self-images) is hardly designed to attract a wide public. So it is unfortunate, but unsurprising, that Walser's plays are almost unknown outside and, however respected, seldom performed inside Germany.

6. *Dialectics*

Brecht's approach, if not the details of his theory, has been perhaps the most significant single influence on world drama since the 1960s. Apart from the frequent productions of Brecht's major plays, and specific borrowings of his techniques by Osborne or Arden, Joan Littlewood or Roger Planchon, the indirect influence of his work can be seen everywhere on the general level of performance. For example, as Ronald Hayman has pointed out, it is largely the standard set by the Berliner Ensemble that changed English acting from Stanislavski's psychology or Shakespearian romanticism to Brechtian unheroic materialism.[1] Equally significant, it can also be seen in the way productions are prepared – the dramaturge, whose function of providing factual data for a play determined its interpretation in Brecht's productions, has recently become a familiar figure in English and American theatre, reflecting a new need to research the political, historical and aesthetic aspects of a play. With this international effect it is hardly surprising that on the German-speaking stage Brecht's influence has been so dominant that even dramatists with totally different political viewpoints are forced to define their aims in his terms. As an 'instant classic' he stands like a rock in the mainstream of German drama, forming stylistic eddies even in work that has no connection with his 'theatre of the scientific age'.

However his plays themselves have not proved particularly useful as dramatic models, and the drawbacks of direct imitation can be clearly seen in the overloaded metaphors of Günther Weisenborn's *Babel* (1947) where images drawn from *St Joan of the Stockyards* (*Die Heilige Johanna der Schlachthöfe*, 1931) and *Jungle of Cities* (*Im Dickicht der Städte*, 1923) have become substitutes for reality, or in the overstretched parallels of Hartmut Lange's *The Murder of Ajax: or a Discourse on Wood-Chopping* (*Die Ermordung des Aias oder ein Diskurs über das Holzhacken*, 1971) where Odysseus equals Stalin, Ajax – Trotsky, and the weapons of the dead Achilles, which they guard, are Lenin's control of official communist theory – interpretations carefully specified by 'subtitles' on placards. Brecht's distancing and 'historicising', illustrating the essence of an issue in strange (even exotic) forms to break the audience's unthinking acceptance of

social conditions as 'normal' and therefore unchangeable, becomes a straitjacket of allegory, and forces didactic simplifications
even onto such material as Kleist's *Marquise von O...* which in
Lange's adaptation, *Die Gräfin von Rathenow* (1969), is turned
into a political metaphor.

The story of the chaste widow, who is forcibly seduced, then driven to
sacrifice her happiness to the man who wronged her, has analogies to the
Franco-Prussian war, which broke with similar violence on the Elbe-
feudal State and left a political child behind, very much against the will
of the officious Prussians: Hardenberg's and Stein's reforms.[2]

(And for Lange this nineteenth-century parallel in turn is only an
analogy to the modern situation, the humane French seducer and
the rigid Prussian father who shoots him being – again – Trotsky
and Stalin. The original story has lost all intrinsic significance.)

The 'force and innocence' of plagiarism is not always, as Brecht
liked to claim, a sign of great literature, and taking over Brecht's
material together with Brechtian techniques has turned what was
substance in his approach into pure formalism in Helmut Baierl's
work. *The Finding (Die Feststellung*, 1958), which presents the
re-education of a peasant couple who fled to the west after
collectivisation to escape (in their view) the repression of individual
initiative or (the official view) the healthy discipline of working for
the common good, and who have now returned disillusioned to
their agricultural cooperative, imitates the structure of *The
Measures Taken* (1930). The action is a replay, played out as a story
before a chorus (the cooperative) by the leader of the cooperative
and the returned fugitives, each acting their own and then the
others' roles; a learning process in which conflict is overcome
since each is taught to respect the contrary view. Unfortunately
this 'dialectical' resolution of opposites is only superficial. This
is partly due to the way Baierl substitutes personal differences for
moral principles, so that an apparent conflict of ideas is revealed
as mutual misunderstanding, the peasant's dissatisfaction being
with the leader's lack of sympathy, not with socialism. But it also
comes from an over-literal transcription of the qualities in Brecht's
work. Where *The Measures Taken* ends with a 'Judgement', even
if the revolutionaries' actions have already been approved at the
opening of the play, Baierl entitles his final scene 'The Justification'. Similarly, the propaganda intentions that Brecht disguised
are only too obvious here. Brecht is always careful either to make
his plays open-ended, avoiding a conclusion which would impose

a decision on the audience, or to present his characters critically
so that the audience are forced to evaluate their actions – even
though this 'objectivity' is no more than a didactic technique and
his list of epic qualities, which stresses that his theatre 'enforces
decisions...drives to the point of recognition...determines
thought',[3] betrays the authoritarian premises of his drama. But
where Brecht is oblique Baierl is direct, as the way he copies
The Exception and the Rule in the prologue to *The Finding*
demonstrates:

> Observe the conduct of these people closely:
> Find it estranging even if not very strange,
> Hard to explain even if it is the custom...
> We particularly ask you –
> When a thing continually occurs –
> Not on that account to find it natural
> (Brecht)

> But we ask you, regard
> the attitude of the players critically,
> find it extraordinary...
> Much is unclear.
> Therefore the talk here
> is of the power of persuasion and not
> of persuasion through power.
> (Baierl)[4]

Brecht claimed that his approach, with its 'scientific' analysis
and clear lighting, materialism (expressed as much in his use of
puritanical colours, worn and grimy costumes, or well-handled
props as in his mockery of religion) and dialectical structure, was
specifically designed to embody a Marxist view of the world; and
it is the political connotations of Brecht's style as much as its
theatrical effectiveness that attract playwrights like Lange or
Baierl. But the focus of Brecht's plays is seldom simply political
and the 'straight' use of his techniques to portray the Marxist
viewpoint leads to plays like Baierl's *Frau Flinz* (1961). The
central figure is based on a mixture of Mother Courage, Frau
Carrar and Brecht's other mother, Pelagea Wlassowa, and the play
was first performed by the Berliner Ensemble, where Baierl was
acting as dramaturge. With Helene Weigel in the title role the
comparison with *Mother Courage* – an unsatisfactory play for
Marxists since its heroine learns nothing from experience[5] – was
unmistakable. Baierl simply inverts Brecht's play, setting his

cynically egoistic and mistrustful character in a humane society (the DDR in its post-war period of socialist construction) so that when she loses her children it is to the benevolent state, not to war. His basic situation is a variation on Brecht's opening scene in which Eilif is persuaded by the recruiting officer to leave his family for the army while Mother Courage is distracted by the prospect of a sale. But here Frau Flinz' five sons recognise the difference between enlightened self-interest and selfishness, instead of sacrificing the imperative of self-preservation for false moral virtues, while Flinz herself comes to see the inappropriateness of her conventional folk-wisdom in the new society, and appears in the final scene as the representative of an agricultural commune at a Party Congress. Brecht's astringent irony is what gives his dramatic situations their particular effectiveness, and Baierl captures much of the same humour and paradoxicality in his characterisation. But the 'positive' situation submerges the sharpness in sentimentality, and strikingly realised perceptions, such as the peasant woman's relationship to her field, represented by an isolated figure bent over potatoes laid in long rows on sackcloth converging to the miniature outline of a village against a stark white backdrop, turn into clichés: the flag-waving euphoria of the ending, or the (unfortunately) unintended comedy of a scene in which the fifth son has built a radio with parts smuggled in from the west. He turns it on, a west German station signal is heard, and one of his reformed brothers bursts in with a choir of handsome youths in scout uniform who drown out the crackling of the radio with a Party anthem.

There are equal disadvantages in using Brecht as a stylistic pattern independent of his ideological perspectives, as examples in English drama show. When applied as techniques rather than springing naturally from a playwright's intrinsic vision, Brecht's distancing and objectivity can become a confusing lack of commitment, as in Arden's *Serjeant Musgrave's Dance* where the irony undercuts the point and the poetry, which is intended to comment on the action, works on an unrelated level. Alternatively, a borrowed Brechtian style can distort a playwright's own strengths. Osborne's *Luther* takes its chronicle structure of self-sufficient scenes from *Mother Courage* and its plot treatment from *Galileo*; but where Brecht's approach is epitomised in the scene of Barbarini's personality being overlaid by hierarchy and history as he disappears beneath the papal robes, Osborne's rhetoric is the individualistic and heroic isolation of monologue. As a result of this conflict between form and content, *Luther* is neither epic nor convincingly emotional, but anecdotal. Osborne's other 'Brechtian' play, *The Entertainer*, is far more successful because, instead of borrowing directly from Brecht, he develops equivalent techniques out of the theatrical conventions of the Music Hall which, as the play's central symbol, is an integral part of its material.

Like any classic, Brecht's influence is double-edged. His example acts as a catalyst while the significance of his achievement has a stultifying effect, and there would seem to be an inverse ratio between the value of a play that follows Brecht's approach and its closeness to his actual work. Dürrenmatt's *Frank V*, for instance, the opera of a private bank which he had hoped would have the same 'wildness' and impact as Schiller's *Sturm und Drang* play, *The Robbers*, fails because it is too near to its model, *The Threepenny Opera* (*Die Dreigroschenoper*, 1928). Dürrenmatt takes his theme from Polly's business reform of Macheath's criminal organisation, 'romance is over – serious life begins. One can rob a bank, or rob the public with a bank...what is robbing a bank compared to founding one?', and extends Brecht's basic question of 'Thieves are citizens – are citizens thieves?'[6] In Dürrenmatt's formulation, apparently respectable citizens are gangsters, whose traditional methods of luring customers into the bank with richly-clad prostitutes, who loiter outside its imposing portico, and murdering them as soon as they deposit their money (see Illustration 8) have become unprofitable; and the reforms introduced by Frank VI bring the business into line with the (even more inhuman) scientific and statistical exploitation of the computer age. This technique is typical of Dürrenmatt. But here, instead of magnifying a social situation to bring out its moral essence, the exaggeration is based on literature which is already a satiric distortion of life. In consequence the reversal – the liquidation of Frank V by his son in the interests of efficiency, and the State President's refusal to allow any admission of crime because justice would 'destroy the whole world order...The faith in our banks must not be shaken'[7] – loses contact with the reality it is intended to illuminate. The same effect can be seen in Dürrenmatt's use of songs, although Brecht's musical techniques are copied in detail (songs to epitomise the 'Gestus' of a scene, singing against the music to create an effect of 'incorruptible rationality'[8]); and the end result is the opposite of everything Brecht achieved:

137

8 Dürrenmatt, *Frank V*, 1959. 'The Bank': epic staging.

Through the music . . . the stage events are removed from any conceivable realistic frame, for it reveals and corroborates the nature of everything that happens on the stage as play. What might appear unendurable in the text becomes bearable, and it does so precisely because the music does not support or point the content and tone of the speech but characterises the harshness [of the dialogue] by contrast.[9]

Like Brecht, Dürrenmatt intended *Frank V* to be 'opera for ACTORS' and wrote songs with 'a dramaturgical function'. But instead of the songs being points of stasis reflecting on a fast-paced plot, as in *The Threepenny Opera*, Dürrenmatt composed the lyrics first and arranged his 'plot' as a contrapuntal series of monologues to support them. As a result there is too little contrast for the music to counterpoint the action, and it is forced into fantasy by the literary nature of this 'model of a power-system and its disintegration from internal contradictions'.[10] Brecht, not life, becomes the only reference point. The presentation of the characters as 'no less great and bloody than Shakespeare's heroes' (p. 201) and the parallels to *Richard III* reflect *Arturo Ui*. The final Schiller-parody

echoes *St Joan of the Stockyards.* Even structuring the plot by
'such improbable chances' as the lightning which strikes a hotel
and turns an insurance swindle into a real loss, although it
corresponds to Dürrenmatt's principles of 'coincidence' (*Zufall*)
and 'puncture' (*Panne*), takes the form of a rejection of Brecht's
theory of economic determinism; while Böckmann's deathbed-
recognition that

> in every hour we could have turned around, in every moment of our evil
> lives. There is no inheritance that could not have been declined and no
> crime that had to be committed. We were free...created in freedom and
> abandoned in freedom (p. 261)

which for Dürrenmatt sums up the theme of the play, is simply
a reversal of

> To be a good man, yes I'd be so glad...
> But sad to say our earth is far from heaven
> Our life is mean and sordid – man is low.
> Who would not like to live in peace for ever?
> But the conditions here, they are not so![11]

Sufficiently adapted, however, Brecht's techniques can be
highly productive, as where Dürrenmatt uses familiar situations
from his plays as starting points for defining his own approach by
contrast, instead of borrowing an overlapping perspective which
(as in *Frank V*) turns the artifice of comedy into literary artificiality. The positive aspect of Dürrenmatt's relationship to his
work is indicated by a certain type of Brechtian allusion. *An Angel
Comes to Babylon* (*Ein Engel kommt nach Babylon*, 1953) uses
ironically inverted situations from *The Good Person of Setzuan*;
the ending of *The Anabaptists* parodies Shen Te's final speech to
the audience; the transformation of Strindberg's *Dance of Death*
into a boxing-match in *Play Strindberg* (1969) reflects Brecht's
concept of an anti-naturalistic, boxing-ring theatre.[12] Here the
parallels become practical ways of demonstrating the distinction
that Dürrenmatt draws in his theoretical essays between his own
grotesque comedy of protest and the political implications of
Brecht's dramaturgy.[13]

Even the directors who were Brecht's closest collaborators have
adapted his dramaturgy rather than imitating it. For Manfred
Wekwerth Brecht's anti-individualistic characterisation was
appropriate to 'a time of visible class war. The enemy could be
shown on the stage with name, rank and face'. However in the

contemporary situation where 'disguised' economic exploitation causes the alienation of the individual, although epic drama 'should show the individual as the sum of his social relationships', following Brecht, yet 'we also ought to show that this sum results in something new, unique, not interchangeable, even – with good old Freud – driven by instinctual urges, so as to show the contemporary form of exploitation and class war in the way it destroys these qualities'. Brecht's concept of 'scientific' theatre is also reinterpreted. The 'objective' techniques developed for presenting factual material on the stage are used as 'scientific ways of getting at [psychological] impulses', or to gain credibility for 'romantic symbols of revolution' as in *Frau Flinz*.[14] Precision, demonstration, the presentation of an alterable world remain Wekwerth's criteria. But instead of preventing empathy these are now used to focus the emotions aroused by the audience's identification with the characters, who are portrayed psychologically. Thus in Wekwerth's interpretation Coriolanus' reason for retreating from Rome became his Oedipal relationship to his mother rather than, as in Brecht's original intention, the arming of Rome's citizens by the Tribunes.

Peter Palitzsch also sees 'the exposure of direct human relationships' as the primary task of an updated epic theatre, and rejects the detailed methods that Brecht developed while following his basic principle, which he sees as the dialectical treatment of reality. This term 'dialectic' that recurs constantly in contemporary German theatre was developed by Brecht to replace the 'epic' label he had given his theatre in the 1930s, and Palitzsch has defined it as 'a way of thinking that uncovers contradictions, takes account of qualitative changes'.[15] In theory it brings theatre into line with the Marxist perception of history as a dialectical process. Interpreted in practical stage terms, it becomes a way of using the traditional basis of drama – conflict, a shifting pattern of tensions – as a powerful analytical tool, and directs the audience's emotional responses through balance, counterpoint, the creation of contrasts in a play's structure, or opposing perspectives from which the action is presented. Brecht used Erwin Strittmatter's *Katzgraben*, produced by the Berliner Ensemble in 1953, to test and demonstrate this new concept: 'Our play is a dialectical play. We have to cultivate the contradictions, oppositions and conflicts not only on the social, but on every other level.'[16] What made this play particularly suitable from Brecht's viewpoint was its structure, which developed the independent scenes of his earlier epic dramaturgy into self-enclosed acts, each divided by a gap of several years so that the same group of characters were seen in different postures. Covering the period of extensive social change from 1945 to 1953, each episode showed individuals and behaviour in different circumstances so that their final attitudes were a complete reversal of their first positions. Each act therefore modified the perception of the preceding one, and the spectators were made aware of the way social processes work precisely because the convention used allowed the characters to accept each social state as static. On its own each act is drawn naturalistically, and Brecht's rehearsal-notes show that he was concerned with creating emotional involvement in a conventionally naturalistic way – in socialism 'the human face must once more·become a mirror of feeling...then you have your proletarian hero' – but taken together the play as a whole created what Brecht saw as a *critical* empathy which was intended 'to stimulate conscious, not blind, imitation'.[17] Two other examples show the way this dialectical approach was both a natural extension of Brecht's earlier stress on an alterable world, and a reversal of his original separation of passion and objectivity. In his 'Short Organum' the metaphor of 'a man standing in a valley and making a speech in which he occasionally changes his views or simply utters sentences which contradict one another, so that the accompanying echo forces them into confrontation' illustrated that dialectical materialism 'regards nothing as existing except insofar as it changes, in other words is in disharmony with itself';[18] and his essay on 'Dialectics in the Theatre' (1953) applied the same principle to audience response.

Let us imagine: a sister weeps because her brother is going to war, and it's a peasant war, and he is a peasant on the peasants' side. Should we sympathise completely with her sorrow? Or not at all? We must be able to both sympathise and not to sympathise. Our actual emotion will result from the recognition and following of the double action.[19]

The concept of dialectical theatre has influenced even such un-Brechtian playwrights as Peter Handke, who attributed his exploration of 'the functional possibilities of reality' to Brecht's 'conceptual model of contradictions', while at the same time rejecting the methods of the Berliner Ensemble as fake, 'setting up contradictions simply to show their possible resolution in the ending'.[20] But its major effect has been on the production-work of leading directors.

Unlike the English and American system where star actors form the main attraction, German theatre is based on the ensemble and it is directors who are significant. This remains true even when the ensemble is run on democratic lines, as in the Berliner Ensemble where the principles of Brecht's productions were established in discussion, or in Peter Stein's 'commune' where in theory performances are group productions. While the history of the English stage is summed up in the names of performers, Irving, Guthrie, Olivier; the equivalent figures in Germany are the Duke of Saxe-Meiningen, Appia, Piscator. (Significantly the few English directors who have achieved an independent importance, Gordon Craig, Littlewood, Brook, all did so through work with ensembles.) One result is a greater emphasis on style in the German theatre, and the practice of inviting leading directors to mount 'guest productions' for other theatres outside their ensemble makes it easier for an individual style to become standard. Another is that directors work more closely with playwrights, encouraging a greater range in the types of plays, an author's style frequently being moulded by a particular director. Hochhuth's work, for instance, was shaped by Piscator, while Hans Hollman's rediscovery of Horváth provided a model for the new 'folk plays' of Kroetz and Martin Sperr, and Claus Peymann has gained acceptance for Handke and Thomas Bernhard. But it is in productions of the classics, particularly Shakespeare, that directors test and demonstrate their styles – perhaps because new qualities are shown up by the immediate contrast with traditional expectations – and these form the clearest examples of the main ways in which Brecht's dialectical theatre has been developed.

The dialectical approach has an obvious relationship to Brecht's principle of 'historical distance', preserving the forms and concepts of a historical era so that those issues or characteristics of a situation which are common to both the past and today's society emerge clearly. Relevance is gained by contrast, highlighting the shared nature of essential qualities precisely because of the superficial differences. As Palitzsch put it, 'the stranger the period [of a play] appears to us, the more immediate its topicality. We say: indeed – even then, when there was none of this, that or the other, the same questions were appropriate.'[21] This was the basis of Palitzsch's production of *The Wars of the Roses* (*Der Rosenkreig*, 1967) which was recognised as a turning point in the Shakespeare-tradition.

Elizabethan drama always had particular significance for Brecht as a model of epic theatre, and Shakespeare is a continual reference-point in his theoretical essays. In his view, a historically accurate production of Shakespeare's plays would seem a 'report', and the attitudes of a character like Lear could be 'presented as eccentric, conspicuous, remarkable, as a social phenomenon that is not a matter of course' without any additional alienation effects; while Shakespearean tragedy was analysed as

a tragic view of the decline of feudalism. Lear, tied up in his own patriarchal ideas; Richard III, the unlikeable man who makes himself terrifying...they are all living in a new world and are smashed by it...how could there be anything more complex, fascinating and important than the decline of great ruling classes?[22]

Palitzsch put these theories into effect, turning Shakespeare's Histories into a study of the dialectics of history. The three parts of *Henry VI* were reduced to two, and the action was simplified to give a clear outline of political events at the expense of character. The presentation was analytical, a demonstration in which the theatricality was undisguised, avoiding stage illusion and reducing everything to pure action. The only commentary came from parallels and contrasts in the structure, and Palitzsch's notes follow Brecht very closely in stating that the story should illustrate

the collapse of the tyrannical power of a late feudal family, who necessarily fall victim to the mechanism of the socially destructive power-struggle that they themselves set in motion...a politically educative fable.[23]

What made *Henry VI* particularly suitable for Palitzsch's treatment was the panoramic view of history that makes the trilogy so difficult to perform in conventional terms. There is no linear progression, the plot does not revolve around a central figure so that the focus is not on character, and the ironies arise from events rather than the fate of a hero. The action is not rounded off with a reconciling moral, and the ending is the hollow triumph of those momentarily on top. The principles in Palitzsch's adaptation were concentration, clarification, intensification; reducing each scene to its essential point, a specific perception, which sharpened the breaks and contrasts in the action. The result was an impression of unstable flux, a rapid sequence of battles, betrayals and murders, in which intrigues became unsubtle power-ploys. Everything was related to the political struggles, even Cade's rebellion being interpreted as a plot directed by York. The pointlessness of the struggle was underlined by altering the sequence of Shakespeare's scenes so that the flight of the English is immediately followed by a French defeat, or by creating verbal parallels so that the list of titles and honours awarded to Talbot (already made deeply ironic, Lucy's 'rise Earl of Shrewsbury...' being read out to a 'rotting' corpse) is echoed in Cade's incongrous claim to nobility. At the same time in contrast to the reductive compression of the action, poetic 'set speeches' were kept in full, so that Shakespeare's poetry signalled either the characters' flight from reality or the rhetoric of propaganda.

The constant change revealed a senseless, monotonous continuity in which everything remained the same, a mechanical process which was shaped by two contrasting lines of development. Intrigues, initially disguised under artificial ceremony, led to secret assassination, indirect violence in the manipulation of a popular uprising, armed rebellion and finally open murder – revealing the true qualities beneath the social forms and moral attitudes as they are progressively discarded. At the same time a war of conquest between nations is superseded by internecine struggles, group against group, family against family, and ultimately (with the opening monologue from *Richard III* which is used as the closing speech) between members of the same family – so that as the conflict becomes more inhuman it is progressively individualised. The schematic patterning of fragmentary actions was a correlative for Palitzsch's theme, 'the universal fragility of human society', and the same approach of parallels and contrasts was used to relate the historical action to the present. The abstraction of the ordering principle beneath the extremely concrete sequences of violence was designed to focus on 'what is still existent today', encouraging the spectator to complete the picture from his own experience, and the programmes contained two complementary lists which set the performances in the modern context: a summary of monarchy from 1848 ('abdicates... murdered...shot...deposed on account of madness, later drowned...stabbed') and of revolutionary history from 1848 ('failed...beaten down...defeated').

Palitzsch not only heightened Brecht's dialectical structure into a demonstration of process *per se*, he also transformed the stage into a dialectical instrument and the difference can be seen in the type of set. Caspar Neher's designs for Brecht were overtly anti-illusionistic. For *The Wars of the Roses* Wilfrid Minks created a manipulable, neutral playing space – a wall of sliding panels revealing inner stages, which could be opened to form a wide perspective, present a scene as a miniature or a fragmentary glimpse, split an action into sections, or show different scenes simultaneously (see Illustrations 9 and 10). Cinematic montages could be achieved or images counterpointed, as in the scene of Talbot's death. A single centre section opened in the wall to show Talbot and his son riding hobbyhorses toward the audience: 'To rescue England we give our lives'. The panel closes, reopens. Talbot reappears, still riding but now carrying his wounded son: 'Together we will tear the Fury, war, from her throne, hack her to pieces.' The panel opens again immediately to show Talbot on foot, wounded and carrying the body of his son: 'Death is invincible, plays with us'. Then in the final image the wall is completely opened revealing 'a field of death'. The instant transitions and continual transformations created patterns of dark and light (sombre clothing/brightly coloured symbols, dark groups of figures/the blank white wall) within a frame of skeletons enclosing the stage, which made the restless action seem frenetic, pointless by contrast to their menacing stasis; a continual motion without movement which interpreted the objectively presented scenes by rhythms. A brilliant realisation of Palitzsch's dialectical ideal:

the grouping and gestures of the actors presents the story so that even if the words were inaudible the events would be understood, the shifts in the dialectic being marked on the stage by alterations in the groupings.[24]

Peter Stein's work represents a second major development of Brecht's concept, extending Palitzsch's dialectical rhythms of action into what could be called a dialectic of perception. In his adaptation of Gorki's *Summer Folk* (1974), for instance, microscopic attention to detail turns a *trompe l'oeil* naturalistic surface into patterns of visualisation. Almost all of Stein's sixteen characters are on stage throughout the performance, sequential or separated scenes are amalgamated or played simultaneously, and

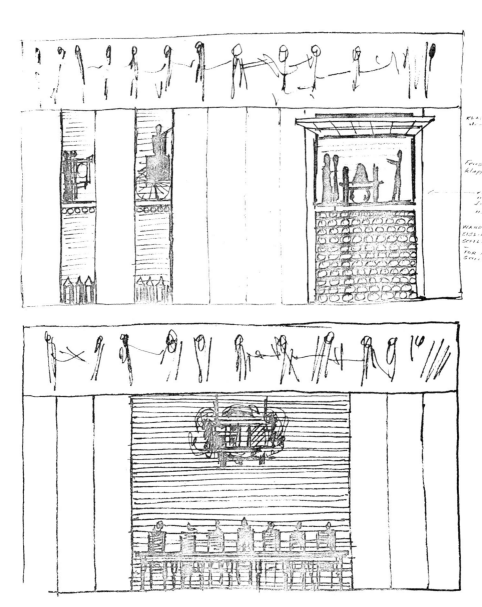

9   Palitzsch, *The Wars of the Roses*, 1967. Scene sequence.

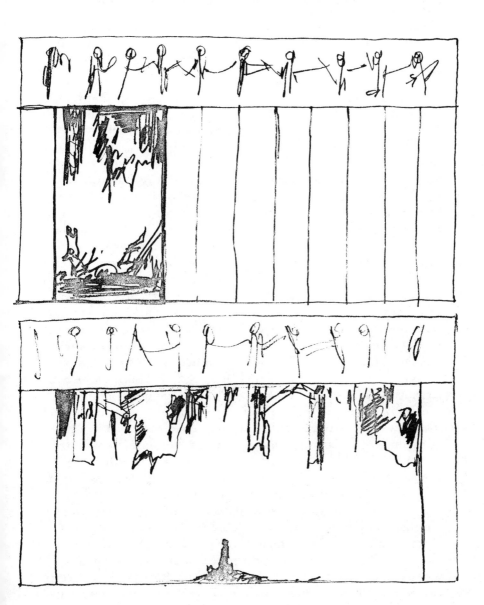

the production is designed to introduce the characters to the audience

just as one gets to know real people in social situations where the most fleeting contacts arouse the most obstinate suppositions and fantasies about them. And from this confusion of observation and imagination come moments of exhaustion in which one loses all perceptive handholds and experiences one's immediate environment as a distant apparition.[25]

Elements that marked the play's environment as historical and foreign were emphasised to create a shock effect, spectators being induced by naturalistic techniques to accept as alien moral and intellectual attitudes which were presented as clearly outdated – only to recognise them as their own – and this recognition was intended to increase self-perception, rather than giving the conventional insight into characters, since 'the rejection of an uncomfortable political vocabulary as outmoded' is seen as 'a topos of petty-bourgeois conservatism'.[26] The nature of the performance as an exploration of the audience's awareness was echoed in the critical self-consciousness of the characters: a poet who despises himself for his conversational platitudes, women who break out of the social conventions that had defined their personalities through determining their behaviour. Similarly the interweaving of the scenes into a continuous and communal action embodied the values of the production as well as conditioning the audience's manner of seeing. While the overall rhythms illustrate the aimlessness and despair of Gorki's characters, the multiplicity of individual conflicts are presented as inseparable parts of the whole, so that self-realisation becomes self-defeat, demonstrating that the ideal of a unique and independent personality is a futile illusion. The potential strength of the collective contrasts with 'a picture of the history of our society that mirrors the completely destroyed and helpless " I " of our days and is therefore unendurable'.[27] At the same time the orchestration of simultaneous scenes in which individual incidents dissolve into a communal continuity, or freeze into symbolic attitudes on one section of the stage while the emphasis transfers to another, not only provides a double and triple counterpointing focus but forces a bewildering freedom onto the audience. Instead of being told where to look, the spectator is given a ceaselessly changing choice, and the structure is like the setting of 200 real silver birches – the myriad real details forming a frieze in which one can't see the trees for the wood.

10 Palitzsch, *The Wars of the Roses*, 1967. The divided stage: dialectical structure.

One of Stein's latest productions, *Shakespeare's Memory* (1977), is a model demonstration of the same qualities, overtly exploring the theatrical possibilities in this type of dialectic drama as well as epitomising the scientific research on which it is based. A mammoth, multi-stage, two-evening display of background material for a planned Shakespeare production – either *As You Like It* or *Richard II* – this is an attempt to encompass the whole ethos of an age. The anti-individualism of *Summer Folk* with its implication for art that 'only through the imaginative continuity of a whole folk is it possible to create such broad generalisations and inspired symbols as Prometheus or Satan'[28] is expressed directly here. Shakespeare's characters, presented through the monologues alone and thus isolated from their context in his plays, are related to popular archetypes and communal images drawn from court masques, folk dancing, philosophical disputations, acrobatic and conjuring tricks, fencing displays, historical events, or scenes from Tourneur, Kyd, Marlowe – and these separated stage events, worked up by individual actors and groups within Stein's ensemble, gain their significance in the context of the whole. And the whole here is not a social grouping, as in *Summer Folk*, nor even an era, but a museum of consciousness which takes 'All the world's a stage' as its theme, and presents the mind as theatre. Ideas are given dramatic form – Machiavelli and Erasmus arguing on the definition of a good ruler before Elizabeth. Or communication is analysed as acting, meaning presented as identical with sign, in a demonstration of Cicero's system of rhetoric. And the illustration of the Elizabethan anthropocentric cosmos by a reconstruction of Leonardo da Vinci's sketches and zodiacal diagrams against the background of a planetarium is extended by variations on two figures from opposite ends of the scale: Queen and Clown. Elizabeth as heroic embodiment of her people in the speech to her troops at Tilbury, as symbol of political glory and personal divinity in a masque, as a puppet of her own power in a speech to Parliament describing herself as a sacrifice to her office, as an aging and emotionally starved grotesque; together these scenes and stereotypes form a commentary on the mechanisms of ruling and its ideological legitimation through public symbolism. The clown as the irreverent rogue of *The Second Shepherd's Play*, as Lear's 'bare, forked animal', Mad Tom, or the 'bitter fool' whose jesting is a cry of protest against 'heartstruck injuries', as the donkey in the Revesby Sword Dance who is killed and

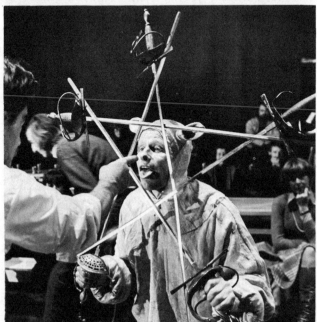

11 Stein, *Shakespeare's Memory*. Contrasts (a) The Queen (Triumphal Procession). Contrasts (b) The Fool (Revesby Sword Dance).

resurrected by turning the circle of swords around his neck into a mirror; together these represent the irreducible, irrational side of human nature and the anarchic defiance of authority by its victims. And one realises that the two series of contrasts create a fundamental identity, with the Queen as a prisoner of her position and the chained Fool as free, the Queen as a fool in sacrificing herself for a crown and the Fool in the final analysis as dominant. And this exploration of reciprocal relationships takes the dialectical structure of *Summer Folk* to an extreme in which the spectator is both forced to be selective and to make logical connections for himself. The setting for the production was a huge cinema-studio, filled with separated stages, acting-areas and displays, around which the audience walked and on which different scenes were simultaneously performed. No spectator could see all the events and each therefore created his own counterpoint from the variety of possible contrasts. Stein's dialectic of perception is subjective theatre, which has moved from the Marxist analysis of history to practising the audience in dialectical thought.

Brecht's concept of dialectical drama as a 'report' which highlights contemporary issues by showing identifiable forces at work in a different context, distanced in time or space, has also had a continuing effect on German playwrights, as Dürrenmatt's rationale for his adaptation of *King John* (1968) shows: 'a political play...only revised in argument, but kept in the old style, so that the possible applications to our time become that much more terrible. That *King John* is still as relevant as ever underlines our problems'.[29] But the innovations based on this approach have diverged widely from Brecht's original intentions, and Peter Weiss could almost be said to have founded a new school with *The Marat/Sade*. This play is normally considered to be a unique step in Weiss' idiosyncratic development, but although its theme is indeed the working out of a personal ideological standpoint, the style has an independent validity. Weiss has employed it for a different subject in *Hölderlin*, and the same mixture of epic and Artaudian approaches characterises the later work of Heiner Müller, as does a similar thematic opposition between reason and irrationality (a contrast that also recurs in Stein's *Shakespeare's Memory*).

In his theoretical essays and commentaries Müller extends Brecht's dialectical concept. It becomes an image for 'the contradictory nature of the epoch' and therefore typifies contemporary drama in which 'the vitality of a text comes from the contradiction between intention and material, author and reality'.[30] Where Brecht worked for a Hegelian synthesis, Müller's antitheses are presented as unreconciled opposites, for example in his linking of two short plays, *Slaughter* (*Die Schlacht*, 1976), and *Tractor*. The first depicts the murder of others as imperative for personal survival, while the second is an agitprop hymn of praise for a man who risks his life to save others. Yet these are designed to be performed as a pair. The distance from Brecht is indicated by Müller's description of his structural principles as 'billiard ball dramaturgy', in which each scene collides with another and the original impetus is converted into diverging movements, and 'collage', which has a similar function to Stein's work: 'not that one thing is presented after another, as was still a rule for Brecht. Nowadays as many points as possible must be presented simultaneously, so that the spectators are compelled into choice'.[31] Müller's collage is formed of dynamic systems rather than objects, and the same kind of structural opposition is also reflected in his dialogue. Prose 'alienates' verse, as in the emotionally charged monologue of *Tractor* which contrasts with the rhyming doggerel of soulless dialogue in *Slaughter*, and in Müller's poetry rhythms are designed to conflict with the metre. Müller still sees himself as working within the Brechtian convention, his latest work being a new version of *The Measures Taken*, but his aim is 'to swamp' the audience rather than to convey information. He defines his 'altered form of teaching play' as 'not simply presentational, but only effective when the audience are swept into the action from the start',[32] stresses the nature of drama as 'process' by 'fragmenting the action', and interprets Brecht's scientific theatre as a 'laboratory for social fantasy'.[33] This corresponds to Artaud's ideas, which are the opposite of all that Brecht stood for, irrational and mythic, creating an emotional and subliminal identification of spectator and action with the aim of cathartic release. Dialectical oppositions have found their most extreme form.

Müller's vision is tragic – 'in the century of Orestes and Electra that is upon us, Oedipus will seem a comedy'[34] – and it is appropriate that the Shakespeare he chose to adapt was *Macbeth* (1972). This was the play that Jan Kott picked out in *Shakespeare Our Contemporary* (1961, translated into German 1964) as the archetypal modern tragedy, based on a perception of existence as absurd, a state in which poetic justice becomes savage irony, guilt irrelevant; and Müller's version follows the line already set by Ionesco's *Macbett* and Marowitz's *A Macbeth* (performed at Wiesbaden in 1969), which treat history as a nightmare farce or as a hallucination controlled by demonic forces. In the context of Marx's bland optimism, epitomised by a notorious paragraph of *Die deutsche Ideolgie*, artistic endeavour is seen as no different from dairy farming (with the drudgery removed), sport (without effort) or the relaxed self-expression of well-fed conversation; and the idea of the artist as a man struggling with a difficult discipline or driven by an imperative vision has no place in the perfect world:

> In communist society, where no one has an exclusive sphere of activity, but can perfect himself in any branch that pleases him, society regulates general production and thus makes it possible for me to...hunt in the morning, fish in the afternoon, raise cattle in the evening and go in for criticism after dinner, as I please, without ever becoming either hunter, fisherman, or critic.[35]

Marx's vision of the future may have been intended ironically, parodying the anarchist ideal, but its celebratory mediocrity has become the orthodoxy of contemporary communist states like the DDR, whose credo is the promise (already officially achieved within its borders) of freedom from problems, oppression, suffering – in short from the motives that have inspired a significant proportion of the world's art. Some authors, like Peter Hacks, have adapted successfully to the new requirements. The work of others affirms artistic values in a radical denial of the Marxist paradise, even when the ideological frame is retained; and Müller's existential pessimism reflects a not-uncommon artistic position among communists: Jan Kott, for example, whose literary criticism expresses the view of a 'revolutionary' who has 'no illusions', for whom the most humanitarian politics is no more than a lust for power and 'life is cruel, cruel and hopeless. The only hope is to know that it is hopeless. The only dignity of man is in his consciousness of things.'[36]

Following the same line as Kott, Müller cuts Shakespeare's verse to the bone and piles on incidents of horror to create an Artaudian image of cruelty – Macduff's sword nails the Porter to the door he was slow to open, a peasant has his tongue cut out, others are tortured to death, Banquo is castrated by his murderers, a lord is skinned alive on stage. The theme that

> The world has no exit but the knacker
> With knives to the knife is life's course[37]

is presented in action, not in metaphor, and the irrationality of
human nature is stressed in the witches, who end the play by
hailing Malcolm with their opening greeting to Macbeth, and
whose dominant role is epitomised by their power over Macbeth,
'tearing his hair out and his clothes to shreds, farting in his face,
etc. Finally they leave him lying half naked, screeching they throw
the crown to one another until one of them puts it on' (p. 45). But
this accentuation of violence and this verbal compression is in
response to the urgency of political action, and the emotional effect
is intended to be directed rather than vicarious: 'the time for
intervening to alter something is always less. Consequently there
is really no more time for discursive dramaturgy, for a calm
presentation of factual content.'[38]

Unlike Ionesco's 'Jeu de Massacre', Müller's sadism and
slaughter has a political aspect. There is a qualitative difference
between the rulers murdering each other in power struggles and
their casual killing of the peasants they prey off. The undertones
of violence are full of repressed class conflict, as in the scene where
the peasant soldiers, ordered by Macbeth to execute a lord, flay
him alive to learn 'how a lord looks underneath his skin'. One
of them perceives his victim in class terms, declaring the flesh to
be the same as a peasant's, and Macbeth, seeing the danger of
rebellion, orders the other soldiers to kill him: 'A long silence.
Then the soldiers carry out the command' (p. 46). This feudal
society is directly linked to modern fascism. Macbeth quotes Ovid
while watching the Lord being skinned, echoing the classical
string quartets outside the gaschambers in Nazi concentration-
camps; and this is made a keynote for the play, questioning the
audience's aesthetic responses by the contrast between the
brutality on stage and its frame of pictures, Botticelli, Michelangelo, Rubens, which line the proscenium.

The theme of fascism is treated directly in *Slaughter*, a series
of five short 'scenes from Germany' which starts with a variation
on the Night of the Long Knives in 1934 and ends with the
Russians handing out bread to the defeated in 1945. As in *Macbeth*
Müller analyses the mechanics of terror by which an unjust order
perpetuates itself, and again society is presented as a slaughter-
house. But here it is the psychological effect on the powerless

that is the focus rather than 'the meat-grinder of power' itself. Both plays assault the audience with shock-effects which are heightened by a dry use of incongruous clichés – after Macduff has murdered the Porter the only comment is

MACBETH: Work is work.
MACDUFF: Work which we gladly do is none...(p. 41)

After three soldiers starving in the snow on the Russian front shoot and eat their comrade in a parody of the Last Supper, they justify their cannibalism with

now his comradeship strengthens our fire-power.[39]

but where 'power is cold' in *Macbeth* and horrors are presented factually, the images in *Slaughter* are surreal. In the fevered mind of a man who decides to emulate his Führer's suicide and prepares his personal *Götterdämmerung* by shooting his wife and daughter, Hitler steps out of the portrait on the wall. The mental state of a butcher who kills an American airman and reluctantly drowns himself in fear of reprisal (his head being pushed under by his wife, who has sold the American's body as pork to her customers) is externalised in a grotesque dream:

The inside of an animal/man. Forest of guts. Rain of blood. An overlifesize doll hangs from a parachute, clothed in the stars and stripes. Boar masks in SA uniforms shoot at the doll...sawdust runs out of the bullet-holes. The shots make no noise...when the doll is empty it is torn down from the parachute and ripped up. Dance of the boar masks. They stamp the rags into the sawdust (p. 131).

In these fantasies of seductive fear, the SS appear as angels of death, moving with black wings to the music of Wagner. Even the Red Army, figures whose normality is emphasised by their gift of bread and inability to speak German, the language of sick dreams and slogans in Müller's intentionally defective verse, appear as symbols. They freeze into a victory tableau, and their arrival hardly acts as an intrusion of reality. It is men who have just betrayed one of their number to the SS whom they greet as 'brothers', and the behaviour patterns of the 'dreamers' are unchanged – they fight each other for the bread over the body of their betrayed comrade.

Müller's problem is that the visceral impact of his presentation overpowers his political theme. Feudalism and fascism may be intended as models (in the epic manner) of specific power-relationships, murder as a metaphor for social exploitation which reveals the intrinsic terrorism of contemporary capitalism. But the Artaudian 'cruelty' transforms history into nightmare, and the emotional overwhelming of the audience gives an impression of determinism, reinforced by the completeness of Müller's condemnation which denies any possibility of an evil political system reforming itself. (Thus the butcher drowns himself, while in *Macbeth* a peasant, threatened with execution by both the English and Scots soldiers, hangs himself as the only release from fear. More explicitly, Macbeth's death 'makes the world no better', and Malcolm's first act as king is to show what he has 'learnt from his example' (p. 47) by having Macduff murdered.) The negative parable is so forceful that, instead of leading to the rejection of specific social evils, the impression is of cruelty as a universal, unchangeable human condition.

Similar difficulties occur in *The Marat/Sade*, the best known and most successful example of dialectical theatre. Weiss outlined his intentions in terms taken straight from Brecht – 'to depict the situation in which we live so forcibly that people...on their way home say: "We must change that. It can't go on so. We won't be a party to that any more"...' – and stressed his influence: 'I learnt most from Brecht. I learnt clarity from him, the necessity of making clear the social question in a play.'[40] At the same time he rejected Brecht's 'pedagogical means', stressing like Müller the need for 'strong emotional effects', which could only be achieved by 'Antonin Artaud's theses. The violent and cruel attack on the spectator.'[41] In the play this contrast is reflected by setting intellectual argument against sexual excess, ideas against acrobatics, and summed up by the opposition announced in its shortened title. Sade, the advocate of instinctual, passionate involvement and anarchy, as Artaud – versus Marat, the rational technocrat of impersonal revolution, representing Brecht's approach. The thematic antitheses and the stylistic contrasts, though more extreme than anything envisioned by Brecht's definition, place Weiss' play firmly in the category of 'dialectical drama' – but these oppositions are only superficially the dialectic of argument.

Weiss, who has always been attracted by historical figures whose situation parallels his own inner exile, saw a symbol of the modern intellectual in Marat, the French Revolutionary isolated by his skin disease in a bath that became his coffin. But Marat's physical stasis presents obvious theatrical difficulties. To solve these Weiss linked this figure with another revolutionary outsider, the Marquis de Sade, whose years in prison had cut him off from his contemporaries; and the imaginative basis for a play was formed by juxtaposing three unconnected historical facts. Charlotte Corday killed Marat while he was drafting 'a call to the people of France'; Sade spoke Marat's funeral oration, forced by the precariousness of his own situation to praise the achievements of a man whose politics he opposed; and while imprisoned in a lunatic asylum Sade wrote and directed plays for the patients. The basic approach was also drawn from Sade, who set analytic philosophical discussion against scenes of sensual excess in the dialogues of *La Philosophie dans le Boudoir*. The full title, *The Persecution and Assassination of Marat as performed by the Inmates of the Asylum of Charenton under the Direction of the Marquis de Sade* (a deliberately undramatic, pseudo-acdaemic listing of contents which became standard for Weiss' later documentary dramas), relates all the elements to the play-within-a-play framework.

The effectiveness of the play comes from this complex texture in which time, place and action each work on three different levels. Plot – the murder of Marat, set in Paris in 1793 – is separated from argument – the debate between extreme individualism and social dictatorship in the Charenton Asylum in 1808 – and both are set in question by the theatrical present. Here the actors become visible in the constant switching between their roles in the Marat-story and their characters as lunatics, and the awareness of the play as performance is emphasised (*à la* Genet) by having the Sisters in charge of Charenton played by men. Each circle of the play is turned into overt pretence by its framework, which in turn is theatricalised by a network of correspondences between the different levels. The psychosomatic symptoms of Marat are identical with those of the paranoid who plays his role, while apparent improvisations and interruptions are openly scripted. Even Coulmier, who as the director of the asylum is outside the context of both plot and argument and identified with the audience, speaks in rhyming verse, so that the whole play is based on an alienation effect: stage illusion is shown to be theatre on the principle that 'the stage has its own reality, and the impression it creates is most realistic when it holds strictly to the laws of this reality. The starting point for these laws is always: this is the stage...'[42] In conventional Brechtian terms this theatricality would focus on general issues by making the surface transparent, but here the use of structural complexity to strip away stage illusion relativises the issues instead of distinguishing them. The ideological debate becomes part of the pattern of oppositions instead of the dialectical subject, and the form itself becomes the content, the clash of styles representing the modern world that Weiss sees as 'mad and far too complicated to be understood'.[43]

The two poles of the play are not the intellectual positions of Marat and Sade, but anarchy and artifice. The rhythms and movements of lunatics are contained in highly formalised patterns of litany, liturgy, military march, dance of death. Loss of control is set against static tableaux. Even copulation, the expression of animal violence on the stage, is abstracted to a principle of order in the structure by breaking an orgasm down into its component phases, which are presented in symbolic terms, foreplay as whipping and climax as murder, with historical developments as an 'interruptus'. This formalisation, which becomes one of the hallmarks of Weiss' later documentary dramas, is also reflected in an arbitrary mathematics of threes. Apart from the three levels of theatre, the Marat-play of assassination within the Sade-play of discussion within Weiss' image of a mad-house world, there are the three alternative revolutionary lines: equality, psychological liberty and Corday's liberal idealism. The play has thirty-three scenes, the murder is divided into three episodes, and the symbolic religious reference is spelt out in 'the Passion' of Marat, 'heading straight for Calvary', crowned with imitation laurels as thorns and 'crucified' to found a 'new religion' for those who 'believe' in him.[44] Although on one level this is ironic, a sadistic perversion equivalent to the prayer to Satan (Scene 14), on another Marat is indeed intended 'as a visionary from whom the line runs to future revolutions'.[45] This interpretation relates to the original concept but, in spite of the way Marat's voice is strengthened by echoes in Roux and the four singers, the perspective is still Sade's as the author and director of the inner play. Traces of the initial radio-version, a vision of revolution set in the mind of the historical Marat, remain in Marat's dream (Scene 26); but the stage framework of history and the lunatic asylum make it surreal. The revolutionary vision becomes grotesque, and the audience are presented with an ambiguous balance of negatives.

This ambivalence is reflected in the five different versions the play went through between 1963 and 1965. Originally an

exploration of Weiss' political doubts, the changes express his
growing socialist conviction, and the range of possible interpretations is indicated by the three major productions by Swinarski,
Brook and Perten, each of which Weiss approved in turn. Swinarski, who worked with Weiss on the text for the première,
emphasised the theatrical stylisation. The scene, designed by
Weiss, was neutral, a flat grey wall of immense stones with tiers
of stalls into which the inmates could be locked and in which they
sat as an audience until the final march. Representing 'the
masses', they were treated as a unified and anonymous group who
provided a background of limited, carefully organised responses
to the Sade/Marat debate. Rhythms and musically choreographed
movement ritualised the inner play as a formal performance, while
the framework became a symbolic extension of the philosophical
argument. In the opening a naked man, his back to the audience,
was sprayed with white-grey liquid by two sisters – a parody of
both the make-up and costuming of the patients and the ingestion
of the individual into society. In the epilogue the wild dancing was
orchestrated into a disciplined march with the figure of Napoleon
rising out of the prompter's box to take the salute; and the
performance was brought to a stop by the figure swinging round
to reveal himself as Death (see Illustration 12), freezing the
cheering marchers into a tableau of shock while Sade's approving
laughter showed his authorship of the surprise and reduced it to
a dramatic 'trick' – a demonstration that the whole is a theatrical
statement not historical reconstruction, which emphasises that
there is 'a lesson', a consequence to be drawn from the action,

namely that the unhindered dialogue between right and left within a
society corresponds to a situation which could be called democracy. If
this possibility is removed [by violence], society is at the mercy of
dictatorial power.[46]

Where the Swinarski production cut the revolution/copulation
verse (Scenes 30 and 33) and used the patients as part of the
scenery, even drawing a curtain across to hide them during the
conversation between Sade and Marat so that there should be no
distraction from the dialectic, Brook placed the patients in the
foreground of the action. Instead of balanced, polished choreography giving an impression of rationality, Brook's madmen were
individualised, a range of spiritual distortions, each with its own
physical deformity. The image of the madhouse world dominated
the debate, which then became simply another symptom of the

12   Weiss, *The Marat/Sade*, 1964. Swinarski's production, the final scene:
Napoleon revealed as Death.

disturbed intellect, and the focus was the revolution/copulation parallel. Shock effects were multiplied by accompanying the descriptions of atrocities with grotesquely comic mimes of disembowelling and the guillotine. Sade was made the central figure by underlining his role as the creator and director, arranging every detail of the action for his own self-indulgent entertainment, epitomised in the brilliant voluptuousness of Corday whipping him with her own hair. Again, the frame summed up the intention. The opening provided two alternative audience-representatives – Coulmier and his family, seated as in a box at the edge of the forestage and identifying themselves with the public in the auditorium, or the madmen who wandered onto the stage while the audience were finding their seats and sat waiting for the play to begin, a grotesque mirror-image of the spectators. The ending was the culmination of the visual and emotional shock treatment in which the obscene and convulsive hysteria, repeatedly inflamed and restrained by Sade during the performance, threatened to spill out into the auditorium as Sade stood back relinquishing his control, and the forward surge of madmen was only halted by the stage-manager's entry with a whistle – turning the whole into a monstrous version (for the audience) of the pyschotherapy that Coulmier intends the inner play to be for the patients. Total theatre – in which the audience were drawn into the action by a pattern of emotional tensions, and the illusion based on fear was so powerful that it could only be released by breaking out of the theatrical convention altogether. In this interpretation the audience were given a negative choice, to side with Coulmier, the discredited representative of authoritarian repression, or to identify themselves with the lunatics, who underlined their interchangeability by lining up to applaud the audience who were applauding them. The Swinarski version achieved a Brechtian balance between equal alternatives by simplifying and separating the different levels of the play; Brook's presentation of all the multiple levels simultaneously created an irrational, Artaudian illusion from Sade's perspective.

Perten's production in Rostock a year later made Marat the dominant figure, reflecting Weiss' new Marxism. The patients became a disciplined, organised proletariat whose interventions were not the excesses of insanity but protests against the social repression represented by the straightjackets of Charenton, and the copulation dance was forced on them against their natural

inclinations by warders under Sade's direction. Sade was presented as degenerate, his individualism reduced to egoism, and
allied with Coulmier's authoritarianism, so that the ideological
opposition in the play was transferred to two social groupings:
politically aware revolutionaries versus the forces of the establishment. In this interpretation the structure becomes Marat's
increasing independence from Sade as the author of the play (i.e.,
from the control of the counter-revolution, which then has no
option but to kill him because 'Marat's truths. . .penetrate so that
what Sade says appears ever more threadbare. Sade undermines
himself in confronting Marat.')[47] For the ending Weiss restored
the original epilogue of his first draft, in which each figure steps
forward and recapitulates his position. The patients were whipped
into marching order by warders, marched on-the-spot in silence
while Coulmier, Sade and the warders sang the song glorifying
Napoleon, and were shot down by an immense cannon pushed
onto the stage. Roux encourages them as they lie on the stage with

> Learn to see, show that you are not beaten down.

They rise and Roux's 'When will you finally understand?' is
spoken direct to the audience, in the light of which Marat's
summation becomes an unequivocal forecast of certain success for
future revolutions

> until each is an equal
> guard of communal goods.[48]

While praising this production as 'the only interpretation
grasping Marat's true revolutionary mould', Weiss also commented that 'although Perten's black/white depiction was extra-
ordinarily consistent in execution' it destroyed the dialectical
oppositions: 'the effect would be stronger if [Marat's] victory had
been presented in a more complex manner'.[49] In other words the
form precludes limiting the play to any single interpretation, and
even these three major productions by no means exhaust the
possibilities. More recently Weiss has redefined the basis of the
Marat/Sade conflict in terms of the dichotomy between ideals and
action in *Hölderlin*, and any contemporary interpretation would
have to take this into account:

It is always the same conflict – the dualism of utopia, ideal, dream,
poetry, humanism, the urge to change versus external reality, dogma,
paralysis, force, compromise, repression.[50]

What is exciting about this type of dialectical drama is that the conflicts are embodied in the form itself. On the negative side the contradictory styles and clash of theatrical approaches make a play like *The Marat/Sade* thematically confusing. Each of these major productions was forced to simplify, and Weiss' repeated attempts to clarify the play's political meaning not only reflect his personal uncertainties at the time. They are also symptomatic of a basic stylistic problem. The strong Brechtian elements and the serious level of intellectual argument lead an audience to expect a statement or at least a clear conclusion. What they get is a self-cancelling balance of negative oppositions. But it is precisely this complexity that has made *The Marat/Sade* one of the most electrifying experiences on the postwar stage. Paradoxically then the main flaw in the dialectical approach is on the political level, even though the original rationale for developing such a style was primarily ideological. However as a structural form it seems inherently theatrical, as Weiss has recognised in re-using it in *Hölderlin*.

7. Documents

From *The Marat/Sade* Weiss moved to a very different style –
the documentary – and his *Investigation* (*Die Ermittlung*, 1965)
and *Discourse on Vietnam* (*Vietnam-Diskurs*, 1966–8) are the most
complete examples of this genre. Together with *Song of the
Lusitanian Bogey* (*Gesang vom lusitanischen Popanz*, 1967) and
theoretical essays where Weiss analysed his achievements in the
light of his political intentions, these plays set the standards for
a whole theatrical movement. At the same time Weiss' movement
away from the strict documentary of 'investigation' towards the
mixed form of 'discourse' and 'song' highlights the problems of
this type of drama.

The document characterises German theatre in the 1960s, but
it was not originated by Weiss. Erwin Piscator had already
developed the various elements in the 1920s, and it was his
appointment to the Freie Volksbühne in 1962, together with the
overwhelming impact of the Eichmann and Frankfurt war-crime
trials in 1961 and 1964, that acted as a catalyst. Indeed Piscator's
work as a director provided much of the driving force behind
modern German drama. His concept of a 'political theatre'
became a basic assumption for all serious playwrights – one reason
why politics forms the core of German theatre while remaining
on the fringes in England and America – and his early productions
also shaped Brecht's epic style. Piscator's aim was to transform
the stage into an instrument capable of dealing directly with the
complex anonymity of twentieth-century economic and political
issues, to create techniques appropriate to the modern world of
mass movements and technology. His experiments used simultaneous stages to manipulate the audience's perspective by playing
one action off against another, introduced factual commentary
through placards and projections, and brought in film to provide
authentic backgrounds or present the wider implications of an
action in terms of the masses. This mechanisation of the stage
made new dramatic structures possible; montage instead of plot,
fluid action instead of scenes, ways of compressing material to
extend the range of theatre. Now an accepted part of the director's
armoury, it provided the technical basis for documentary plays,
and Piscator's *Rasputin* (*Rasputin, die Romanovs, der Krieg und das*

Volk, das gegen sie aufstand, 1927) was the prototype. Here events were re-enacted rather than acted. The actors were made up to resemble historical figures and the scenes became extensions of documentary film sequences, while the dialogue was taken from letters or historical speeches. Instead of a conventional plot following through the motives of the protagonists, there were four distinct centres of action. As the full title indicates these were split between individuals and 'the people' in the guise of a historical force; and the different levels were related by juxtaposition – as when the Tsarina ridicules reports of mutiny while photographs of revolutionaries storming the Winter Palace moved across the screen and a calendar emphasised that the two events were mere months apart, or when comments from the Tsar's personal correspondence ('The life I lead at the head of my army is healthy and has an invigorating effect') were projected together with pictures of Russian corpses. The setting, a global construction with opening segments for interior scenes, on which figures could stand and over which film could be projected, allowed the characters to be presented in a double perspective, separating their historical role from their limited significance as individuals. It functioned both as a symbol and a means of drawing thematic connections, and its value was such that, in spite of its mechanical complexity which made it liable to malfunction, Piscator re-used it for staging his adaptation of *The Officers' Uprising* (*Aufstand der Offiziere*, H. H. Kirst) in 1966:

the 'global stage' allowed me to show the World War in its internal and external relationship to men...while simultaneously demonstrating its political and economic effect on society. Thus the sequence of vital and fundamental situations appeared on the main stage level, while the personal, sexual, anecdotal stories, which in the main provide the reason why people go to the theatre, played on the side stages or in the [opening] segments.[1]

The apparently objective treatment of authentic material – combined contradictorily with a clear political bias (the audience were expected to join in singing 'the International' at the end of *Rasputin*) – the broad treatment of global events, the overt use of technology together with presentational methods taken from film and news media: these became the principles of documentary drama. Piscator employed a staff of historians, economists and statisticians to provide the groundwork for his productions and justified his theatrical approach on sociological grounds, for instance citing Arnold Hauser:

Everything that is immediate, contemporary, integrated with the present moment possesses a particular meaning and value for the people of today...their mental world is attuned to actuality and simultaneity, as that of the Middle Ages was to eternity and that of the Enlightenment to the future. They experience [their world]...in the juxtaposition, in the unity and interconnection of objects and actions.[2]

The same standards of factual accuracy, immediacy and 'the presentation of the whole' characterise the work of all documentary playwrights; and the first of the new wave of German drama in the 1960s was very closely linked with Piscator, who directed the premières of not only *The Representative* but also *The Investigation* and *In the Matter of J. Robert Oppenheimer*, and worked with Hochhuth, Weiss and Kipphardt on revising and restructuring their scripts to suit his methods of production.

Critics have tended to class drama as documentary on the basis of subject or the use of recorded words and events. But Büchner's inclusion of speeches verbatim from Thiers' *Histoire de la Revolution française* or Hochhuth's listing of sources does not put *Danton's Death* (*Dantons Tod*, 1835) or *The Representative* in this category, any more than Aeschylus' use of accurate historical background makes *The Persians* a documentary. The elements that define this genre are qualitative: how material is treated, not its factual nature. A subject like Vietnam can be dramatised as an agitprop revue (Chaikin's *Viet Rock*) or a hallucinatory fantasy (Gatti's *V comme Vietnam*). Even a play scripted according to documentary principles can be reduced to conventional satire, as in Peter Stein's production of *Discourse on Vietnam* which presented Weiss' representative figures as caricatures. Diem became a puppet with his arms and legs moved by strings from the flies; Eisenhower, Kennedy and the American generals were given immense and grotesque heads, and their debates were turned into clown slapstick. Stein cut the text by almost half, and the actors not taking part in any given scene became 'students', cheer-leaders for the audience who accompanied each 'number' with cheers, boos and chants of 'Ho-Ho-Ho Chi Minh', while a slogan across the back wall of the stage declared 'Documentary Theatre is Shit'.

Similarly, certain traditional dramatic qualities disqualify a play as documentary. *The Representative*, normally considered the first of the documentary plays of the 1960s, has none of the stylistic qualities of the genre. The structure is that of a conventional tragedy; the protagonists are heroic, indeed mythic, the plot explores personal motivation, the theme is the moral responsibility of the individual, and the blank verse with its traditional associations heightens the dialogue, giving emotional significance even to banalities. Although the impact of the play came from the carefully researched accusation against Pius XII and the public controversy centred on questions of factual accuracy and objectivity, the intended effect is cathartic. The significance of the issues raised by the play meant that its actual form was largely ignored, in spite of the fact that in terms of the action and 'superobjective' Hochhuth's indictment of the Pope for complicity in the death camps is of secondary importance to the redemptive self-sacrifice of a fictionalised protagonist. *The Representative* is indeed a 'significant attempt to come to terms with the past' by 'objectifying, exploring human behaviour as a totality, history not a story'; but as Piscator also realised it is 'a historical drama in Schiller's sense', a drama of 'ideas'.[3]

The formal elements of documentary theatre first reached the postwar stage with *In the Matter of J. Robert Oppenheimer*, produced a year after Hochhuth's play. Kipphardt set up very different standards of authenticity, basing his action directly on transcripts rather than imaginary scenes or symbolic re-creations of events, and using film, tape-recording, news clips, tabloid-placards to comment or to integrate factual details in the play (where in Hochhuth statistics, dates, quotations and factual evidence are limited to stage directions). With factual accuracy, not imaginative truth as a primary criterion, he emphasised that the documentary dramatist had a 'duty' to define the exact relationship of the play to its sources so that 'anyone has the opportunity to check if the author has caught the historical reality in his work against the historical documents'. However, whenever this is actually done (as with Bernd Naumann's comparison of the text of *The Investigation* against the Frankfurt trial-transcript) any play must inevitably be judged lacking, if only because of the necessity for compressing days of hearings or years of events into the time span of a stage performance, and Kipphardt's foreword is rather an apologia for altering the 3,000 page record of the Atomic Energy Commission's proceedings than a documentation. Referring to oneself in the third-person as '*der Verfasser*' (literally 'the compiler') as Kipphardt does, is no more a guarantee of impersonal objectivity than the qualification 'only' – 'the author exercised his freedom only in the selection, the arrangement, formulation and condensation of the material'.[4]

Certainly the wider significance of the stage action is portrayed by recordings of McCarthy's speeches or newspaper headlines as well as photographs of cloud formations caused by atomic explosions, of the radiation shadows cast by victims of Hiroshima, of Truman and Malenkov; and the impression of actuality can be indicated by Oppenheimer's threat to sue Kipphardt for libel, demanding that the play be withdrawn. Yet the points made by the play are contained in fictional monologues inserted between the courtroom scenes, rather than rising directly from the material itself, as Kipphardt implicitly admits when he describes his aim as being 'to strip away the circumstances and aspects that are of merely secondary importance, and to replace them with such that allow the essence of the matter to appear' (p. 5). One result is a clear bias in the characterisation of secondary figures, such as Griggs and Pash whose evidence is discredited in advance by presenting them as ignorant philistines from their first words, and this is one of the major weaknesses of the play. The polemic of a dramatist like Bernard Shaw is theatrically effective because he takes care to give his inquisitors, social reactionaries – even the Devil in *Man and Superman* – convincing arguments. Here the crude channelling of sympathy through caricature removes much of the drama from the conflict of principle, which is limited almost entirely to the self-questioning doubts of the protagonist. The dialogue concentrates on Oppenheimer's motivation, his moral problem as the man primarily responsible for developing the American atomic bomb, and the issue of individual freedom. However, the texts projected as scene headings and the monologues focus on the nature of man and his political responsibilities, the distortion of scientific advances for social repression, or the principles of democracy. The personal and general levels are never completely integrated, but this frame does transform the question of an individual's security clearance into an indictment of the state, and in the summing up by Oppenheimer the scientist on trial becomes the judge of individual and social responsibility, revealing the play as a topical version of Brecht's *Galileo*. The particular miscarriage of justice is only a stalking-horse for wider issues, and Kipphardt's intention is not to justify Oppenheimer, whose moral surrender is ironically confirmed by the texts projected during the final speech, which discredit the moral stand where he rejects his former conformity as a betrayal: 'December 2nd, 1963, President

Johnson presented J. Robert Oppenheimer with the Enrico Fermi prize for services rendered...' (p. 107).

In theory documentary drama gives us as the audience sufficient facts to reach political decisions for ourselves, selecting well-known contemporary situations so that we concentrate on the implications of an event and the reasons for it, rather than being caught up in the superficial suspense of what comes next. In practice the facts presented are not naked but fully clothed in interpretation, even where direct comment is avoided, the evidence being usually selected to invalidate the 'official' version of a story. This is partly due to a lack of confidence in the audience's discrimination. Since any topical event suitable for documentary treatment would have already been received through the mass media controlled by the Establishment (automatically assumed to be safeguarding their position by falsifying the facts), any reinterpretation had to be spelt out. For Kipphardt it was therefore 'insufficient to reflect the world in the spiritual reflex of an individual'. What had to be shown was 'not just the [human] effect, but also the [political] cause'.[5]

At the same time factual accuracy is not important as a quality for itself but for its impression, an objective tone being an effective means of persuasion. Significantly Kipphardt originally wrote both this play and *Joel Brand* (1965) for television, and the use of media techniques is as much a tool for creating the illusion of reportage as a way of structuring dramatic material. It not only allows information to be communicated without slowing the tempo of action, but can be used to gain a deceptive effect of authenticity, particularly in the case of film. That the camera cannot lie may be an exploded cliché, but it automatically gains in verisimilitude when juxtaposed with the artifice of the stage where an actor necessarily exaggerates emotional values to project across the proscenium. This becomes particularly clear at one point in Kipphardt's play where a tape recording is introduced as evidence, and a film sequence of the original interview is projected on the screen above the actors' heads. The film adds no extra information. It does condition the audience's attitude to the security officers' testimony by a subtle counterpoint between their apparent openness as witnesses and the underhand way their evidence is collected, but its primary function is simply to reinforce the sense of factuality, and Kipphardt therefore calls for a deliberately poor quality of definition:

the interview PASH–OPPENHEIMER–JOHNSON, on an 8-mm film, is projected, reasonably synchronised with the tape recording...JOHNSON ...surreptitiously manipulates a tape-recorder. PASH sees to it that the microphone is close to OPPENHEIMER. The whole film should look rather the worse for wear, in order to look like a genuine documentary. On no account must it give the impression of being a sound film (p. 47).

Facts as such are undramatic, and the playwright's perennial problem is how to integrate his exposition with the action. This becomes acute in documentary theatre. Kipphardt's solution, selecting a trial as his subject, became almost standard since in the trial form tension and conflict comes from the unfolding exposition itself. It is one of the few contemporary situations where social issues are still given a formalised, quasi-theatrical expression and the acts of individuals are set in a public dimension. Within this framework, commentary and judgement gain the status of evidence, rhetoric is accepted as natural, symbolism merges with reality. In addition, justice has been used as a political tool from the trial of Socrates to the Moscow show-trials, and it is always this type of court from which documentary dramatists draw their material – the Oppenheimer hearing in which the legal processes themselves reveal the true nature of an unjust society, or the Warren Report (Walter Jens' *Dallas 22 November*) where the subject of the enquiry is the social ramifications of an assassination, not the act itself; the Eichmann case (Kipphardt's *Joel Brand*, Shaw's *The Man in the Glass Booth*) where an individual had been tried as the symbolic representative of a political system, the Frankfurt Tribunal (*The Investigation*) or the questioning of Cuban prisoners after the Bay of Pigs (Enzenberger's *The Havana Hearing/Das Verhör von Habana*) in which the defendants were a group, a cross-section of society. Apart from these stylistic and thematic advantages the trial form also changes the relationship of the audience to the actors. Instead of vicarious empathy or emotional identification, we are cast in the role of a jury, expected to evaluate and led by the evidence to share the prosecuting dramatist's judgement. Kipphardt, for instance, deliberately sets up a contradiction between the decision of the Commission and the audience's judgement by reversing the standards of right (national interest for the commissioners/the individual conscience for the audience) and wrong (putting humanity as a whole before patriotism for the commission/duty to a paranoid state for the audience). Thus although Oppenheimer is guilty of delaying the development of the H-bomb as charged, his 'crime' is a proof of conscience. At the same time he is not presented as a figure for emulation. He has sold out and still cannot bring himself to the same outright condemnation as Brecht's Galileo. The spectators are made to feel they have been put in the position of making up their own minds (a deceptive impression since they can only decide on lines laid down by Kipphardt): 'The question is, what authority is independent and powerful enough to prevent nations, or groups of nations from committing suicide' (p. 74). The answer is militant civil disobedience, and for the spectator to make the judgement that national loyalties are inferior to individual values is the first step.

This use of a trial to question or invert accepted criteria of justice is also typical of documentary drama, forming for example one of the underlying themes in *The Investigation*. In the death camp, where crime from theft to mass-murder became a norm, survival was the only moral imperative. What is revealed by the events is that conventional standards of right or wrong are inapplicable and artificial. This is also the argument of the Defence Counsel. The indifference to inhumanity which characterised the camp remains the attitude of the accused, and the Frankfurt Tribunal is shown to be as much a 'mock trial' as that presided over by one of the witnesses in Auschwitz itself, since the prosecution of minor individuals only serves to legalise the system that made the crimes possible. The assumption behind this type of play is that the audience is directly involved, and in different productions of *The Investigation* they were either associated with the witnesses (who rose from an unseen row of seats right down stage in front of them – Piscator) or the accused (seated among the stalls – Palitzsch). In Piscator's production the play was opened by an usher who announced 'The Judge. All rise please!', a direction reinforced by a projection – 'The investigation: Court in session: Please rise' – and cued by members of the theatre company in the audience with the specific aim of 'bringing the spectators to their feet in the same way that prisoners and law officers have to rise in court'.[6] Following this line and in sharp contrast to normal theatre, applause was not wanted. How often do the victims, condemned criminals or jury clap in a court of law? So placards were even hung in the auditorium requesting the audience not to applaud at the end. This reflects the real aim of documentary drama: to produce political action, if only in the form of discussion, rather than aesthetic appreciation – and indeed several plays have achieved this effect, although not perhaps quite as the authors intended. For instance at the Frankfurt première of *Discourse on Vietnam* students armed with Viet Cong flags occupied the stage, broke up the performance and substituted a teach-in, objecting that art – even in the deliberately 'unartistic' shape of documentary theatre – distracts from real political involvement.

Karl Jaspers has pointed to what he considers a recent revolution in historical thinking. Instead of the past being seen as an object sharply separated from the present by progress, the concept of a 'continuous now' means that history is a subjective confrontation, a tool for analysing contemporary actions[7] – and this is the key to Weiss' treatment of Auschwitz in *The Investigation*, produced simultaneously by seventeen major theatres throughout the Bundesrepublik in a deliberate attempt to emphasise the relevance of the stage as a 'moral institution'. The trial itself had a traumatic effect in Germany, bringing the public face to face with a guilt they believed buried beneath the intervening twenty years (Walser's point in *The Black Swan*) or paid for in reparations; and as Piscator commented in his production-notes, the general attitude was well represented by the characterisation of the accused, an arrogant self-assurance which rejected the charges as irrelevant – corresponding exactly to the viewpoint Jaspers discredits – history as alibi:

> Today
> since our nation has once more
> worked its way up
> to a leading position
> we should concern ourselves with other things
> than reproaches
> which must be seen
> as long since outdated.[8]

The apparently objective, neutral surface of *The Investigation* is in its own way a demonstration of the effectiveness of the documentary approach, since the spur to writing the play was intensely emotional and subjective. Weiss' response to visiting Auschwitz can be seen in his essay, 'My Place' ('Meine Ort-schaft', 1965), a powerful imaginative reconstruction of the death-life of the prisoners, in which Weiss identifies with the slaughtered so strongly that he feels an accomplice simply because he is a survivor and uses the obscene irony of the slogans carved on the gateway of the camp – 'Obedience, Industry, Cleanliness, Honesty...Love of the Fatherland' – to evoke the same guilt feeling in the ordinary reader. The picture and perspective of *The Investigation* is the same, but the personal involvement has disappeared. Here Weiss is concerned with the complicity and guilt only as catalysts for political change. The recitation of appalling conditions and inhuman actions is intended to create a revulsion against the present social system, which is seen as containing exactly the same seeds as fascism. The state-approved extermination of Auschwitz is not presented as an aberration, but as the 'logical and ultimate consequence' of economic exploitation (p. 89). And the cool, clinical tone, the substitution of neutral, quasi-scientific words for any emotive terms from the transcript, together with the radical simplification of the original syntax is intended not only to intensify the audience's abhorrence by contrast, but to give the impression that the events described are absolutely and horrifyingly normal. For this reason the only images of any kind that Weiss takes over into the dialogue are two similes describing atrocities in everyday clichés: Kaduk's 'I watched like a hawk' and 'the transports followed one another like warm rolls' (pp. 47–8). Weiss' aim, outlined in his programme-notes, was specifically to 'brand capitalism' as 'the customer of the gas chambers', and his additions to the transcript (almost all of which occur in the speeches of Witness 3) emphasise that the firms who profited from the concentration camps are still prospering, and that these accused are only subordinates:

> Others are over them...
> who live unreproached.
> They hold high offices
> they multiply their possessions
> and continue to operate in the same factories
> in which the prisoners of those days
> were consumed.[9]

The functional language, presenting genocide (as here) in terms of production and consumption, reinforces the political point on a subliminal level and, like the consistent transfer of active tenses into passive, focuses on the system rather than individual responsibility.

This generalisation is most obvious in the depiction of the

characters. Witnesses are referred to as 'anonymous', 'mouth-pieces' rather than people, while the accused are only superficially personalised to indicate the spuriousness (from a Marxist per-spective) of bourgeois concepts of individuality. They have names, but react in their protests and approbation as a group. In Piscator's production the accused all wore dark, single breasted suits, a social uniform differentiated only by signs of status and income, such as a chic black briefcase or a noticeably elegant pair of spectacles, and pin-stripes for the professional class, checked patterns for shopkeepers, plain material for workers. The actors were instructed to present the mentality of individualism rather than a particular face – as one commented, 'one doesn't assume a "role" here, one takes on a communal guilt'[10] – and though each of the accused had a nameplate on his desk these were deliberately made too small to be legible. The three groups were related by the restricted gradations of the colour-scheme from a neutral grey for the witnesses through the darker clothing of the accused to the black robes of the judges, and by the setting in which each formed one side of a triangle and the witnesses rose from a bench sunk below the stage to accuse society ranged in ascending tiers (see Illustration 13). In other productions the essential unity of the formally opposed groups ('...all equally dedicated to the same nation/...and if they had not been designated prisoners/ they could equally well have supplied the guards')[11] was made even more explicit, Palitzsch for example having actors switch roles between witness and accused.

On the surface at least Weiss appears to make no distinction between factual accuracy and imaginative truth, unlike Kipphardt whose characters refer several times to the relativity of facts during their end of scene monologues. The only 'plot' to *The Investigation* is the historical progress of prisoners from the gates of Auschwitz to the crematoriums. The spare vocabulary and neutral style transfer attention from the speakers to the events described, the staccato and irregular free-verse lines are designed to inhibit emotional expression, and the culminative effect of lists and repetitions is substituted for conventional conflicts and climaxes. The impression of factuality is so dominant that Naumann, whose reports of the trial Weiss listed as his primary source, considered that demonstrating how Weiss had 'falsified' evidence by intro-ducing interpretation as if it were testimony and by altering the sequence of speeches or their tone was sufficient to invalidate *The*

Investigation as a play. Not altogether unjustifiably – because Weiss had stated categorically that 'documentary drama abstains from all invention'.[12]

Such a claim, of course, is deliberately ingenuous since beneath the reportage Weiss has created a highly artistic structure which he refers to in the subtitle, 'Oratorio in 11 cantos'; and it was as a 'Third Testament' that Piscator conceived his production of the play:

Here the theatre re-enters the realm of religious ritual, which it had left. It turns back from the regions of the purely aesthetic . . . and becomes the ritual exorcism of an incomprehensible fate; the most moving and meaningless Passion in world history. The cultural experience that this aims at is no longer fear of the gods, but man's fear of himself.[13]

This is not to be confused with the religious vision of *The Representative*. The eschatalogical perspectives which seem to arise almost spontaneously out of contemplating such horrific events are deliberately avoided by Weiss' factual language which limits reference to man and the material world. The 'exorcism' is intended to be a political one; the 'religious ritual' is used as a formal and structural principle, not an explanation. While working on *The Investigation* Weiss published two articles on Dante in which he discussed the 'comprehensive allegory' of the Renaissance, claiming to 'have something of this totality in view';[14] and the eleven sections of his play are each divided into three scenes so that their total corresponds to the thirty-three cantos of *The Divine Comedy*. The 'perfect number' – three – with its religious connotations reappears in its prime form or in multiplications throughout the play. There are three judges, nine witnesses, eighteen accused, and the third witness is the key figure who spells out the political significance of the facts. On one level this symbolic numerology seems in bitterly ironic contrast to the realities expressed within it. But, if the camp is seen as literally 'the Inferno', this structure has a utopian function that shifts the weight of the play decisively from the past to the future. Unlike Dante's metaphysical vision, this is a secularised reality. If hell exists here and now, paradise is also a material possibility and political revolution substitutes for spiritual purification (purgatory). One state implies the existence of the other two and the ending of the play is left open, no judgement being given. This interpretation is indicated by Weiss' choice of words in one of his Dante essays where he refers to exploring situations in such a way

13 Weiss, *The Investigation* (Piscator), 1965. Neutral tone, hierarchical structure.

as to incite action that will change them and be 'an absolution'. It is also backed up by the idea of the play as an oratorio (which in musical terms is a celebration of the Passion) not a requiem, since the significance of the Crucifixion lies in the Resurrection – in Weiss' terms the social ascendency of the masses to a heaven on earth.

The symbolism is even clearer in *Discourse on Vietnam* where the same structure is repeated but left incomplete. Each Act has eleven scenes, but only two 'phases' are given. The first presents Vietnamese history as a repeated pattern of oppresssion and exploitation corresponding to the inferno of Auschwitz: 'All that changed in thousands of years/the names of the rulers.' The second, dealing with the struggle against the Americans, represents the revolutionary purgatory, and the final speech points to the missing third 'phase', the communist ideal of triumphant world revolution, the paradise which will complete the numerical pattern:

> the aggressor
> is divided.
> The front line runs
> through his own land.
> The voice of protest
> ...grows louder...
> What we have shown
> is the beginning.
> The fight goes on.[15]

The aim of this play is wider than *The Investigation*; not an enclosed event as the image of society, death camps epitomising an economic system, but history as revolution. The emotional range is also more ambitious, celebration as well as indictment, and the problems of the documentary style become correspondingly more obvious.

As in *The Investigation* a retrospective subject is transformed into a perspective on the present, but it has far less immediacy being taken from half a world away and representing a culture alien to most audiences. The action is still based on official records, statistics and news reports – Weiss published a whole book of interviews, historical analysis and sociological observation to back up the play, *Notes on the Cultural Life of the Democratic Republic of Vietnam* (1968) – yet when, as in the first half of the play, 2,500 years of events are compressed into eleven scenes, each on average containing less than 100 sentences, many of which are merely single phrases, then documents are reduced to unsubstantiated generalisations. This tendency to abstraction is paradoxically one of the major dangers of the documentary, and here it becomes intensified by the need to avoid the 'folklore' attitude (an apolitical interest in strange customs). Costumes and props, which were very detailed in Palmstierna–Weiss' first sketches, became emblematic. Each historical situation is reduced to the same elements in order to reach a level on which the Vietnamese experience becomes analogous to European events. A world-view is substituted for the world, ideology for objectivity, and historical conflicts are simplified to the greed for power versus the desire for freedom.

This generalisation is partly due to the limitations of the stage, and even the second 'phase' which presents such familiar figures as Eisenhower, Kennedy, Johnson or Rockefeller must necessarily seem a random and arbitrary selection if facts are in the foreground. Compared to say even the selected *New York Times* excerpts from the official forty-seven-volume analysis of the war, 'Vietnam Archive: Pentagon Study Traces Three Decades of Growing U.S. Involvement' (1971), any compression of the same material into a dramatic form must appear fictional and its conclusions therefore questionable, no matter how accurate the dramatist's perspective may really be. The logical conclusion is that only certain subjects are suitable for documentary treatment. But the focus on abstract issues is an essential principle for Weiss: 'Simultaneously with the exposure of [historical] actions, the development of which they are the symptom is shown and attention is directed to consequences that are still to come' so that 'what is sketched in is always how a political trend gives rise to a counteraction or how different movements interact'.[16] As a result, the authentication through media techniques that normally characterises documentary drama is relegated to very secondary importance in *Discourse on Vietnam*. In the production that Weiss oversaw himself, photographs of each speaker were projected in the second half together with a label defining their official function, while an impersonal loudspeaker listed their economic position or described the rhetorical gestures that accompanied the actor's words to give the audience an objective perspective. Originally Weiss had intended the American policy discussions to be accompanied by documentary film of the carnage and destruction in Vietnam, but the graphic detail contrasted too radically with the abstraction of the stage action.

It brought out the artifice instead of backing up the interpretation and, after unsuccessful attempts to integrate it during rehearsal, this film was finally separated from the performance and screened in a different area of the Frankfurt theatre. The same problem was encountered in *The Investigation* where film was also considered, first of Auschwitz itself then of endless lines of prisoners, individual faces, the instruments of murder, smoke from factory chimneys. But finally all visual illustration was rejected in favour of a classic simplicity, 'the hard cold light of sober space',[17] and only the scene-titles were projected, white onto black drapes enclosing the stage.

As these productions showed, extreme plainness of presentation and the absence of all conventional stage illusion are sufficient to gain an effect of authenticity, and the economy of *Discourse on Vietnam* is one of its most noticeable qualities. The setting is starkly functional, a bare stage and moveable white podiums against a white backdrop, white banners lowered from the flies with black lettering giving dates, one for each scene, culminating in a single red flag at the end of the first 'phase' to signal the founding of the Democratic Republic. The actors wear close-fitting, severe dress, a formalised version of rehearsal suits rather than 'costuming', plain white for the rulers, colonial figures and Americans, unrelieved black for the peasants or Viet Cong. The music for *The Investigation* was a complex illustrative composition combining electronics with a recorded children's choir. *The Song of the Lusitanian Bogey* had a small orchestra to 'support the actors'. Here however the instrumentation was reduced to two hand-drums which accented movements and stressed line-endings in the speeches: rhythm without melody. Carried to this extreme, simplicity becomes an image of ascetic rationality rather than merely a mode of authentication, and Weiss' notes to the play stress 'uniformity', 'meticulousness', 'precision', 'discipline'.[18]

Intellectual signification replaces naturalistic illusion on every level of the performance. The characterisation corresponds to Weiss' principle that

Individual conflicts are not presented but socio-economically determined modes of conduct. The documentary theatre . . . does not work with stage characters and depictions of milieu, but with groups, force-fields, currents[19]

– and the movement of the 'figures' is therefore along 'prescribed paths'. The acting area is conceptually divided into points of the compass, North, North-East, East, etc., and these 'geographical directions' come to represent power relationships as repeated situations of conquest, economic interest and rebellion proceed along the same paths across the stage. Patterns of movement stand for Hegelian patterns of history, and, since the actor is the only means of communication in this stripped-down drama, 'single gestures, attitudes, reciprocal coordinations, groupings and re-groupings' are required to symbolise global events. A stylised choreography was developed for the Frankfurt première to replace more traditional acting techniques which express personality, but this proved to be only partially satisfactory. It offered no opportunity for identifying with any characters, and the deliber-ately analytical structure of repetition was hardly compelling enough to substitute. Weiss is caught in a basic contradiction between the twentieth-century experience that 'great men' can neither be seen as the driving forces of history nor held personally responsible for events on a global scale, and dramatic conventions which present conflict in terms of individuals. As a result he places impossible demands on the actors:

Although the figures in this play contain no personal characteristics and private development, their nature must still not appear abstract; the actors should rather strive to show them as if they were active agents who cause historical changes, interpreting them in living and tangible terms.[20]

But no style could be evolved to present conflicts as simultaneously personal and collective. The actors found that simply the continual change of roles ruled out emotional or psychological depth, and Weiss tacitly admitted the difficulties by subsequently reverting to traditional characterisation in *Trotsky* and *Hölderlin*.

It is not only the characters that are two-dimensional. The black-and-white staging symbolises the way Weiss treats his material, and the apparently rational position of a documentary dramatist as 'an observer and analyst' who 'lays out facts for appraisal' is replaced by open propaganda. Objectivity is defined as 'a concept which serves to excuse the actions of a power-group', 'fairness and understanding' are seen as tools of political domi-nation. Referring to the subjects of *Song of the Lusitanian Bogey* and *Discourse on Vietnam* as 'one sided crimes', Weiss makes his approach explicit:

In depicting spoliation and genocide the technique of a black-and-white drawing is justified, with no reconciling traits for those who commit atrocities and every possible solidarity with the exploited side.[21]

In terms of the play this not only enforces a level of abstraction on which such categorical judgements are undisturbed by individualities, but transforms any real conflict into a static opposition between mutually exclusive moral absolutes. Since the correct reaction is held to be self-evident the logic of persuasion is discarded, and with it the possibility of structural development in terms of argument. What is left is the insistence on a single statement through reiteration, the same situation duplicated eleven times in miniature, and then repeated again (phase 2, the American neo-colonial involvement and defeat) as an expanded picture of its component phases. The dialogue emphasises this repetition by reusing the same words or verbal patterns – 'slay', 'seize', 'prison', 'tribute', 'famine rules the villages/we're fleeing to the hills' – to form comparisons between different historical situations; and the only development in the first half of the play is a purely formal one. More and more 'whites' gather on the stage with every entry of a foreign oppressor.

For Weiss Vietnam is a test case:

> Our struggle here
> ...will decide
> whether revolution
> can be brought back
> to the international plane (p. 74).

But the outcome of history is predetermined by his ideological belief, so that on this level too the conflict is artificial. The aim is not to allow the audience to weigh evidence but to create emotional commitment, and the function of the repetition is to evoke an automatic, almost Pavlovian response. The collection that was taken 'for weapons and the Viet Cong' at the end of Peter Stein's Munich production, the actors coming down into the auditorium and passing plates along the rows of spectators, is a logical extension of Weiss' approach – as was the subsequent dismissal of Stein from his post as director of the Kammerspiele, on the grounds that his production was a gratuitous provocation of the US forces in Germany. This type of play aspires to be a political act, negating the intrinsic distinction between art and actuality so that, as he commented referring to *Song of the*

Lusitanian Bogey, 'it is a direct intervention into a current political situation'.[22] Weiss spelt out his premises in 'ten working points of an author in a divided world':

The guiding principles of socialism contain the only valid truth for me...my work can only be fruitful if it stands in direct relationship to those forces which signify for me the positive strength of this world.[23]

The result in *Discourse on Vietnam* is a complete absence of subtlety or ambiguity. Even the title, in contrast to, say, Brecht's scene-titles which are deliberately out of phase with the scene itself and challenge thought by indirection or ambivalence, outlines not only the subject but the political standpoint, and even indicates the lesson to be drawn from the play: *Discourse on the Background and the Progress of the Prolonged War of Liberation in Vietnam as an Illustration of the Necessity for Armed Struggle of the Oppressed against their Oppressors as well as on the Attempts of the United States of America to Destroy the Foundations of Revolution.* There is no room left for interpretation, and the 'Solidarity' demonstrated by the politically aware chorus must be reflected in the audience's reaction if the play is to be counted successful by its own standards.

To achieve this, the starkness of the presentation and the stasis of thematic repetition is offset by the creation of what Weiss has called 'a dynamic reality',[24] involving the spectator through physical rhythms. Movements are highly formalised, a mimetic ballet, and the structure is conceived in musical terms emphasising tempo in the relationship between the different scenes.

Reports and parts of reports in exactly measured segments of time, rhythmically ordered. Short moments, consisting of a single deed or exclamation, open into longer, more complicated units...Single speakers are set against choruses. The composition is created out of antithetical pieces, rows of similar examples, contrasting forms, changing proportions. Variations on a theme. Gradations of a trend. The insertion of dislocations, dissonances.[25]

It is significant that Weiss emphasises the artistic nature of a form of drama which specifically breaks away from aesthetic categories and justifies itself as a political catalyst. In this he follows Brecht who had already stated the necessity for heightening 'artistic factors' in dealing with material taken directly from reality.[26] The result is a noticeable split between content and form, and although this is common to all didactic drama in some degree – as T. S.

Eliot commented, his drawing-room comedy plots were equivalent to the burglar's 'bit of nice meat' that keeps the watchdog of the spectator's mind 'diverted and quiet', while the message is slipped into his subconscious[27] – here the contrast is intensified by the purely aesthetic quality of the presentation. In effect the performance has the same status as 'ritual action' that Weiss had required for *The Marat/Sade*,[28] and indeed some of the most powerful theatrical movements in *Discourse on Vietnam* are directly comparable to those of the earlier play – for instance the mime of mass-burial, which has a striking resemblance to the image of guillotined heads formed by the patients of Charenton.

Exactly the same qualities characterise *Song of the Lusitanian Bogey*. The subject, Portuguese rule in Angola from its discovery by Diego Cão to the revolutionary situation of 1966, is presented as a broader version of *The Investigation* with colonialism substituted for the concentration camp as an image of the capitalist system. Weiss defines the play as functional drama where 'plot has been dissolved into the depiction of a historical process',[29] and reduces particular situations to their abstract essence, as in *Discourse on Vietnam*, in order to form images of basic political relationships. The same numerical structure also appears in the division of the action into 11 scenes, though here it is a formal arrangement without even indirect thematic significance, and representational decor or costuming is equally avoided. Again the intention is to shape the audience's political commitment in the context of their own society, and the actors' clothing is required to be 'everyday' while the statistical tables that accompanied the scenes of exploitation listed the overseas profits of US firms in the New York production, west German firms in Berlin. In New York too all the actors were Negroes to stress the parallels to the 'internal colonialism' of American society, while in the Swedish production a direct call to action was substituted for the final lines: 'There are many oppressors/There are more oppressed/Free them!' At the same time Weiss outlined his approach in (perhaps deliberately) naive terms: 'By gaining as much knowledge as possible about the conditions in those countries that are most heavily oppressed by the "Rich" we can...develop our solidarity with them.'[30] Again what is communicated is not so much information as an ideological attitude. Every speech is given a one-sided interpretation and the relationship to agitprop theatre becomes clear when the 'Bogey' is dismantled with ease at the end:

All accompany the song with calls, shrieks and leaps. They approach the Bogey.

> 2 Just see how he whines
>   give him what he deserves
>   five centuries too long
>   he has been served
> 5 Strike down this pallid man
>   strike this corpselike man

All rush at the Bogey. They tear away the sash of honour, sword and crucifix, form a chain and pull at the huge figure. From behind 6 releases the mechanism of the construction. The huge figure tumbles over forwards with an immense crash . . .[31]

The Bogey, built of old iron and sacking and with a huge, hinged 'mouth' through which the actors who speak its lines stick their heads, not only stands for Salazar but symbolises the inhuman and monstrous nature of capitalism, and its destruction implies that the social structure can be knocked down with equal ease – a utopian view that recurs in *Discourse on Vietnam* where will and desire alone are said to be enough to overcome all political or practical obstacles:

> Russia was backward . . . the number of revolutionaries small . . .
> But their passion and their courage were great
> And so they established their rule (p. 71).

As the use of the Bogey image indicates, no argument is put forward in *Song of the Lusitanian Bogey*. The conclusion merely states the premise on which the preceding action has been based, a circular logic in which scenes derived from an ideological position become the justification of the thesis they illustrate – and because there is no intellectual development, physical dynamics are even more significant than the stylised patterning of *Discourse on Vietnam*. 'Song' in the title becomes a literal description of the text, which is divided into aria-like speeches with strong rhythms and stressed doggerel rhymes; echo-effects are created by different actors speaking in counterpoint; duets are accompanied by refrains; almost every sequence culminates in a chorus. The presentation is emphasised as a performance by fox and vulture masks, situations acted out in shadow-play while other actors speak the lines of the participants, and stage directions which describe the tone as 'heroic', 'ceremonial', 'heightened'. Tableaus alternate with dance and gymnastics, and the 'historical processes' that have been substituted for plot 'should appear in

the choreography',[32] concepts being expressed in physical movement. The result is frequently vivid, but inevitably oversimplifies
– for instance the mime of performing animals going through their
dressage as an image of economic and socially conditioned behaviour, 'closing with a communal "Hup!" as after a successful
circus act'.[33] For the first performance Weiss prepared 'very
precise stage directions about the gestures – longer than the text
itself. My aim is physical theatre and the musical stage is total
theatrical expression'; and commented that both this play and
Discourse on Vietnam were 'conceived visually and in movement'.[34] Even so the lively surface activity has no intrinsic
relationship to the political theme, although on a basic level it
could be said to express 'the freedom/that is coming' which the
final lines celebrate.

What is most revealing about these plays is their idealism. Acts
of 'brute force' are set against 'passion and courage', a 'system'
in which 'permanent crisis' can only be disguised by 'armaments
and war' versus a utopian solidarity.[35] The ascetic or acrobatic
surface covers sentimental pathos, and the ending takes on the tone
of a consecretion ceremony. Weiss in effect transforms history to
mythos. Factual situations become transmuted by the mythology
of revolution into emotional magnets with a communal, quasi-
religious significance which goes far beyond the actual events. As
Piscator commented with reference to *The Investigation*, Auschwitz and Hiroshima are not events but images, and any dramatic
treatment becomes 'the ritual exorcism of an incomprehensible
fate'. For Weiss any revolutionary moment has the same archetypal value, and his most recent work, *The Aesthetics of Resistance*
(*Die Ästhetik des Widerstands*, 1975), transforms history into a
passionate iconography of 'heroic communism'. Rosa Luxemburg and the International Brigade in Spain, the Russian Revolution and the defeat of fascism are seen as the culmination of a
struggle against exploitation that goes back to Spartacus and the
slave revolts of Rome. It is a celebration of violence under the
motto of 'action is beauty', in many ways comparable to Gottfried
Benn's proto-fascist essay on 'the Doric World', counterpointing
war and torture with descriptive interpretations of famous art-
works from the Pergamon Altar through Breughel and Géricault
to Picasso's *Guernica*, in order to transfigure human suffering into
noble archetypes of eternal struggle. In this book, again based on
documents – diaries, news-reports, letters (to be published in a

second volume) – Weiss makes his approach in *Song of the Lusi-tanian Bogey* and *Discourse on Vietnam* explicit. He also implies that, like *Guernica*, such plays are themselves intended to have the status of documents, which perhaps helps to explain the clumsy and sloganeering language for which *Song of the Lusitanian Bogey* has been criticised. The banality seems a deliberate attempt to give the text the character of a pamphlet. In one sense Weiss' evaluation is accurate. His work can be analysed as a sociological expression of the 1960s, just as *A Doll's House* or *Dance of Death* have become source material for studying the late Victorian era. But as iconography it is essentially illogical, and even Marxist critics have attacked Weiss on this point, commenting that his over-valuation of the subjective factor in revolution leads to 'an illusion of missionary-belief'.[36] Interestingly, the only criticism that pro-voked Weiss into a direct reply came from Enzensberger, whose *Havana Hearing* (1970) has exactly the same quality in a more disguised form. His points were that the emotional nature of Weiss' work substituted art for political activism, rhetorical declarations of solidarity for actual commitment, creating a 'vicious circle of the metaphorical', and that the result falsified reality by simplifying complex political problems to 'pictures of a world free from contradictions'.[37]

The naivety of Weiss' idealism can be ironically illustrated by the general communist reaction to these plays which are designed to promote their cause. Every DDR production has been accom-panied by attacks on Weiss' style as 'formalistic', leading him to complain that 'if the artistic development that began in the Soviet Union after the Revolution had been allowed to develop, then authors today would have much more solidarity with Socialism'.[38] And, not unexpectedly perhaps, the conflict between communism as a system and its propagandist came to a head with *Trotsky in Exile*. The Stuttgart acting ensemble refused to produce the play, calling it 'crude ideological sabotage', and in 1971 Weiss was refused entry to east Berlin as an 'undesirable visitor', while Hartmut Lange wrote a counter-version (*Trotzki in Coyoacan*, 1971) to demonstrate that Trotsky's 'revolutionary experience decayed to "pure idea" in his fight against Stalin', making him the 'hero of late-bourgeois idealism, for the more he proclaimed Marx's axiom that "social being determines consciousness", the more clearly his egoistic consciousness determined his political position'.[39] And Weiss is not the only artist in this slightly schizophrenic situation. In much the same way Enzensberger dedicated *The Havana Hearing* to Heberto Padilla as 'the Poet of the Cuban Revolution', only to find that less than a year later Padilla was under arrest for writing 'counter-revolutionary' verses.

Documentary theatre does not, as is sometimes assumed from taking the name literally, transfer documents direct to the stage. Its presentation is highly critical of 'the facts', and if Weiss' list of 'authentic materials' is examined it becomes clear that, except for the first two categories, these are not primary sources at all but interpretations which have already been edited and scripted for public consumption:

Legal transcripts, official documents, letters, statistical tables, stock exchange quotations, shareholder's reports of banking and industrial corporations, governmental declarations, debates, interviews, opinions from public personalities, newspaper and radio reports, photos, journalistic films and other testimony of the present.[40]

This emphasis on the news media is ambivalent. On the one hand Weiss attacks 'news' as manipulative, distorting or disguising the truth for the advantage of social power-groups. As a result one of the primary functions of documentary drama becomes the critique of reportage, and *Song of the Lusitanian Bogey* or the second half of *Discourse on Vietnam* are based on the contrast between the nature of an action and its official justification. The Viet Minh are depicted as founding their revolution on the ideals of Liberty, Equality, Fraternity, a graphic way of revealing French and American actions as hypocritical by their own rhetoric. The labour camps and brutalities of Portuguese colonialism are presented in the context of traditional claims that the Europeans are 'civilising' savages, that it is their 'duty to spread the word/of God on earth', and the crucifix reversed to become a sword is a major image in the heroic tableau of Diego Cão's conquest. The technique is shown at its clearest in one ironic song where the words repeat an interview given by the West German Minister of Justice on his return from an international investigation after an unsuccessful African insurrection in 1963, in which he described Mozambique as 'an island of peace', an example of how race problems could be successfully solved.[41] Similarly *Trotsky in Exile* was based on 'the extreme discrepancy...between the infamous image Stalin created of Trotsky and his actual ideas, principles and forecasts' so that 'the play is really an attack on this [official] picture'.[42] On the other hand, at the same time as discrediting the content of the media, its forms are used both as authenticating conventions and as rhetorical structures. The techniques of reportage are not just used for communicating information or commentary, but as articulations of consciousness. Flashbacks, montage, superimposed images, pictorial rhythms correspond to the relativity of time and place, the variability of vision in, say, Godard or Resnais; and Weiss has referred to the perspective of several of his plays in film terms – comparing the 'collision of ideas and images, the juxtapositioning of appearances' to Eisenstein, or commenting that 'by means of an unrealistic arrangement of time Trotsky's career is critically illustrated, in flashbacks somewhat like a film'.[43]

At one extreme this trend in documentary theatre results in a play like Peter Brook's *US* (1967). Here the overt subject of Vietnam became secondary to an attack on the media industry with its commercialisation of culture, and the structure of the play presented an image of debased consciousness that implicitly ruled out the possibility of meaningful commitment called for in the speeches.

A very different approach can be seen in *The Havana Hearing*. Eight years before he wrote this Enzensberger published a series of essays on the manipulative effects of the 'knowledge-industry' ranging from advertising to news-reels (*Specifics/Einzelheiten* 1962). Here in the play the subject, counter-revolution, is analysed by exposing the manipulated consciousness of 'counter-revolutionaries', but the form is that of a media-event. The script is stated to be 'reconstructed' from the tape-recorded transcript of a show-trial organised by the Cuban regime, at which forty-one selected survivors from the Bay of Pigs invasion were questioned by politically approved journalists in front of television cameras, the hearing being broadcast live as a highly effective publicity campaign. The situation was dramatic, the prisoners still wearing torn and dirty battle-dress, unshaven and bandaged with field-dressings, a graphic picture of defeat, while sounds of the continuing battle filtered in from outside the building. And Enzensberger's stage directions not only reproduce 'the theatre in the Cuban Trades Union Building', but even cast the audience as part of the original scene: a bare stage hung with banners, '¡Muerte al Invasor! ¡Viva la Revolución Socialista!' and

TV cameras left and right, in the auditorium and the proscenium-boxes. At the door and on the rear stage armed sentries in militia uniform. The heavy beat of marching music while the audience take their seats... Atmosphere of a political meeting. The audience is restless and excited.[11]

This extreme of illusionistic realism, paradoxically achieved by the total absence of conventional scenery, is accompanied by a complete rejection of any literary reworking of the script. In deliberate contrast to Kipphardt's sacrifice of word-for-word accuracy to reveal intrinsic meaning in *Oppenheimer*, or Weiss' inconspicuous compression, linguistic simplifications and inter-polated speeches in *The Investigation*, Enzensberger leaves his cuts as obvious gaps. There are no bridging speeches or inserted conjunctions, 'every word and every sentence of the dialogue was spoken in Havana', and an attempt is made to set it outside all literary categories. Even though designed for 'stage or television presentations', it is claimed to be 'neither a court record nor a theoretical discussion, no stage play, no film script, no radio play', but the reconstruction of a revolutionary act (p. 53).

Apart from the utopian naivety of classifying a play as a political act rather than art, this extreme and anti-literary realism conflicts with Enzensberger's intentions on several levels. Its value relates to 'the total publicity of the proceedings' (p. 24), a guarantee of authenticity that is particularly important for an analysis of intangibles such as consciousness. But the reproduction of a propaganda exercise makes the truth of what is presented ques-tionable. The same disadvantage applies to the theme. The play focuses on the structures of thought by which a system survives, even when the individuals within the system can find no intellec-tual or moral justification for its existence, and on the unques-tioned assumptions that disguise the user's real interests from himself. In other words the play exposes our concept of 'reality' as fake, as a product of ideology which camouflages the true effects of that ideology – an insight which is automatically undermined by a 'realistic' presentation. Still more damaging is the way this 'reproduction' distances the analysis from the audience. The surface of the play with the Cuban slogans, the references to Batista and Trujillo, the opening lines which transpose the spec-tator into the Bay of Pigs context – 'the Revolutionary Govern-ment requests all present to keep complete silence and to avoid all expressions of approval or repulsion. The public gathered in this hall has unaminously promised to obey this request...' (p.

14   Enzensberger, *The Havana Hearing*, 1970. Media techniques and documentary reproduction.

54) – refers to an alien situation half a world and almost a decade away. These specifics distract us so much from the real aim, which is to reveal a general truth about the audience's own society, in 'the attitude of a collective...the character of a class', that in his introduction to the play Enzensberger has to repeatedly emphasise that it is not 'material towards the understanding of Cuban history', but an 'exemplary event, i.e., an event whose meaning extends beyond the occasion', that namely 'the *structure* which comes to light in it recurs in every class-society' (p. 21). The reorganisation of the original forty-one interrogations into ten, gradated from 'The Saviour of Free Elections' through 'The Man between the Millstones' and 'The Big Landowner as Philosopher' to 'The Murderer', is specifically arranged 'to offer the public possibilities for identification' (p. 22). To underline that these 'prisoners are exchangeable, [that] they can be recognised in any West German, Swedish or Argentinian state', an overtly theatrical device (which had to be discarded for the Recklinghausen première as too incongruous in the surrounding realism) is called for:

all the prisoners can be represented by the same actor, who is provided with a new face [mask] after each hearing, perhaps by the guards. This is no director's trick, but a procedure which makes...that totality, in denying which the prisoners sought to save themselves, tangible (p. 53).

The problem is the same as in the use of Vietnamese or Angolan history; how to point out the relevance of strange material. Weiss' solution was abstraction – 'no milieu depiction. No indication of geographical position. The stage space is provisional'[45] – which left his general theses unsupported since the audience were unable to fill in the picture from their own knowledge. Enzensberger avoids this, but at the expense of disguising the immediacy altogether. As a result he finds it necessary to draw the comparisons explicitly and to spell out their significance for a German audience in a foreword which is almost a quarter as long as the play; so that the play itself then becomes a documentary appendix to this essay. In the Recklinghausen production an effective equivalent was provided by introducing short interviews with actors who came up from the audience between each interrogation as German doubles of the prisoners, a parson following the Priest, a landowner's son after the Son of a Big Landowner. But the conclusion is inescapable: the nearer documentary drama comes to the documents, or the more presentational techniques drawn from the

media turn the play into a media event, the less such a 'reconstruction' can stand on its own. Even with the addition of double
interviews and generalising slogans, such as the projection of a
quotation from Eldridge Cleaver – 'Either you are a part of the
problem of imperialism or a part of its solution' – the discussion
following the Recklinghausen production concentrated solely on
what the situation in Cuba really was, which made the play
(according to the standards set up in the introduction)
'meaningless'.[46]

In spite of the surface objectivity, *The Havana Hearing* betrays
exactly the same iconographic idealism as Weiss' plays. The
impression of impartiality which comes from selecting the prisoners' self-justifications from the trial transcript rather than the
accusations against them, allowing them enough verbal rope to
hang themselves and leaving the judgement open at the end of the
play, is offset by the openly black/white moral perspective.
Counter-revolutionaries are here, almost by definition, 'scum...a
totally functionless, parasitical elite of corrupt politicians, military
and big landowners together with their retinue of professional
murderers, torturers and police-spies' (p. 11) while 'the ques-
tioners treat the invaders with a liberality and patience which are
without example. The moral superiority of the revolutionaries is
clear' (p. 25). Cuba in fact appears not as a real country but a
utopian state, where the population has been transformed into
'new men' *à la* expressionism by a socialism which has avoided
the errors of bureaucracy and the evils of Stalinism, and where
policies are decided by people not programmes, the existence of
the revolution depending (in true Latin-American fashion) on
Castro rather than a bureaucratic Party. It is this idealisation
which leads to the syllogistic nature of Enzensberger's attack on
'bourgeois-parliamentary proceedings'. Parliamentary elections
under Batista were manipulated to keep a dictatorship in power;
West Germany is a parliamentary democracy; therefore west
Germany is a class dictatorship and

the insistence on free elections is aimed not at extending but at limiting
political freedoms...The people have to be given the opportunity at
regular intervals to assent to their own oppression. Nothing else concerns
the voters.[47]

The play in fact is a prophetic paradigm of revolutionary victory,
based on the 'dangerous stupidity' of 'counter-revolutionary'
arguments (p. 21). And the irrationality beneath the apparently

logical and objective form, which results for instance in the presentation of a sadistic murderer as 'the typical representative of representational democracy and American freedom', is made explicit in Enzensberger's preface: 'At the moment of truth the "enlightened" rationalism of the *raisonneur* shows itself as what it always was – mere ideology' (p. 44).

Taken to its logical conclusion the rejection of all artistic criteria in *The Havana Hearing*, the double use of the media, and the attempt to reproduce documented facts which expose ideological attitudes – in short, the total merging of theatre and revolutionary politics – leads to the kind of approach that Günther Wallraff has developed. Wallraff deliberately sets out to break down conventional artistic boundaries and his 'work' is not limited to literary expression, even though it may take the form of reports on working conditions, interviews, or a quasi-drama like *After-Play* (*Nachspiele*, 1968). Here the documentary is not an end-product, a self-enclosed study, but becomes extended to include the research process itself. Wallraff not only 'performs', being forced by the antipathy of employers to his reports to adopt a pseudonym and false persona in order to gather his material, much of which has come from taking short-term employment in factories. His observation is also a form of intervention which is designed to alter the consciousness of all involved, making the workers aware of the everyday injustices in their position by interviewing them, and using his presence to give the experience that he reports a structure corresponding to 'the formal element in literature...the arranging, the preparation, the leverage to force others to react, to speak, particularly those [the authorities] who otherwise do everything to escape notice'. In this way his 'role-reporting' becomes the acting out of a situation for an audience, although they are normally at one remove from the 'drama' – as for instance in his 'study' of Greek fascism. Here he provoked his own arrest (filmed by a friend) by carrying out an act of sabotage, and persuaded the police to torture him by refusing to answer questions, characterising himself in such a way as to illustrate his perception that the impersonality of contemporary society has reduced the individual to a cypher, a conclusion arrived at in his investigations of industry: 'there are no individuals any longer... I made myself anonymous, a principle of my other work. I cut out the label "Made in Germany" from my jacket, carried no papers...didn't speak a word'.[48] Then on his release he used his experiences and the film as the basis of a television programme. Wallraff's approach, combining 'the happening' with documentary interpretation, lends itself to dramaturgical analysis, and its relationship to documentary theatre can be seen in *After-Play*. This play, commissioned on the first article of the west German Constitution which deals with 'the Dignity of Man', has the same quality as his extra-theatrical work. It measures the theoretical rights enshrined in the constitution against the practice of German courts, and contrasts a montage of quotations from the right-wing press and politicians to the shootings of radical student leaders such as Rudi Dutschke, the student spokesman, and Benno Ohnesorg, who became a student martyr for the radicals, so that the rhetoric undermines itself by its distance from reality. As the title indicates, this play was written to be performed *after* a discussion among the audience (initiated by the director) which would catalyse their awareness of their true political position by using recorded comments from the discussion as the starting points for each scene – if they showed an approved political position – or by taking those viewpoints which were 'false' and contrasting them with 'scenic documentation'. Wallraff's aim is 'political provocation' through creating 'a confrontation with the immediate experience of reality', and his success in creating 'functional literature' is indicated both by the way his books are reviewed in the political/news columns of daily papers, not the literary supplements, and by the criteria he has been forced to adopt by the court-cases that have followed his work:

An author of fiction can put what he knows and believes right in the strongest form; I can only put it in a form which at need I can also support in a court of law – and so must often renounce the closest, strongest instance.[49]

Paradoxically it is precisely this restraint which gives his indictments their effectiveness.

If Wallraff takes the documentary approach to an extreme at which all the formal qualities of art disappear and dialogue is a selection of quotations, where character is non-existent (the individual being seen as a blank which has no distinguishing qualities once the label of a name is removed) and the conscious acting out of a situation is a real event, the work of one of the newcomers to the German theatre-scene provides an interesting alternative. Where the direction taken by Enzensberger and

Wallraff leads off stage, away from any form that could be classified as drama, Dieter Forte has developed an approach which offers the documentary a theatrical future.

One of the limiting factors in this type of drama is contemporaneity. The subjects of all the plays so far discussed in this chapter had immediate public relevance, using this to inject a straight factual presentation with the emotional involvement necessary for holding an audience's attention; and significantly, when the facts were drawn from even the recent past, as in *The Investigation*, they are set in the frame of current events like the Frankfurt trials. Forte has succeeded in extending the range of material open to documentary treatment by taking the vision that Jaspers defined as peculiar to modern consciousness as his theme as well as his perspective. Our consciousness of facts rather than the facts themselves is his focus, and his first play, *Martin Luther and Thomas Münzer or The Introduction of Book-keeping* (*Martin Luther und Thomas Münzer oder Die Einführung der Buchhaltung*, 1970), gives history an immediate political relevance by challenging something taught to every German schoolchild: 'That this play, which holds so self-effacingly to the facts, stands our social picture on its head should make us mistrustful of what we have been told up to now.'[50] Starting from the realisation that the theological aspect of the Reformation fills libraries, while what he calls 'the social secretions' hardly rate a footnote, Forte applies a scientific-historical method to his material. Where there is only one witness to a scene it has either been struck from the play or is presented in openly unrealistic terms as a hypothesis. Much of the dialogue is taken straight from letters and contemporary writings (in modern translation), or even account books, all of which are kept in their original context; but the effect is peculiarly modern. The themes that emerge are the relationships between finance and revolution, power and ideas. Fugger, the financier who invented double-entry bookkeeping, the basis of capitalism, is revealed as the true revolutionary because it was his ideas that transformed society; while Luther's Ninety-Five Theses are proved to have been plagiarised, and his refusal to recant at the Diet of Worms is shown to be due to spineless subservience, the princes (who had borrowed heavily against the expectation of expropriating Church lands) being able to put greater pressure on him than the bishops.

But however effective as a revolutionary, Fugger hardly counts as a positive figure since the social changes that follow from his career make more men less free than even under the superseded feudal order; and on the surface this supports Forte's overtly apolitical attitude. However, in spite of his claim to a 'neutral' viewpoint ('to illustrate nineteenth-century ideologies is simply boring') this 'sceptical' play 'without heroes' contains a sentimentalised ideal in the figure of Münzer, a proto-communist who provided the intellectual leadership for the Peasant's Revolt. This is presented as 'the first great German revolution' and stands for positive values in the play as a conflict 'that runs like a red thread through the centuries: always the call for freedom and self-determination on one side and bookkeeping on the other'.[51] Apart from Münzer, all the characters are reduced to bank-balances, and the only motivation is that of the cash-register. The Emperor Maximilian's asceticism comes from being too poor to afford anything but water, the sale of indulgences is due to the Pope having been bankrupted by the high fees charged by Michelangelo, Raphael and Titian, while Fugger is prepared to finance anything for profit, whether votes for the Holy Roman Emperor or arms for the Peasant's Revolt. As Forte correctly remarks, 'accounts make fascinating reading. What appears complicated and unclear, often disguised as purely personal, suddenly reduces itself to a pair of sober columns of figures, to a pair of basic facts.'[52] But clarity is gained at the expense of oversimplification, and this effect is reinforced by Forte's treatment of history as polemic farce. The action, presented in eighty-two short scenes, is reduced to a series of punch lines, while the Pope, played by a mini-skirted actress, finds it comic that Luther's discovery of the Bible occurs just when the Vatican has lost its belief and prefers Plato. The serious point that Luther's example is responsible for the Church's return from a humanistic liberalism to repressive attitudes is presented as high camp – the 'Pope' exclaiming 'Back to the bosom of the church. We'll wear a maxi and become Christian again. Beautiful uniforms. Do any of you know the Mass?'[53] – and the ending culminates in a chorale by Fugger and the princes parodying Luther's hymn 'Ein feste Burg' as an ironic counterpoint to Münzer's brutal execution. The serious intentions behind this farcical presentation hardly come across in performance, and in the Basel première most of the more fantastical elements were cut, including the petticoat-Pope. This figure in fact epitomises the flaws in Forte's stylistic approach, and rehearsals showed that, however it was portrayed, the transvestite joke trivialised the effect of the whole, in spite of Forte's claim that this represented 'the institution – the feminine emancipated culture' and 'symbolises the contrast between Mediterranean and German civilisation, between barbarians and the Popes who read Plato'.[54]

Luther and Münzer hovers as uneasily between a pamphlet and a revue as *Song of the Lusitanian Bogey*, but it has immense theatrical vitality. As Patterson points out, 'it makes John Osborne's *Luther* seem as conventional as a Sunday School play';[55] and even if it runs the danger of reducing its historical material and social criticism to slapstick, it is a useful corrective to the sombre sententiousness of *The Investigation* or *The Havana Hearing*. The comedy is carefully balanced against the casual brutalities of the princes, the psychological repressiveness of Luther's protestant work-ethic, or the inhumanity of Fugger's sacrifice of everything to economic power. Even the humour is a serious attempt to respond to the twentieth century, which in Forte's view, like Macbeth, has become over-satiated with atrocities: 'One can no longer weep for horror. I want to make the spectator laugh so that he doesn't forget.'[56] Although Forte's approach is only a partial solution to the stylistic problems of documentary drama, and his treatment of history as farce tends to undercut his serious political aims, as a method of popularising contemporary issues this variation on documentary techniques is theatrically successful. It can also be applied with equal effect to different subjects, as Forte has shown by repeating it even down to the detail of the title-formulation in his latest play, *Jean-Henri Dunant, or The Introduction of Civilisation* (*Jean-Henri Dunant oder die Einführung der Zivilization*, 1977) which focusses on the founder of the Red Cross organization and his involvement in the revolutionary disaster of the Paris Commune.

8. *Traditions*

To an outsider the major characteristic of postwar German drama appears to be the development of new theatrical approaches, the constant search for new forms which would reflect and express a qualitative change in the way reality is perceived. To the ordinary German theatregoer, however, the greater part of the repertoire would have seemed comfortably conservative, and many of the most successful productions continued to be classics – Schiller and Goethe, Shakespeare, Hebbel and Hauptmann, with Brecht's plays from the 1930s and 1940s reaching the stage as 'modern classics' in the late 1950s, Sternheim and Wedekind being rediscovered as period pieces in the mid 1960s. Yet perhaps because of the influence of the Volksbühne which, from Otto Brahm at the turn of the century, had brought radical theatre to a wide public, German drama never suffered a split of the schizophrenic Broadway/off-Broadway kind between experimental and conventional stages. On the one hand Shakespeare and Wedekind became the basis for stylistic experiment (Peter Zadek's pop-art production of *Spring's Awakening*, 1965, or *Measure for Measure* along the lines of the Living Theatre, 1967; Hans Hollman's absurdist *Coriolanus*, 1970, or Peter Palitzsch's 'dialectical' *Wars of the Roses*). On the other hand the same contemporary themes that had sparked radical stylistic innovations were also handled in a conventional manner. Beside *The Physicists* or *In the Matter of J. Robert Oppenheimer* must be set Zuckmayer's mix of Mata Hari melodrama and Shavian discussion, *The Cold Light*; beside *The Black Swan* or *The Investigation* a play like Helga Zinner's *Ravensbruck Ballad*, where the atrocities of the death camps are treated as background for an unrealistic story about the escape of disguised Russian 'freedom-fighters' through the self-sacrifice and political solidarity of the other prisoners. Only too frequently in fact a conventional style embodies the most conventional of ideas, and whatever the ostensible theme the result is unmemorable entertainment. But there have been three significant exceptions which, at least initially, reconfirmed the continuing value of traditional forms. The Schillerian heroic 'drama of ideas' gained a new impetus from Hochhuth. Peter Hacks has achieved an impressive mythic and poetic theatre. The 'folk play' has been re-established by Sperr and Kroetz in distinctively modern terms. These have provided striking and effective drama, although their success is problematic and it is indicative that much of what goes under the label of the 'folk play' is cheap, exhibitionistic sensationalism, while Hacks stands alone, an example with no competent imitators, and Hochhuth has never been able to duplicate his first success.

Hochhuth's work, initially mistaken for documentary theatre and hailed as a new stylistic breakthrough, is striking testimony to the problems of presenting contemporary material in anachronistic forms. Perhaps more than any other single play, *The Representative* established postwar German drama on the international stage. The controversy it aroused caused a major re-evaluation of recent history and, measured by the volume and intensity of public discussion, its production must be counted an equivalent theatrical event to Ibsen's *Doll's House*, providing as it did a dramatic conflict that acted as a touchstone for moral attitudes, even for audiences who had no connection with either the Catholic Church or the 'final solution' for the Jews. In the mind of the public Hochhuth came to represent the new, political drama, shaped by the discipline of fact, and his second play was dedicated to Piscator who had acted as a spokesman for this line of theatrical development.

Now that the controversy has receded, however, the quality of Hochhuth's work as drama can be seen more clearly. In terms of the text what absorbed public attention was actually of secondary importance: the accusation that Pius XII was an accomplice in the Nazi extermination of the Jews since he had the moral authority to stop the murders, but refrained from comment to avoid weakening the German battle against communism, which he considered the greater evil. The real focus of the play was intended to be the deliberate self-sacrifice of Riccardo, whose assertion of personal responsibility, of the possibility of moral choice even in the context of Auschwitz denies the 'alibi for all guilt' provided by the view that individuals no longer have any autonomy in a world of mass movements and technological processes. In Hochhuth's original concept the Pope did not even appear, and he was only introduced as an antagonist to emphasise the significance of Riccardo's moral standpoint.[1]

The major characters are based on historical figures. Gerstein was a chemical expert who joined the SS to expose the euthanasia programme, but became one of those responsible for developing Cyclon B, without which the gas chambers could not have operated with such horrifying efficiency; the Doctor has an obvious counterpart in the notorious Dr Mengele of Auschwitz; and Riccardo is an amalgam of the two priests to whom the play is dedicated, Kolbe who offered to take the place of a prisoner in a group that was to be punished for the escape of one of their number and starved to death in Auschwitz, and Lichtenberg who prayed publicly for the Jews, asked to share their fate when arrested and died *en route* to Dachau. But in spite of the unwieldy length of the play, which was itself taken to be evidence of its epic nature, the inclusion of specific detail, or the historical and bibliographical references, Hochhuth's criteria are not those of fact. History is treated as 'a blueprint from which to construct the behaviour of man in our time', not analysed to illuminate a specific situation. Consequently although the personal attitudes of Pius XII are documented, the point on which the accusation turns – that an official protest from the Church would have been effective in halting the mass-murder – is a matter of opinion. On one hand the protests of the Bishop of Münster resulted in the temporary suspension of Jewish arrests, on the other those of the Dutch Bishops only intensified the SS extermination programme. The true centre of interest is religion not politics, and in terms of this universalisation the indictment against Pius XII is no more than an example of 'a lesson which is timeless'. Yet even on this level the political implications of the indictment actually distract from Hochhuth's intention that the Pope should act as 'a symbol, not only for all leaders, but for all men...who are passive when their brother is deported to death'. In the same way eschatological symbolism removes Auschwitz from the real world, yet the overwhelming facts of Auschwitz invalidate Hochhuth's attempt to present it as 'only one example of the terror which reigns on earth at all times, in all epochs, in every century'.[2] As a result the dramatic climax of the fifth act hovers uneasily between kitsch, the 'human façade' of hut and garden, and abstraction, the 'ghostly' cloud of an 'infernal atmosphere'.[3]

This incongruity between the level of generalisation and the material, the theme and the situation used to present it, is responsible for the major flaws in the play. Not only is the weight of fact such that almost all the scenes are overburdened with exposition and the primary motive for one character confronting another is to inform him of something. Hochhuth's premise – that history is the sum of individual actions, so that each person has the power to determine events by declaring his own moral position – is thrown into question by the need to make his figures equal to their historical background. Instead of drawing individualised characters, the people of the play are weighted with symbolism to counterbalance the mass anonymity of the death camps. In an article attacking Adorno's thesis that individuality is a nineteenth-century concept which was already being outdated by industrialisation at the time when it reached its fullest artistic expression, Hochhuth outlined his approach in a quotation from Schiller: 'Though you honour always the whole, I can only respect individuals. Always and only in individuals have I glimpsed the whole.'[4] But in practice his characterisation shortcircuits the equation of the general with the individual. Even the minor figures are 'representative' – Helga epitomises 'the specifically feminine abilities to adopt the opinions of those who impress her and to see nothing that might disturb her...totally malleable, like most young girls' while all the men around her are summed up in Fritsche: 'we see them daily either on the roller coaster of the German economic miracle or in our own bathroom mirror...as interchangeable as car-tyres. Therefore it suffices to observe one for all' (pp. 183–4). The normal becomes transposed to the typical, and as for the major figures, these are idealised to the point of abstraction. Gerstein is described as so 'modern' in his morality 'that in order to understand him fully it is necessary to read Kierkegaard'; even the Pope is not significant enough to stand on his own personality but, ceremoniously washing his hands, becomes Pontius Pilate; while Riccardo is a walking principle whose opening words state the position he holds throughout: 'Could your Excellency not intervene?' (p. 17). This tendency becomes clearest in the treatment of the Doctor, whom the other characters refer to only in terms of 'an enigma' (p. 42), 'not a man at all', 'the Auschwitz angel of death' (p. 63) – descriptions which reflect Hochhuth's own views. 'He has the stature of absolute evil...to him it no longer seems worthwhile even to play with homo sapiens...an ancient figure of the theatre and of Christian Mystery plays' (pp. 29–30). Such a mythological status is incompatible with individuality, and at this point the superficiality of Hochhuth's attempt to deal with twentieth-century realities in terms of free will and personal responsibility becomes clear. On the one hand the same actors are to play different roles because 'in the age of universal conscription it is not necessarily a question of virtue or guilt or even character which uniform a person wears or whether he stands on the side of the victims or the executioners' (p. 14). On the other hand a 'devil doctor' provides no insight into the economic and political system that created Auschwitz, nor even into human nature:

Since this sinister apparition from another world was obviously only playing at being human, we must forgo any further attempts to trace its human features – for these could contribute nothing to our understanding of such an incomprehensible being or its deeds (p. 30).

That the appearance of personal conflict is an empty front would be relatively unimportant if it did not discredit Hochhuth's stress on individual conscience. But this is not even a 'drama of ideas' in any normal sense, and instead of a developing dialectic of argument there is only an opposition of ethical principles which is static because they are absolute. The final act substantiates the rhetoric of the earlier scenes. Hitler is indeed 'the adversary of the creation' (p. 131), Auschwitz 'the apocalypse' (p. 119), and ideas are transposed into eschatology. The theme is set by surrealistic monologues defining the death camp in religious terms as the state of despair. The self-proclaimed devil recognises Riccardo as 'an angel' (p. 197). The rationale for genocide becomes conscious 'sacrilege' to challenge God: 'to provoke him so limitlessly that he would have to answer. Even if only the negative answer which...can be his sole excuse' (p. 198). Evil triumphs as a consequence of the Pope's passivity, which stands for the apparent silence of God, while Riccardo's sacrifice as his, and so God's 'representative' is an affirmation which restores meaning to life. This is an extreme level of symbolic abstraction, and by contrast the everyday scenes are reduced to a level of utter banality.

Hochhuth's frequent references to Goethe and Schiller are sufficient indication of the ambitious level he is aiming at, and *The Representative* has been compared both with *Don Carlos* and Lessing's *Nathan the Wise*.[5] But the cathartic effect of the play comes from a structure of action that has no intrinsic connection to the theme. Suspense is created by conventional 'rescue' scenes which could have come straight from Victorian melodrama, and the way in which here high tragic pathos teeters on the edge of farce was unintentionally illustrated by the Broadway production of the play. There the poetic pretensions were inflated – as for instance in an antiphonal chant from Gerstein and Jacobson, 'take the star, priest. The light is in the star. The pain is in the star'; a vulgarisation which is not in fact out of line with the text, but rather, simply made the emotional rhetoric of the original gesture explicit – while the Doctor was demoted to a traditional villian, twirling a swagger-stick instead of mustaches, so that a horrified question like Riccardo's 'what sort of – of devil are you?' became reduced to the exclamatory 'what a devil you are!' Even Piscator's production suffered from a similar emotionalism. His director's notes call repeatedly for 'more irony' or 'less pathos', and the only suitable setting that could be found for the Auschwitz scenes were projections of 'the faces of Jews with pleading eyes' behind barbed wire which 'grow fainter until by the ending they are completely transparent in the clear light'[6] (see Illustration 15). The true quality of the play is also reflected in the way the American translation hovers uneasily between over-literary and over-idiomatic expressions. The rendering of Hochhuth's irregular lines into blank verse is equally indicative, and although in one sense this is unfortunate with its artificial Shakespearean overtones, it is really a fair attempt to find an equivalent for the 'Schillerian style' that so many critics have referred to. But if Hochhuth's text is set beside, say, a passage from *Don Carlos*, the impression is one of functional bareness, an avoidance of metaphors and rhetorical devices, even in Riccardo's climactic plea to the Pope. There is none of the driving rhythm that comes from Schiller's regular iambic pentameters, but equally the breaking of rhythm by shorter lines has little of Brecht's emphatic harshness. In fact the verse seems to have no discernible effect, and printing the Pope's dictated statement (a literal translation from *Osservatore Romano*, 25 October 1943) as 'found poetry' by arbitrarily chopping up sentences hardly corresponds to Hochhuth's insistence that 'a subject which is so closely involved with contemporary events...must be transposed, heightened by language'.[7]

To some extent these weaknesses could be disguised by intelligent production, particularly since the length of the text requires drastic cutting for performance. But it was only the sensationalism of the attack on Pius XII that allowed the defects of Hochhuth's approach to be overlooked, and when he tried to repeat the formula these became obvious.

15 Hochhuth, *The Representative* (Piscator), 1963. The Auschwitz projections: classic conflict – protagonist, antagonist, chorus.

The intention of *Soldiers* (*Soldaten*, 1967) is more precisely formulated – to arouse sufficient public opinion to force the member nations of the Geneva Convention to sign an agreement outlawing air attacks on civilian targets. As his programme-notes show, Hochhuth had worked out practical, if over-optimistic tactics for a political campaign in which his play would be the opening blow. Through presenting the fire-bombing of Dresden as a war crime equal to the cremation of the Jews in Hitler's death camps, pressure could be brought to bear on the west German President, and Germany's support would be a moral example that no other country could ignore. As in *The Representative*, however, Hochhuth's method is the dubious one of using the emotion generated by a side issue, again the indictment of an admired public figure, to gain support for the main point. The attack on the Papacy in his 'Christian tragedy' was at least a natural by-product of the action, thematically integrated with Riccardo's redemptive sacrifice. Here the accusation, that Churchill ordered Sikorski's assassination, is not only unprovable (the nature of Hochhuth's 'evidence', a confidential deposition by an unnamed Secret Service agent locked in a Swiss bank and not to be disclosed for 50 years, is dubious, while the available facts show Sikorski's death to be an accident which damaged British interests). It appears gratuitous since it has no direct relevance to the main theme, and in the event did nothing to promote the play's aim. A press conference before the première was attended by six television crews and over 150 journalists, but the only public actions that followed were a historical analysis of Hochhuth's contentions (Carlos Thompson, *The Assassination of Winston Churchill*), the banning of the English National Theatre production and two minor libel suits, one of which challenged the documentation rather than the accusation itself.[8]

Where *Soldiers* is most successful is in the treatment of Churchill. There is a real fascination in this exploration of a charismatic personality caught in a dilemma between ends and means, who finds himself forced by the logic of events which he has set in motion and believes he controls to take actions that are either morally repugnant to him or ultimately self-defeating. Thus Churchill's criminal pleasure in the havoc wreaked by his bombers is balanced against his 'last call to arms as Prime Minister, the Bermuda Conference in 1953: he pressed in vain for a law to protect open cities...by that time he was only smiled at'.[9] Indeed

Hochhuth uses his indictment to deepen this fascination. Even Sikorski is forced, as a stage direction emphasises 'to see the absolute cogency of Churchill's argument' and Hochhuth presents the scale of Churchill's 'mistakes' as in direct proportion to his 'colossal qualities', with the intention that the audience should 'sympathise spiritually and humanly with his conflict'.[10] The result is a highly effective ambivalence in our response, empathy with Churchill clashing against the recognition that his antagonists' arguments make his position untenable, both on the human (Sikorski) and on the moral level (Bishop Bell). Hochhuth's approach to history is unchanged: but here his thesis that 'the chances of survival for mankind lie in the personal choice of *every* man, of each single *individual*' (p. 178) is more credible in the example of a 'great man' who is himself conscious of 'making history' – an awareness stressed in his speeches. The strength and complexity of this characterisation draw on the connotations of Churchill's public image, and it is capable of withstanding even Hochhuth's grandiose equation between Churchill's autobiography and the history of the twentieth century. But it is precisely here that this achievement is undercut by Hochhuth's stylistic aspirations. The title, taken from Lenz's drama about the brutalisation of men under military discipline (1776), indicates the play's relationship to the German tradition of bourgeois realism. But the treatment is nearer that of neo-classical tragedy, and Thomas Mann is quoted to show Churchill as 'a hero from Corneille, wearing the mask of our time'. The result is incongruous – the 'intimate sphere' of a symbol. History is reduced to hubris, and if the imagination is strained by metaphors depicting Churchill as Neptune or Oedipus, the level of symbolisation creates demands that no contemporary concept of man can rise to. What are we, or indeed the actor, to make of an individual who is also elemental, 'the personification of the war drive and bloodstream of the century in which more men have met violent ends than ever before since the beginning of the world?' (p. 127). Even Hochhuth has to admit that language will not carry that far:

This is the point in the play at which the author can do no more, the actor everything, to make the *leap* from the comic moment into myth...There must be magic in the performance. If the actor can awake it, radiate it, then his characterisation will embody what Churchill himself achieved: that the imagination of the public amplifies such a figure of its own accord (p. 126).

This idealisation is also applied to the characters surrounding Churchill, where the links with *The Representative* become clear. Bishop Bell, his moral nemesis, was specifically intended as a protestant counterpart to Riccardo, while Cherwell is the 'devil doctor' in a slightly more disguised form, 'the Grand Cremator' and arch-tempter who is also the epitome of the soulless technological age and sees himself as a perfectly constructed machine. Sikorski too is not simply an individual, but both the personification of Churchill's dilemma and of romantic 'knight-errant' values, Don Quixote in the rocket era. In contrast to Dürrenmatt's demythologising approach in a play like *Hercules*, where the theme is also the hero as monster, these characters add to the daemonic interpretation of Churchill, and it is hardly coincidental that the actor who played the part in the Berlin première had made his reputation as Harras in Zuckmayer's *The Devil's General*. As one critic remarked, this Churchill is 'a Wallenstein who has read Sartre's *Dirty Hands*'.[11] Humanising such symbolic figures is outside Hochhuth's range and, even more obviously than in the earlier play, idealistic inflation is accompanied by bathos. Churchill is a myth who sets his wastepaper basket on fire (reducing the accompanying discussion of the bombing of Hamburg, in which the dialogue is built around the eschatalogical code name of Gomorrah, to an incendiary absurdity) and has it farcically extinguished with a soda-siphon. Similarly the Garden of Eden of the final act, where 'the fall of man has already taken place', is turned into sentimental kitsch by including an Adam and Eve in the shape of two minor figures whose love is destroyed by their knowledge of evil (Sikorski's murder).

This doubling between symbolic ideals and banality is a symptom of stylistic anachronism. Dramatic conventions, which are formalisations expressing perceptions of reality, a socially determined reflex of awareness, are unacceptable if they do not appear as natural as breathing. Here the self-consciousness of the heroic, neo-classical vision is compounded by the use of a framework which is intended to make such a treatment of recent history more plausible by distancing it. *Soldiers* is presented not only as a play within a play, but as a rehearsal. The 'author' is called Dorland after the supposed name of the medieval author of *Everyman*, a dying ex-bomber-pilot turned playwright, and the 'workshop' run-through we witness, which is introduced as his expiation for his war-crimes, commemorates the centennial of the Geneva

16   Hochhuth, *Soldiers*, 1967. 'The Garden': heroic protagonists in a quasi-
documentary context. (Flanking the sundial/compass are two trees, the Tree
of Life and the Tree of Knowledge of Good and Evil.)

Convention in the ruins of Coventry Cathedral, while as the final lines inform us (a cunning inclusion of up to the minute fact) it will never come to public performance since the play 'has been banned' in England. This outer play, which devotes a disproportionate effort to arguing against the view that individuals have no decisive influence on historical situations and that the modern context makes freedom of choice illusory, is deliberately expressionistic and over-written. As a Morality play, it extends the themes of the Churchill drama into a conflict of allegories where Angels (the artists, Dorland and the Sculptor) stand against Death (the projected photograph of a dead woman, mummified by a fire-storm which has left her hair untouched, epitomising the horror of Dresden). The title, *The Little London Theatre of the World* refers back to Calderón's *El Gran Teatro del Mundo* and indicates how the Churchill drama is to be taken – as a metaphoric microcosm. Quite apart from the contradiction of setting a strictly structured action, based on the French three-act form and with a limited number of characters, inside a frame modelled on the psychomachia of *Everyman* and the fluidity of Miller's *After the Fall*, once again the anachronistic nature of the convention means that this Morality play frame cannot be taken seriously if left to stand on its own. Consequently the stage directions suggest it to be either a psychological projection of Dorland's agonised mind or even 'a dream: characters and settings in a trial of conscience are precisely as real and actual as we take them to be and recognise them in ourselves' (p. 13). Presumably if 'the setting is totally freed from restrictions of place and time' this is meant to condition our view of the inner play, which is in theory at one further remove from reality. Paradoxically it has the opposite effect. Even the overt theatricality in the presentation – the indicative, incomplete scenery; the first glimpse of the actors as 'tiny depersonalised shadow silhouettes against the sharp duck-egg blue brilliance...like marionettes in the hands of an unseen director' (p. 50); the stress on Churchill's rhetorical view of himself as 'performing on the stage of history' or his way of 'referring to "the theatre of mankind"...' (p. 97) – cannot remove the empathetic immediacy of the characterisation in the main play. In contrast to the semi-mystical darkness of the framework, the 'blinding white light' brings the spectator back to the documentary reality.

In many ways the most effective part of *Soldiers* is the stage-

directions which have the breadth of insight and wit of Bernard
Shaw's prefaces. The characterisation is on some levels among the
best of contemporary German theatre. The moral conviction
behind the play is irreproachable, and Hochhuth can hardly be
held at fault for his failure to solve the paradox that 'humanising'
war by extending the Geneva conventions might make its out-
break more likely. But the strengths of the play merely highlight
its stylistic flaws, and after the critical reactions Hochhuth announced that he was starting work on a comic fantasy (*Lustspiel*).
This is indeed the direction he has taken, but discarding historical
fact as resistant to 'ideal transparency' is simply an implicit
acknowledgement that his approach is anachronistic. Turning to
totally invented plots and people was no solution since it only
revealed the naviety of his vision more clearly. Suspension of
disbelief applies only to the external aspects of a play and depends
on the intrinsic credibility of the imaginative core. 'Truth to life'
– which basically means reflecting the current view of reality –
remains the audience's criterion even for costume drama, and
although an outdated thesis or style may be more acceptable in a
play set back in history as the expression of the outlook of that era,
Hochhuth's aim continued to be immediate political relevance.
The contemporary background and documentary material, which
he still appends in his notes, merely serve to underline the
incongruity of a fantasy where the premises come straight from
classical drama, as in his most recent work *Lysistrata and NATO*
(*Lysistrate und die NATO*, 1974), and the play that followed
Soldiers illustrates the problem only too clearly.

The Guerillas (*Die Guerillas*, 1970) is a logical extension of the
earlier play, picking up on a speech in the prologue:

Man hasn't changed throughout history. In spite of that aggressions
must be broken down, and this will happen through revolutions.
Revolutions supersede wars. That stands in *Soldiers*. I believe it myself.
I have the sculptor say it.[12]

In the programme to the Berlin production of *Soldiers* an essay
by Marcuse had been printed, proposing the individual conscience
as the only force capable of opposing the total subjection of an
advanced society geared to a military machine. Marcuse used
Vietnam to demonstrate the evil of the system, pointing to the
ability of a 'primitive' self-reliant people to withstand an
overwhelming military technocracy as an example for the student

revolt; and this formed the starting point of *Guerillas*, in which Hochhuth's notes attack dollar imperialism and the US role in Vietnam. Rudi Dutschke and Che Guevara are set up as positive principles, and the plot deals with a coup against the US government.

Even in *Soldiers* Hochhuth had shown considerable scepticism over the value of documents, claiming the gaps, what had been omitted, to be more significant than any known facts. As he makes Churchill point out, the victors write history and can transform any betrayal into heroism. *Guerillas* is therefore a complete fictionalisation of contemporary issues, and the Foreword is both a perceptive rejection of documentary theatre and an attempt to outline a political function for fantasy:

a stage which took its style from [reportage] would 'document' little more than its own technical and spatial inadequacy. Newsreels operate on the conventional error that photographic clippings of reality are realistic...The task of political theatre is not to *reproduce* reality...but to approach it through the *projection* of a new one.[13]

In short, moral ideas substitute for facts, and the utopian tendency becomes clearer when Hochhuth goes on to distinguish his approach from Brecht's parables and Edward Bond's brutal naturalism. Instead of transposing politics into a 'fancy dress' model (Setzuan or Mahagonny), or presenting an image of ordinary life which simply confirms social exploitation by making its symptoms seem natural (the sex and sadism of *Saved*), existing conditions are to be challenged by an alternative vision which still retains immediate relevance. The result is pure Hollywood. Good and evil principles disguised as spies and senators in the shape of Stryker, a power-mad head of the CIA, and Nicholson, an idealised Kennedy-figure, millionaire ex-war-hero member of the political elite, wrestle only too literally for control of the western world's destiny. Freed from the logical restraints of documents, this play reveals the underlying basis of Hochhuth's thesis that great individuals determine the course of events to be the conspiracy theory of history. His notes to the play state categorically that the CIA organised the deaths of Martin Luther King and Kennedy; the plot is a palace revolution – Nicholson, converted to democracy by contacts with South American 'Guerillas', versus the '200 families' who supposedly control the United States – and the climax is a rather over graphic representation of men dominating political developments, the democratic forces in society being defeated by Stryker throwing Nicholson from the top of a skyscraper. Imaginary extrapolations of contemporary political situations into ideal forms become open wish fulfillment in the concept behind *The Guerillas* as well as in the outcome of *Lysistrata and NATO* – and this sentimentality is the real quality in Hochhuth's use of anachronistic styles. Adorno's reply to Hochhuth's attack on his sociological theories may underestimate the effectiveness of some of Hochhuth's achievements in terms of conventional theatre, but his main point is accurate: that the 'personalising' of macro-economic or social forces reduces Auschwitz and Vietnam to incomprehensible and therefore 'unavoidable fates', while the illusory significance given by traditional dramatic conventions restricts an audience's response to a purely aesthetic level.[14] Interpreting politics as high tragic pathos is a form of escapism which runs directly counter to Hochhuth's stated aims.

By contrast the work of playwrights as different as Fritz Hochwälder and Peter Hacks are successful in their own terms. Although no less conventional in approach, they are careful to preserve a distance from contemporary issues and adapt traditional forms to serve their own ends rather than allowing them to condition their vision. Superficially Hochwälder's historical plays are similar to Hochhuth's. His first, *Esther* (1940), is based on the extermination of the Jews under Hitler; *The Strong are Lonely* (*Das heilige Experiment*, 1943) is a drama of ideas based on an ethical conflict; *The Public Prosecutor* (*Der öffentliche Ankläger*, 1948) deals with the question of personal responsibility in an era of atrocities, a reflection on one level of the way morally upright individuals were brought to support the Nazi regime. But the treatment is very different to Hochhuth's contemporary immediacy. *Esther*, 'an old fairy-tale put into a new dramatic form',[15] presented the death camps obliquely as a horrifying fantasy drawn from the Old Testament story of Haman's plan to wipe out the Jews in Persia. The other plays retreat to eighteenth-century South America and the French Revolution; and although the themes relate to the Third Reich they only do so in the abstract as general moral problems. Any direct reference is deliberately avoided, and each spectator must draw the inferences for himself. Hochwälder's aspirations are theatrical, not intellectual or political, his principles are primarily those of craftsmanship, and he was scornful of 'literary' or 'self-important' drama: 'true theatre has always been more closely related to the circus than the seminar, to clowning rather than studying'. As a result the type of question posed is not only timeless but almost self-evident – the intention of *The Public Prosecutor*, for instance, was deliberately downplayed as 'showing in the form of a *Teufelskomödie* how terror flays itself'.[16]

His most serious play, *The Strong are Lonely*, which gained a wide international reputation after the war, shows the qualities of his 'unpretentious anti-anti-theatre' at their best. The utopian Jesuit state in Paraguay and its destruction for political reasons masquerading as superior moral claims gave Hochwälder a 'unique possibility to objectify eternal human problems, the question of social justice and the kingdom of God on earth, and bring them close to the present by setting them in a historical sphere'.[17] The issues are left open. How justified is a pacifist state in using force to defend itself? To what extent are spiritual ideals compromised by materialism? Where does one draw the line between the obedience that is the precondition for a perfectly integrated society and slavery? The characters reach decisions which are overruled by higher authorities, and the final equilibrium is then made questionable by their reconsideration. The King's Deputy, de Miura, concludes that the charges against the Jesuits are false, but reveals that the judgement of his inquiry has been predetermined by reasons of state. The Father Provincial refuses to bow to blatant injustice, has de Miura and his soldiers arrested, but is forced to disown his own troops by the Papal Legate who has witnessed the proceedings in disguise. The Spanish empire cannot tolerate the Jesuit state because its utopian order is subversive, its justice and plenty a standing challenge to social inequality and exploitation. The church cannot allow it because its success undermines religious influence in the established centres of power. Paradoxically, it is precisely because it is right in an unrighteous world that the 'kingdom of God' must be abolished; but in the final scene the Father Provincial rejects his acquiescence (while also rejecting the violence that was his only option) and reaffirms the historical inevitability of freedom.

Although this is a drama of character, the action makes it clear that economic pressures and historical forces make it impossible for individuals to follow their own inclinations, let alone control events, and unlike Hochhuth there is no attempt to present a message. As a dying hero, shot by his own men in trying to stop the fighting, the Father Provincial's last words carry special dramatic weight, but what they leave the audience with is a moral vision which any practical programme would negate. Hochwälder works throughout by implication, presenting theatrical situations rather than thematic statements, and the ending is not so much a commentary which (as in *Soldiers*) restates the moral, but an image of the human situation which is also a challenge to the audience. The eighteenth-century setting vanishes in the growing darkness of nightfall, also symbolising the triumph of injustice and oppression, out of which comes the disembodied voice of de Miura: 'And yet – something...speaks in my heart – "For what is a man profited if he gains the whole world, and loses his soul?"...I confess...I confess'.[18] At the same time the mechanics of surprise and suspense in Hochwälder's traditionally Aristotelian structure of discovery and reversal are almost too perfectly balanced. The craftsmanship seems more designed to create strong situations where actors can display their skill, than to communicate fresh insights into our own nature or our society. This relates to Hochwälder's ideal of a 'folk-theatre', equivalent to Raimund and Nestroy, with 'a prescribed content and form, a theatre for everyman',[19] and the tendency is even clearer in a play like *The Public Prosecutor*. Here Fouquier-Tinville, identified with the Terror which has become politically inexpedient, is too incorruptible to be dismissed, too moral to compromise, and the only way of removing him is to use his ruthlessness against himself. He is to prosecute an unnamed criminal and, if successful in gaining a conviction, the death sentence he is handed will be his own. The irony in the situation is emotionally involving, but the same paradox of good in a social context where right and wrong are reversed is simply used to create theatrical effects, and any discussion of the issues is clichéd and minimal. Theatrical excitement is a valuable quality found all too infrequently on the stage, but here it has become an end in itself. The result is easy entertainment which gratifies the audience without touching them on any deeper level.

The same criticism could be made of Hacks' later work. His first plays, *The Chapbook of Duke Ernest, or The Hero and His Followers* (*Das Volksbuch vom Herzog Ernst*, 1953: première 1967) and *The Battle of Lobositz* (*Die Schlacht bei Lobositz*, 1954: première 1956) are anti-heroic comedies with puppet-like characters whose actions are designed to expose social mechanisms. Interspersed with songs, the scenes are each structured to make a point rather than furthering the plot. The first play is based on a popular epic ballad which dates from 1493, the second on the autobiography of a Swiss soldier in the Seven Years' War, and both contain ironic echoes of the west German rearmament of the early 1950s. Technically these plays derive from the Brecht of *Arturo Ui* or *Schwejk in the Second World War*, but where Brecht's satire is specific and modern Hacks is concerned with broad attitudes. The result is farce closely akin to the 'folk-play' or *Kasperl* (Harlequin) theatre. Duke Ernest's progress through the Holy Roman Empire is typically picaresque as he sacrifices his retinue one by one in order to survive the consequences of his own pride and foolhardiness – a 'hero' whose heroism is the self-styled attribute of the ruling classes, and so diminishes to zero as he loses all his followers and thus moves down the social scale. The reference point is as much past as present, and Hacks specified his intention as 'fully in the spirit of the old chapbook...focussing on significant symptoms of Gothicism: gothic militarism, gothic class structures, gothic sexuality, gothic justice. A gothic revue.'[20] In *The Battle of Lobositz* this demythologising is applied to the time of Frederick the Great, one of Hacks' recurrent *bêtes noires*; again with a folk-play basis. Braeker, the proletarian anti-hero who deserts when he realises that the war (between Prussia and Austria) is of no more advantage to him as a common man than as a Swiss, has a relationship with his officer based on 'a propensity for subordination' which is very close to that between Schwejk and Lukasch. This mix of Brechtian and traditional approaches is highly effective.

After coming into conflict with east German cultural policies over his attempts to dramatise topical themes more directly in *Anxieties and Power* and *Moritz Tassow*, Hacks took refuge in even more conventional types of drama. His next play, *Margarete in Aix* (1965: première 1969) is a retreat into the grotesque. In spite of the claim that 'the historical material is like a prism in which contemporary reality is refracted',[21] the effect is a *Grand Guignol* fairy-tale. The climax is a sequence of shock effects created out of ironic incongruities. Margarete, exiled from England, dies of pure disappointment, happily anticipating that this will make her mark on the world. She chooses a banquet as the occasion, but a courtier covers up her death by dancing with her corpse. The highly mannered style that makes such gruesome improbabilities acceptable illuminates nothing but the artificial nature of the stage, and the satire on the pretensions of the ruling classes becomes confused with a parody of dramatic conventions since Margarete consciously plays the role of a tragic heroine in a situation treated as farce. Unlike Dürrenmatt whose grotesque images are created by a radical simplification of life, this grotesquerie comes from a baroque exaggeration of theatre. Medieval Provence becomes the landscape of art not events, characterisation is reduced to gratuitous caricature, and the only obvious contemporary reference is in the marginal figures of the troubadours who epitomise the impotence of the artist.

The mannerism, the fairy-tale elements, together with an elegance of style which emphasises that the play is a linguistic artefact, point forward to Hacks' subsequent attempts to create drama in the 'great tradition'. This has necessarily meant his complete renunciation of Brecht as a stylistic influence: 'Brecht's reality was the first half of the twentieth century. Our reality is already different, our methods must be different.'[22] The Brechtian alienation of Hacks' early plays is transformed into its opposite (though he continued to interpret his work in equivalent terms, referring to the 'distanced attitude' of aesthetics) and imagistic blank verse replaces the verbal economy of his previous dialogue which was modelled on Brecht's shorter, broken lines. In Hacks' view, since the socialism of the DDR has resolved class conflicts and (apparently) created utopian possibilities for personal fulfillment, the function of art is now affirmative. Hence his use of 'beautiful, great forms' which 'proclaim a good opinion of the world', and his *de facto* rejection of all specifically modern dramatic styles – hence too the unattractive virulence of his attack on Wolf Biermann, which also indicates how much his position is out of phase, Hacks being the only significant east German artist to support the state over Biermann's expulsion –

Up to now in this century there have been two typical trends in drama, that of Brecht and that of the absurd. The absurdists renounce knowledge of the world, Brecht sacrifices all to it. From the scientific point of view the absurdists are wrong and Brecht right; from the dramatic point of view both are equally wrong.[23]

Naturalism (or its east German equivalent of socialist realism) is also rejected as equally limited since any claim to scientific objectivity separates the spectator from what he sees. Drama appropriate to the new age will celebrate the 'totality' of human experience and create a 'unity of subject and object', exploiting abstraction, fantasy and sovereign virtuosity – in short, 'the poetic'.[24]

As perhaps might be expected, his attempts to inaugurate a new era of 'classical drama' have led naturally to grand opera – *Omphale* (1976) for example, which was originally commissioned as a libretto for Siegfried Mattaus, an ex-pupil of Hanns Eisler, adapted into a play for the Berliner Ensemble, then revised back into a libretto. This has the sort of playfully heroic-mythological love affair (Hercules and the Queen of Lydia, role reversals and sex changes) and the simultaneously ironic and verbally sensuous poetry that has become the trademark of Hacks' work in the 'great tradition'. But Hacks has shown that this type of poetic high comedy is also capable of producing highly effective theatre, and his *Amphitryon* (1967) has proved itself to be one of the more successful post-war plays, though the difficulty of translating the densely textured and elliptically ambiguous verse means that it is almost totally unknown outside Germany. The plot follows Plautus, but the opening emphasises that this adaptation is intended to have immediate emotional relevance. Amphitryon enters with a heavily traditional invocation in iambic pentameters; only to break off after seven lines with the comment that such a text is 'stupid', revealing that he is Jupiter rehearsing an unsympathetic role and jolting the spectator out of the reverential attitude all too common in German audiences, who tend to take 'classics' as cultural museum pieces. This sets the comic tone of Olympian theatricality. The story of divine seduction is rendered with wit, elegance, some fine poetic passages and a neatly gradated, if predictable, sequence of farcical confusions after the real Amphitryon's return from the wars. But all it adds up to is the romantic truism that love is the only force that can transform dead social conventions. The real Amphitryon, who measures human greatness by social position, is set against his potential in the shape of his divine double, and there is little to challenge an audience in making a husband the pattern for reactionary politics versus a lover's quasi-revolutionary passion which (literally since the lover is a god) transcends human limitations. The strength of the play lies in our sense of the artist's superiority over his material and the way this echoes the theme that love, as the 'aspiration towards infinity', can reshape the resistant material world.[25] Its weakness is in the uncritical optimism which substitutes an ersatz utopia for real problems; and when – as in *Prexaspes* (1976) – Hacks attempts to deal with contemporary events in this 'great style' the result is a *drama à clef*. Darios may represent Honecker; the moneylender Otanes, who is banished from Persia for criticising his choice of queen, can be taken as Biermann; while the plot may be intended as a comment on the current conflict in communist regimes between strict interpreters of Marxist-Leninist dogma and technocrats. But the mythologising and the formal perfection removes all significance from the issues. Although Hacks, as a far better artist than Hochhuth, avoids the simplifications of a naive approach, the problems of anachronism remain, and his work is open to the same criticism as Christopher Fry's plays. These, equally popular in England during the 1950s, were also characterised by a brilliant verbal surface, idyllic plots and affirmative themes; but the style ultimately expressed nothing but itself. The costumes were colourful but empty.

The retreat to myth or the distant past as the only context in which a traditional style can reach its full expression indicates its basic insufficiency, but there is one variation which has stood the test of contemporaneity. This is the 'folk play'. Although Hochwälder and Hacks both referred to the folk play as a model, Hochwälder's conventional well-made naturalistic drama, or Hacks' intellectually sophisticated imitation of naivety in a ballad style have little in common with the traditional folk form which reached its height in Austria with Nestroy. At first sight these dialect satires on pretentiousness, self-deception, conceit and pedantry with stock characters and clever servants look an unpromising prototype for relevant modern drama. And being written in a stylised convention which has no counterpart in English literature, to say nothing of the formidable difficulties of translating his Viennese idiom, it is perhaps hardly surprising that only one Nestroy play has established itself on the English-speaking stage: *Einen Jux will er sich machen*, which has been adapted by Thornton Wilder as *The Matchmaker* and formed the basis of the musical *Hello Dolly*. Where Nestroy's farces have proved useful to contemporary playwrights is in the techniques they contain for presenting the common man as a subject for drama, notably a special use of kitsch to contrast idealistic concepts of the moral worth of simple people with the often brutal reality, and a concentration on their problems in terms of language.

These were the elements picked up by Ödön von Horváth,

whose plays, written in the 1930s but banned by the Nazis, were almost completely unknown before their revival by Palitzsch and Hans Hollman in the 1960s. In Horváth's mature work his satire, unlike the traditional genre which reinforces accepted moral attitudes by attacking aberrations, becomes a tool for analysing social values; and his definition of the social context in terms of clinically observed individuals has been compared to the modern critiques of Adorno, Marcuse and Reich that formed the theoretical basis for the student revolts of 1968–9.[26] Horváth defined his approach as 'the extension' of the folk play tradition into modern political conditions. A mix of deliberately banal naturalism – 'problems of the people ... seen through the eyes of the people' – and naïvely sentimentalised perspectives that reveal the upper-class, idealised concept of 'the people' (*das Volk*) as the real problem, it gains its effects through a 'synthesis of seriousness and irony'.[27] The best examples of this technique and the ones which influenced younger German playwrights most directly are *Kasimir und Karoline* (1931, staged by Palitzsch in 1964 and Hollman, 1968) and *Tales from the Vienna Woods* (*Geschichten aus dem Wienerwald*, 1930, Hollman 1966 and 1971). Both are deceptively simple stories where images of communal culture represented by the romantic folk song and Strauss waltz of the titles frame pictures of isolated characters, unable to identify with each other in a disintegrating society. Kasimir, an out-of-work chauffeur, and his bride Karoline become separated in the gaiety of the *Oktoberfest*, each ending up with partners to whom they are indifferent, and their emotional emptiness reveals the superficiality of the traditional market-place celebration. The nearest English equivalent to this direct presentation of a social panorama in a broad sweep of short scenes is Ben Jonson's *Bartholomew Fayre*, but here the glitter and laughter of the crowds becomes increasingly false as the individual characters betray themselves by taking the outward forms of gratification for real fulfilment. Similarly in *Tales from the Vienna Woods* the heartlessness of petty-bourgeois morality which condemns a girl to misery, or of a respectable woman who leaves her baby grandchild to die of exposure in the cold to preserve appearances, or the signs of coming fascism in the racist views of a patriotic student, are overlaid with idyllic bathing in an always blue Danube and string music from the local wine-cellar.

Horváth defined his central focus as the equal but always

opposed claims of personal rights as against responsibilities to others, that conflict between 'the individual and society, this eternal slaughter with no hope of peace'; and his techniques are designed to hold the balance between the political plane 'where the times are more significant than the people' and the self-assertion epitomised by the protagonist's plea in one of his first plays, 'I beg you to look on me as a man and not an era'.[28] His characters exist primarily in terms of their language, the grotesque German of the half-educated, and it is also on this linguistic level that political criticism is introduced. Dialect, on the surface a colourful milieu, is shown to be both a psychological problem for those who speak it and a symptom of social conditioning, as limiting and depersonalising as the technical or ideological jargon of the more educated characters. Each cliché in the dialogue unmasks an attitude, and it is the gap between intended and expressed meaning, lack of feeling and emotive words that exposes fake social values for what they really are. This ironic contrast is reinforced by sentimental lyricism, as in *Tales from the Vienna Woods* where the waltz (to be played according to the stage directions by a 'heavenly orchestra' with deep emotion) is heard while a butcher's boy speaks of the quality of his sausages, or when the grotesquely fat and materialistic owner of a toyshop allows himself to be moved by conventionalised thoughts of the approach of spring. The satiric counterpoint undermines the audience's sentimental preconceptions by heightening emotionalism into deliberate kitsch, while presenting the brutalisation of individuals by social pressures in a superficially harmless rosy glow of *Gemütlichkeit*.

This balance is hard to achieve in performance, where overemphasis can reduce the plays to slice-of-life flatness or uncritical gush, and it requires a high degree of stylisation not usually associated with the folk play. The fascist tendencies in society are devastatingly illuminated, but unlike Brecht the political reference is always oblique. Horváth shows us the process of exploitation from beneath in the wilful ignorance and sado-masochism of the victimised that perpetuates their subjection, rather than giving the ideological over-view of a model-situation. In contrast to the objective, intellectualising response that Brecht demands and his behaviouristic characterisation, Horváth deals with his characters in terms of their mental world and aims at his audience's subjective awareness, their complicity through shared attitudes and idealistic self-deceptions, their recognition of the reflection of their own dehumanising turns of phrase. It is theatre which 'appeals to the instinct', and the focus is on scenes which show 'the struggle of consciousness against the subconscious'.[29]

These are the qualities which gave Horváth's work its value for playwrights like Franz Xaver Kroetz and Martin Sperr, who have made the folk play one of the two dominant trends in German drama of the last decade. There are also similarities between their work and Büchner's *Woyzeck* with its loose sequence of short scenes and focus on a character who, unable to express himself, can only react instinctively with a violence that exposes the oppressive nature of society. Particularly in Kroetz, as in Büchner, normal expectations are reversed and what is recognisable as human emotion is expressed in crime, while the ordinary preoccupation about personal reputation or moral standards is revealed as callous insensitivity. Another influence is Edward Bond's *Saved* (German première 1967). It was Sperr who did the translation for Peter Stein's production, and with the alteration of a few naturalistic details – tea to beer, blacks to *Gastarbeiter*, the London slum slang to Bavarian dialect, plus specifying the characters' jobs 'to avoid any impression that these figures, even the "child murderers" were not average citizens'[30] – *Saved* acted as a standard for the new German folk play. Bond's use of anti-social characters to epitomise society recurs in Sperr and Kroetz, as does his theme of institutional violence issuing in gratuitous brutality and his compassionate treatment of those a conventional audience would expect to see condemned. Stein's staging established a precedent too with an ambivalent naturalism which combined open artifice – scene changes carried out by the actors to the beat of music from a juke box at the rear of the set – with extreme realism: 'a sureness and naturalness of attitude in the individual actor...to create an equivocal impression in the spectator which would not always allow him to distinguish between the personality of the actor and his artistry'.[31] A further influence was Marieluise Fleisser, while Werner Fassbinder, though not himself a significant playwright, has acted as a catalyst and populariser. Fassbinder's two best known plays, *Blood on the Cat's Neck* (*Blut am Hals der Katze*, 1972) and *Bremen Coffee* (*Bremer Freiheit*, 1971), pick up on the themes of Kroetz and Sperr, the repressed violence of the underprivileged, the amputation of personality through a deprived language, peoples' rights versus neo-fascist prejudice; but present them 'acceptably' as comic or melodramatic fantasies. His major reputation however is as a film director, and he has produced television and screen versions of Sperr's *Hunting Scenes from Lower Bavaria* (*Jagdszenen aus Niederbayern*, 1966) and Kroetz's *Wild Game* (*Wildwechsel*, 1969), familiarising a wide public with the chilling quality in the modern folk play's laconic treatment of corruption beneath everyday moral attitudes. He also directed Fleisser's updated version of *Pioneers in Ingolstadt* (*Pioniere in Ingolstadt*, 1929: rewritten 1968) after she had protested against him adapting the original play, staged two years before. It was this production that brought Kroetz, who played the role of the Lieutenant, into contact with her work, and Kroetz underlined that he was following Fleisser and Horváth after the public outcry which followed the first production of his plays *Homework* and *Stiff-Necked* (*Heimarbeit/Hartnäckig*, 1971). The qualities in their work that he singled out were the objective presentation which neither denounced nor glorified the characters and the political analysis of society through language: 'Horváth's recognition of...the proletariat of the speechless, that most extreme form of capitalism' and the way 'Fleisser's characters always cheat themselves when they speak, exposing the society in which they live, not ridiculing the characters themselves'. But compared to these models the modern folk play is stripped down, minimal drama. While claiming that his characters 'function on exactly the same lines as Horváth's', Kroetz points out that their 'situation has been changed by social mutation'. After the linguistic influence of fascist propaganda, the uniformity imposed by the production line and the 'total manipulation' of the media, dialect in Horváth's sense is no longer viable and actual silence replaces empty phrases to express 'speechlessness'.[32]

Equally important for younger German dramatists, Horváth provides a working alternative to Brecht. In the light of his 'analytic realism' Brecht's approach and derivatives like Weiss' work appear self-deceptive fictions:

Since Brecht's figures are so fluent [having 'a fund of language...which is not *ipso facto* conceded to them by their rulers'] the way to a positive utopia, to revolution is open. If the workers in Siemens had the verbal ability of Brecht's workers, we would have a revolutionary situation.[33]

But as with the stripping of Horváth's dialect, so too the complex undercutting of sentimentalities in Horváth's ironic counterpoint is limited to a contrast between cardboard settings – the idyllic: 'a path through the open country', 'hillside with cranberry bushes'; the bucolic: 'in the hay', 'in the open air. Beer garden. Beautiful day'; the arcadian: a child 'playing in the sand-box', a man 'decorating the Christmas tree in one corner of the room'[34] – and the crude violence of the action: a girl under the age of consent has her boyfriend murder her father so that she can gratify her sexual urge without interference (*Wild Game*), a homosexual is driven by persecution to kill the girl who is carrying his child (*Hunting Scenes from Lower Bavaria*), a cripple drowns his wife's baby by another man, born deformed after an unsuccessful attempt at abortion (*Homework*).

What makes these sexual and sadistic scenes more than vicarious titillation is the straightforward plainness with which they are presented. Immediacy, literalness, and actuality (on a very basic level) become the criteria. Coitus or masturbation are simple bodily functions for the characters, as natural as defecating or a body-wash; murder is committed or abortion attempted without conscience, emotion, or even any awareness that it might be considered exceptional. All of those acts are performed openly on stage in both Kroetz's *Homework* and his double play, *Dairy Farm* and *Ghost Train* (*Stallerhof/Geisterbahn*, 1972). In *Dairy Farm* a 58-year-old labourer, Sepp, seduces Beppi, the under-age, mentally retarded farmer's daughter. The audience's prejudice against 'dirty old men' is deliberately played on by the circumstances. Sepp is 'rather drunk', his deprivation and frustration has already been established in a striking visual image ('Scene 3: Sepp sits on the privy. While shitting he masturbates', p. 138) and Beppi's total helplessness is emphasised by incontinence:

SEPP: *Cleans her up.* Take your underpants off, you can't go anywhere like that. *Beppi does it.* Clean yourself up with them – let me. *He cleans her up, takes his handkerchief and wipes her with it.* Now we can go on. *Takes her, deflowers her* (p. 142).

But beneath this unsavoury surface is real feeling. The old man is the only character to treat Beppi with tenderness, and the sexual act, though painful and unwanted, is her nearest approach to happiness. The farmer, concerned only with social appearances, poisons Sepp's dog in surrogate revenge and first plans to kill Beppi then to abort her. But face to face with her daughter, the mother feels a pang of female fellowship and the final scene ends

17   Kroetz, *Dairy Farm*, 1972. Idylls discredited by the anti-illusionistic stage,
rhythms of work.

as the birth-pains begin. The complex irony of this 'happy end' is heightened by the normality of the way outrages are discussed and by Kroetz's technique of giving us bare glimpses into the characters' thoughts, which we then have to fill out from our own preconceptions:

On the way to church in bad weather...
WIFE: They say the crazy don't feel death like us.
FARMER: True, a fly doesn't notice a thing either.
Pause.
WIFE: Fifthly thou shalt not kill.
FARMER: Sixthly thou shalt not commit fornication.
Pause.
Long pause.
WIFE: That I couldn't ever forget my life long. That I know...
          (p. 153)

Evening in the parlour...
WIFE: Wash ourselves, that's what we've got to do to get the dirt
          away. Take off your underpants. *Beppi does it.* Because you've
          made so much muck that the dirt must come out the same way
          it went in. – That'll sting a bit, but never mind, it's the soap
          washing it all away. Take your dress off, feet apart. *Beppi has
          taken off all her clothes. Stands there naked.* You're freezing,
          stupid. *Pause, Wife takes the wash cloth...begins to scrub the
          floor...*(p. 155)

In the sequel Beppi joins Sepp in the town with her child after her parents decide to put it in an orphanage. Here violence against the individual is extended into the social sphere. Society at large and in the abstract (a form letter, health officials or policemen who remain offstage anonymous presences) replaces the farmer-father, and wherever there is personal contact – even the minimal relationship between this old and broken-down labourer and the brain-damaged girl who can barely express herself better than her baby – then there is tenderness and the possibility of improvement. Even the parents, threatening embodiments of social values in the first play, are shown as bewildered, wanting the best for their child. But Sepp dies of cancer and Beppi, receiving an impersonal 'Dear sir/madam' letter from the social services committing her baby to an orphanage since she is still a minor, suffocates it to stop it crying, fearing that officials will hear and take it away from her. Even more obviously in this play, personal deprivation or fulfilment is seen in terms of language. Living with Sepp, Beppi finally learns to speak. Not indeed as Beatie in Wesker's *Roots*, who breaks through to full consciousness and 'stands alone, articulate at last', but only in finally learning a meaningless nursery tongue-twister; and the one example of educated full expression in the play is the incomprehensible, dehumanising and alien bureaucratese of the letter from the Child Welfare organisation. Thus it is the use of language that represents social pressures, and these drive Beppi back into an instinctive existence where she has no awareness of what killing her helpless child means, either in moral or human terms. Her first sexual experience having been at a fairground, she takes the body to an amusement-park and throws it off the Ghost Train. She loses her precarious grasp on language, and the next and final scene shows her in prison being visited by her parents, to whom she can find nothing to say.

This type of subject is all too close to melodrama and indeed slips over into it in Sperr's *Hunting Scenes*, where rape, the murder of a pregnant girl and suicide are accompanied by insight into the mental distress of the characters through their ability to express their emotions. *Men's Business* (*Männersache*, 1971) verges on prurience for a different reason. Here Kroetz's objectivity in simply setting out an event as a bare 'fact of life', which depends so much on his characters' speechlessness, provides insufficient explanation to make the actions credible. A woman and her lover take turns to shoot at each other in a grotesque duel-to-the-death to assert their self-respect after the man has accused her of preferring her dog for sexual gratification – and the nature of the violence, the implied perversion are too alien to our experience, too near to pornographic fantasy to be taken on any but a symbolic level. In the 1972 Darmstadt production of the play the final scene presented such difficulties that a prologue was introduced in which an equivalent duel was played out by gigantic puppets in dumb-show, a pop-media image taken from picture-paper headlines. Indeed it is hard to see any way of avoiding melodrama without transforming the play into farce, and this at least made a point about role-determining by the popular press and B-grade movie industry. As a result Kroetz's revised version bears the note, 'Performance of the play is prohibited. The following text has been designed for reading' (p. 85).

As in Horváth, exactly the right emphasis must be kept in production. Conventional treatment too can reduce these plays to melodrama, as in Fassbinder's films. In his version of *Wild Game*, where the girl is attractive enough to be an object of desire for the spectator and the form reproduces the Hollywood style of the early 1950s, or in *Hunting Scenes*, where the focus is on the cruelty of the characters as aggressors rather than their deprivation as victims, the effect is hardly distinguishable from popular entertainment. Sperr has outlined his intentions as 'shock theatre' in a way that emphasises his traditional intentions, comparing his use of crudity to Aristophanes:

If one really got an actor to shit on the stage, completely naturally, it would cause a greater shock than any kneading of bosoms or feeling under the skirt...I expect theatre to have the honesty to actually shit and not to show how amusingly and delicately shitting can be avoided.[35]

The problem is that this can very easily become tasteless for the sake of tastelessness, as in certain other contemporary dialect playwrights, for example Wolfgang Bauer or Peter Turrini, whose *Magic Afternoon* (1968) or *Rat Hunt* (*rozznjogd*, 1971) use Austrian vernacular for colour, not to represent thought processes, presenting sex and sadism as lurid excitements without any deeper significance. *Epâter le bourgeois* comes close to sensationalism that simply panders to the public's baser instincts, particularly when the use of such a 'popular' form as the folk play leads a dramatist like Sperr to declare that 'theatre must...be culinary'.[36] It can also be very dull.

What makes the similar acts in Kroetz's best plays significant forms of social criticism – and therefore by definition unmelodramatic since melodrama is concerned only with voyeuristic thrills, never with new insights – is our sense of dramatic purpose. Sepp masturbating expresses not only the frustration that as a character he cannot put into words, but the degradation of the society that has deprived him of any other fulfilment. No less important to the effect of realism is the way Kroetz presents such actions with a total absence of sentimentality, his use of silences, and the demonstration that these characters are driven to what they do by their inability to resolve tensions through language. They are at the animal edge of the social spectrum, and the cliché 'practice is better than study' is a refrain that recurs in almost all Kroetz's plays, as does the statement 'it's finished. That wasn't proper love. That was only physical.' Social conditioning in the form of incongruous moral sanctions or sentimental ideals (romantic love, for instance, as in the fairy-tale which Sepp tells Beppi at the opening of *Dairy Farm* about a white officer, who won the respect of an Indian tribe by marrying an outcast and so succeeded in bringing peace between settlers and redskins) is what destroys the characters, and this is Kroetz's point of attack. It is the morals or ideals which define certain behaviour-patterns as uncivilised, inhuman, bestial that are challenged by showing the audience's concept of what is 'unnatural' to be only too natural in extreme situations, situations which are more average than most theatre-goers realise – and if we feel revulsion at the play this implicates us in the exploitation of such people. The effectiveness can be indicated by the public response. A teacher in an Austrian school was dismissed for organising a class reading of *Dairy Farm*, while the première of *Homework* provoked the audience to throw rotten eggs during the performance, a bomb alarm in the interval and a mass-protest on the street outside the theatre.

This production of *Homework* and the discussion after the first performance underlined some of the intrinsic qualities in Kroetz's development of the folk play. The surface realism is in fact achieved by a high degree of artifice, and not only because any stage performance automatically contains an aesthetic element (a point made by Kipphardt, who was then acting as dramaturge at the Munich Kammerspiele) or, as Kroetz commented, because of the practical limitations of theatre – 'how can one demand that an actor should get a hard-on every evening at precisely ten-to-nine?'[37] The action is given an overall aesthetic structure, beginning and ending with the same visual image of Martha washing herself in her underclothes. The speech is not a repro-duction of the Bavarian dialect, but simplified and stylised (a point explicitly made in Kroetz's stage direction to another play: 'modelled on south German, so relatively free...actors must observe and reproduce the language as an artificial one', p. 384), while the naturalistic actions which fill the pauses are equally rhythmic and patterned, as the director's notes show: 'staples 5 packets shut; drinks, cup away, puts basin underneath; staples 5 packets, 10 packets, basin out.../walks, bends, shovels 5 times, picks up watering can, moves crate, shovels 5 times...10 times...'[38] The tempo is used to express emotions which contrast with the basic clichés that form the characters' vocabulary, so that the detailed minutiae of manual labour are not there to authenticate the action, but to state the major theme of inarticulacy:

The most marked characteristic of my figures is in their silence; for their speech doesn't function. They have no good will. Their problems lie so far back and have progressed so far that they are no longer in a position to express themselves verbally.[39]

Communicating the characters' personalities through gesture gives the dialogue its general level of political implication, for example in the way the repetitive nature of their movements creates a powerful image of stasis in deliberate contrast to usual assumptions about contemporary social mobility. The concentration on minutiae also gives this kind of folk play the quality of an anthropological field-study, and the weight of what is unsaid is shown by the stage directions to *Homework*, which specify that the eighteen pages of text require a performance time of over one hour and forty minutes.

These elements are taken to their furthest extreme in *Family Favourites* (*Wunschkonzert*, 1972), an hour-long depiction of the suicide of a single woman in which not a word is spoken throughout. Here a naturalistic reproduction of the evening ritual of an ordinary person is used to show social conditioning, and the way Kroetz achieves his effects through indirectness is clearer than in the violence of his earlier plays. Excessively normal actions become pathological as the woman rinses out her washbasin 'particularly thoroughly' each time she uses it, 'smokes slowly and attentively' and 'puts out the cigarette with care', 'eats with deliberation', cleans the lavatory 'very neatly and as pedantically and hygenically as imaginable' and makes her toilet 'uncannily painstaking'.[40] In this light the repetitive washing in plays like *Dairy Farm* and *Homework* gains a political dimension: for Kroetz 'the complex about cleanliness' is a form of deliberate propaganda 'so that Vietnam can't be seen for the spot on a skirt'.[41] At the same time normal signs of satisfaction, a smile, a few dance-steps to the radio, the glance of approval at her workmanship as she finishes hooking a rug, are what reveal the frustrated emotional needs and empty boredom that lead her to take an overdose of sleeping-pills once the narcotic distractions of a popular radio programme and physical routine are finished for the night. As in other folk plays the apparently atypical action is intended to be representative, and the 'incredible orderliness' of this suicide is based on police reports, just as Kroetz also justifies the attempted abortion in *Homework* by reference to official figures of the annual 600,000 to 1,000,000 illegal abortions in West Germany. Kroetz also makes his political point explicit in the foreword. The manner of this suicide, epitomising petit bourgeois attitudes and virtues,

says much about the lives of some among us, about their unfulfilled expectations, their futile hopes, their small dreams; it can document their inability to free themselves from the slavery of production...Like animals these people project the extremity of their plight in their attitude of dumbness which contains a strong element of discipline, of patience, of 'declaring themselves in agreement without being asked', of exploitation and prohibition to the point of weakness and collapse. If the explosive force of this massive exploitation and oppression were not, unfortunately, directed against the exploited and oppressed themselves, then we would have a revolutionary situation (p. 185).

These conclusions are little more than vulgar-marxist over-simplifications. But the picture of a comfortably-off, apparently rational, middle-aged person putting an end to her life out of unsatisfied emotional tendencies which she herself cannot define carries far greater conviction than the conventional stage image of Ophelia-like distraction, or a General Harras' noble protest, and corresponds closely to Durkheim's classic sociological analysis of 'anomic suicide'.[42] Luckily the form of the play itself, the silence which objectifies the character and limits the dramatic statement to the concrete details of physical action, precludes any overt message; and in general Kroetz's dramatic sense is subtler, and the implications of his plays wider than his ideology. Where his politics are transferred directly into stage terms, as in his 'Ballad from Bavaria', *Münchner Kindl* (1973, performed at an election meeting of the west German Communist Party), the result is undigested agitprop, mixing abstract factual details with slogan emotionalism.

Horváth drew his characters from the petit bourgeoisie whose position in the social structure had been destroyed by inflation and an increasing polarisation in politics. Kroetz's concentration on inarticulacy limited him initially to the lowest level of the rural or urban proletariat. But his audience remained intellectuals in spite of his aspiration to 'go into the country and create critical peasant-theatre (*Bauerntheater*). My plays are proper folk drama, and intended for the people about whom I write, for peasants and workers'[43]. So he was forced to find ways of extending his range. The signs can already be seen in *Family Favourites*, where the woman disguises her physical unattractiveness with 'better than average' clothing and lives surrounded by consumer goods and advertising material. *Oberösterreich* (1972) and *Das Nest* (1975, a title with an untranslatable double meaning, *The Nest/The Awful Hole*) have better educated characters, people integrated in the supermarket society of a modern economy. The 'folk' of the folk play are no longer 'common' but average: one is saving up to complete his schooling, the other a well-paid truck driver. In Kroetz's earlier work the violence is only credible where the characters are completely helpless, and as soon as they move above the poverty line, like the woman of *Men's Business* who owns her own butcher's shop, then expressing the mechanics of oppression in naked brutality seems forced. In *Oberösterreich*, although abortion is discussed, the couple resign themselves to the birth of the child, and violence is only present as a possibility in an item read from a newspaper:

ANNI: ...Murder in Desperation...Furrier Franz M battered his sleeping wife to death in the marriage bed...because she was pregnant, refused to agree to an abortion although it was the only sane way...
HEINZ: Takes all kinds. That's much the same as us. We could add a thing or two (p. 415).

The whole play demonstrates their nearness to self-destruction beneath the prosperous surface of material possessions and outings to beauty-spots, evenings in the cinema or bowling. In one scene they add up the cost of a child. Everything they own is on hire-purchase, and once Anni has stopped earning they work out that they will have only '3 Marks 54 Pfennigs [under £1] for each of us per day' (p. 390) even after the car, television, all entertainment, Anni's new furniture, Heinz's accordion and plans for self-improvement have been given up. The situation here is one that the average audience can identify with, but the difference to Sepp and Beppi is only one of degree. The materialistic ideals of advertising brochures are just as empty as the idyll of simple country life, and the advertising slogans or newspaper clichés that form the basis of Heinz and Anni's conversation ('the sky is "steel blue" [this year's colour on new-model cars]', 'there are much too many people in the world')[44] is just as much a form of speechlessness as the stock maxims of Kroetz's peasants.

At the same time the ending is left open: 'The baby is an exception. It must be different from us, otherwise there's no point in it all. From the beginning on – full of hope' (p. 416). In *The Nest* this equivocal optimism becomes almost facilely positive, with the protagonist, a truck driver whose job is dumping toxic industrial waste in a lake, going through a radical change of consciousness after a practical lesson in ecology when his child receives chemical burns from bathing in the water. Kroetz called this a 'revolutionary leap' in his artistic development. But, fortunately for the dramatic quality of the play, the truck driver's recognition that he has been acting as 'a trained ape' and his final enthusiastic statement that although a single man may be powerless to change society 'the union, that's many' is accompanied by an 'insecure' smile.[45]

Another approach used by modern folk dramatists to extend their dramatic range is to take situations from traditional drama. Already in *Ghost Train* there are literary parallels for the situation of a young girl, abandoned by a much older lover, who murders her child and ends in prison (Goethe's *Faust*, Heinrich Wagner's *Die Kindermörderin*) while Sperr's *Tales from Landshut* (*Landshuter Erzählungen*, 1967) is loosely based on *Romeo and Juliet*. But Kroetz's *Agnes Bernauer* and *Maria Magdalena* (1973) remain deliberately close to Hebbel's original plays. The details of the plots are identical, even though transposed from the tragic to the economic level, and the content of many of the speeches is similar, even if Hebbel's eloquence is replaced with mean media-jargon and impoverished slang. Unlike Hochhuth's use of heroic conventions or Hacks' classical adaptations, the value of Hebbel for Kroetz is primarily ironic. The updating of a well-known mid-nineteenth-century play makes the point that social conditions are basically unchanged very concisely, and with no need of elaboration or explanation which might be rationally questioned. Thus not only the basic action of the original is kept, but also the vision of Hebbel's foreword to *Maria Magdalena* in which he proposes a theory of history as a process where the individual is destroyed by a self-motivated adherence to cramping moral principles. This is quite in line with Kroetz's views, and the elements in Hebbel's play that demonstrate this are taken over intact. However the parallels are also used to deflate traditional pretensions. The metaphysical implications in Klara's sacrifice of herself for her despicable father are rejected, and Hebbel's moral grandeur is turned into parody. Ironic subtitles are appended to each scene – 'What is Right and Proper', 'Mon Chérie' (sic), 'Swan Song' or, for the last scene, 'Final Reckoning'[46] – and Hebbel's duel becomes a farcical boasting-match, each lover listing the influential public figures who will support him socially or ruin the other financially. The most decisive change is in the ending where Marie's father sits playing cards with her two ex-lovers, and when she announces that she has taken poison the only response is:

PAPA: Stop play-acting.
MARIE: Help!...
   Save me!
   Ring one one one
   the firebrigade!
KARL: One one two is the firebrigade...
PETER: First you've got to be dead
   then we'll believe you!
   They laugh. Pause.
   Fetching a beer'd be brighter (pp. 474–5).

Instead of the individual coming to grief through the operation of inexorable and immutable laws in society, as in Hebbel's domestic tragedy, the audience's cathartic expectations are reduced to black comedy.

This treatment of a classic might almost be seen as a natural derivative of the folk play form, since Kroetz is following an established pattern in his adaptations of Hebbel. Horváth, who originated the modern folk genre, had set the precedent in using a well-known traditional comedy as the sentimental side of one of his ironic equations in *Figaro Gets a Divorce* (*Figaro lässt sich scheiden*, 1936), an example Turrini has followed directly in *The Most Fabulous Day* (*Der tollste Tag*, 1972). Like Kroetz's treatment of Hebbel, this latter adaptation gives Beaumarchais a tone typical of the updated folk play – though here with the social elevation of the characters the sexual aberrations and brutalities seem gratuitous, as in so much of Turrini's work. The count buys a divorce from a corrupt court and is strangled by Figaro, who finds him whipping Suzanne into submission after he has blackmailed Figaro into marrying Marcelline. Kroetz's choice of domestic tragedy as a model is thematically more appropriate, but the need to fall back on the classics indicates the limitations of the straight folk play approach, while the ease with which classical material and plot-lines can be incorporated demonstrates its essentially traditional nature.

9. *Dialogues*

The way Horváth's linguistic analysis dovetailed into the concerns of Group 47 made his work equally significant for one of the most original and controversial of recent German dramatists: Peter Handke. At first sight Handke's highly philosophical and abstract drama has little in common with the proletarian figures and instinctive actions of the contemporary folk play, but a popularising work like Fassbinder's *Blood on the Cat's Neck* shows the connection. Though the setting and structure are typical of such folk plays as Jochen Ziem's *News from the Provinces* (*Nachrichten aus der Provinz*, 1967) or Wolfgang Diechsel's *Leave it Be* (*bleiwe losse*, 1971), a series of close-up scenes forming a survey of social attitudes, the symbolic nature of Fassbinder's protagonist brings the focus very close to Handke's *Sprech-stücke* or 'speaking plays'. An extra-terrestrial reporter analysing democracy, Phoebe Zeitgeist finds herself unable to comprehend what people say, although she knows all the dictionary definitions. Consequently our attention is drawn to speech as a functional web of autonomous clichés. Differences in social position or distinctions between individuals are reduced to words, and what appears on the surface to be a sociological study is transformed into pure linguistic analysis.

For Handke, as for Kroetz, Horváth represents a viable alternative to Brecht, an inductive model for analysing political structures that avoids simplistic generalisation. Handke's attitude to Brecht is ambivalent. Although he acknowledges the theatrical value of the 'epic' approach as a way of exploring 'the functional possibilities of reality' to show apparently 'given and natural' situations as artificial and so alterable,[1] he rejects its rational assumptions, its political overview, as a form of facile optimism which distracts from the real issues. In particular, Brecht's use of alienation techniques to 'disillusion' an audience is seen as imposing illusion on another level since the distancing effect substitutes slogans for scrutiny and turns specific problems into wish fulfillment, making his plays as irrelevant as 'Christmas fairy tales'. Horváth, on the other hand, measures up to the complexities of modern existence which 'can no longer be clarified by sentence-length wisdom...The confused sentences of his characters' not only act as 'microcosms...of the disorder in a particular society' but also 'show the leaps and contradictions of consciousness'.[2] These two qualities that Handke singles out in Horváth's work define his own central concern, and by way of tribute the point at which the protagonist of his first full length play, *Kaspar* (1968), gains a delusive linguistic control of his environment is marked by a quotation from *Faith, Love and Hope* (*Glaube, Liebe, Hoffnung*) – 'Why are there so many black worms flying about?',[3] the dying cry of the Horváth character who holds most rigidly to verbal fictions.

Handke's starting point was a radical questioning of theatre as an art form in *Offending the Audience* (more literally *Abuse of the Audience* – *Publikumsbeschimpfung*, 1966), which is 'a prologue', a preparatory exercise to heighten the audience's 'self-awareness'.[4] The Experimenta Festival where it was first performed was hardly an appropriate setting since its effectiveness depends on the four 'speakers' facing an unsuspecting audience who have totally conventional expectations. These assumed expectations are played on by a carefully exaggerated build up – noises of scenes being set and whispered conversations between stage-managers and stagehands, elegant programmes, the refusal of admission to those inappropriately dressed, formal even ceremonious gestures by the ushers, a very gradual dimming of the lights – before the curtain opens to reveal an empty stage and the casually dressed speakers, who at first ignore the public altogether (see Illustration 18). As a prologue to the audience's future theatregoing, the play not only avoids all the familiar dramatic elements of plot, situation, character and even dialogue (in the sense of conversation between the figures on stage) but explicitly points out that these are absent. It presupposes a 'standard idea of theatre', defined by oblique references to Shakespeare and naturalistic 'keyhole' plays (p. 19), and rejects the symbolic relationship to reality that is the imaginative basis of all the various traditional forms of drama as 'impure' on the grounds of pretence:

The theatre played tribunal. The theatre played circus ring. The theatre played moral institution. The theatre played dreams. The theatre played tribal rites. The theatre played mirrors for you. The play exceeded the play. It hinted at reality. It became impure. It meant...(p. 31).

18 Handke, *Offending the Audience*, 1966. Choreographed abuse on a bare stage.

This attack on conventional theatre through the reversal of expectations leads up to the direct attack on the audience referred to in the title, a surreal sequence of abuse which modulates from insincere praise to a diatribe that vilifies every possible social position or attitude; and at the end (instead of the spectators being allowed to applaud) roaring, whistling and taped audience reactions to pop concerts are directed at them through loudspeakers. As Nicholas Hern points out in his perceptive study of Handke, this is a one-time-only, non-repeatable practical joke, while the claim to 'purity' through negation is itself delusive since the play has a conventional structure of exposition, development and emotional climax, uses traditional devices and cannot avoid a degree of role-playing ('actors acting actors and not the ordinary people they are required by the author to say they are').[5]

If 'using the theatre to protest against the current theatre' were the sole rationale for *Offending the Audience*, then it could be dismissed as provocative but facile. As a reminder that 'every expression on the stage is dramaturgy not realism' it must necessarily include itself as artifice, but on another level this negation of stage illusion, behavioural conventions and personal attitudes sets up language as the irreducible basis of reality by reducing all things to words. This gives additional significance to the label of a 'speaking play', which is underlined by the way Handke has defined his focus: 'enmeshing the spectators with words...to bring them to defend themselves with words...to free themselves by interrupting'.[6] This is not so far from the intention of a play like *Look Back in Anger*, where the major attack is against pusillanimity – the indifference which is symptomatic of an inability to feel – and Osborne noted in the acting edition that success could be measured by provoking the audience to walk out of the performance, in other words forcing them into an emotional commitment which broke accepted behaviour patterns. In a very real sense Handke's play is not on the stage but in his audience's responses. The statement 'you are the theme' is repeated five times, and the references to traditional theatre are all concerned with varieties of actor/spectator relationship. The emphasis is on what it means to be 'an audience' as an example of social roles and conditioning. Our dress is assumed to be a costume, and at the end our 'performance' is evaluated ironically in typical clichés from drama reviews. Our uniformity is stressed at the expense of

individuality, the ushers' ceremonial treatment is designed to
persuade us that the group has more significance than its component parts, and the actors relate to us as a unit, addressing 'the
public, but...no one person in particular'.[7] The whole play in fact
is based on the traditional metaphor of 'All the world's a stage'
– while rejecting the converse that the stage is all the world – and
since the audience 'are not someone here but something. You are
a society that represents an order' (p. 23), the play is literally 'the
prologue to your practices and customs...to the plays and to
the seriousness of your life' (p. 24). The structure is therefore
a manipulative sequence, moving from what the audience are
(present time – defined by our expectations) then reminding us of
how we came to take up our role (the immediate past of prepara-
tions and physical actions that brought us to the theatre), and
finally projecting the conventional follow through, applause acknowledged by the actors, which the play explicitly disallows.
Acoustical patterns are as important as meanings, moulding the
listener's response by rhythm, tempo, shifts in key, which Handke
compared to Beatles and Rolling Stones music in his 'rules for
actors' and later explained in greater detail:

a frequent bravura phrase in beat is a very particular sound sequence
which can be pictured like this: a train...slowly pulls out of the station
becoming softer and softer. And at the same moment a second train pulls
in becoming louder and louder.[8]

The sense behind the cross-fire aimed at the audience is communicated indirectly by the repetition of motifs, while any given
sentence is contradicted or varied to the point of fallacy. Apparent
statements become evasive regressions, which expose the audience
to the subliminal effect of rhythms by making it impossible to deal
with a separable content intellectually, and throw our attention
back onto our own responses. This is made explicit in the short
sequences which are used to divide the different thematic sections,
punctuating the play by forcing each spectator to concentrate on
himself, to become aware of his automatic body functions
(blinking, salivating, breathing). And the final section of abuse
is comparable to the dismantling of the central figure's personality
in Harold Pinter's *The Birthday Party*, replacing all the varieties
of social role that we, the audience, could be identified with,
however unlikely, with the positive of 'fellow humans'. Handke,
however, is hedging his bets. The polysyllabic profusion of the

insults removes their affront, and indeed, since the abuse is directed at the audience as a 'role', as individuals we can enjoy it as a demonstration of expertise.

This attempt to 'sensitise' the audience is, like Pirandello or the Living Theatre's work, too dependent on an unrehearsed public's willingness to act out a precise part. When after the first performance some spectators ignored their 'cues' and invaded the stage, the actors' inability to deal with the interruption or alter their lines to make use of it revealed the fiction behind the play, and Handke's subsequent work is less direct. The other 'speaking plays' focus on different aspects of daily language. *Self-Accusation* (*Selbstbezichtigung*, 1966) explores the concept of individuality as a verbal abstraction through a circular structure, which undercuts the proposition that personality is something stable and consistent by classifying the 'I' according to the whole conceivable range of human actions and attitudes. Change and growth are the definition of life, and the opening lines apply this to consciousness: 'I moved...I came to my senses. I made myself noticeable' (p. 43). But as a form of movement, the self-awareness that creates individuality simultaneously exposes it to possible destruction, and the final sentences return us to the starting point in a circular pattern of negation: 'I offered an easy target. I was too slow. I was too fast. I *moved*' (p. 57). In *Cries for Help* (*Hilferufe*, 1967) it is the basis of society that is defined by setting up a rudimentary form of group cooperation, again in purely verbal terms. All varieties of statement are spoken as appeals for help, and the audience are expected to suggest words they might be searching for until the speakers finally find the word 'help' – at which point 'they no longer need help...the word HELP has lost its meaning'.[9] In reducing action to words and separating syllables from sense, these plays turn drama into a type of linguistic analysis that has been compared to logical positivism, and there are indeed points of similarity with Wittgenstein's *Tractatus Logico-Philosophicus* where verbal 'propositions' are used to demonstrate that thought is determined by language and that reality has no absolute metaphysical existence, being dependent on the definition of words. But although 'the inherent reality of words' is the premise for Handke's plays, they are not dramas of ideas in this narrow sense. His aim is political: 'using linguistic disclosure, grammatical analysis to reveal to people that the way domination is perpetuated is neither divine nor statutory'.[10] This is the rationale for examining theatrical conventions as forms of rhetoric in *Offending the Audience*, and for the inversion which makes the audience the subject of inquiry, separating a social event from its accepted conceptual frame and so putting it in question.

The self-imposed limitations in the 'speaking plays' tend to oversimplify the picture of society, reducing seriously intended criticism to word-play. At the same time they can be seen as ground-clearing exercises and initial formulations of themes which reach their full expression as Handke developed a more complex dramaturgy. *Kaspar*, for instance, is still conceived as a story of words, and Kaspar's use of a single sentence to express all varieties of emotion is simply the reverse of *Cries for Help* where all sentences have a single meaning. It also elaborates elements from *Offending the Audience*, turning the speakers – who at one moment in Peymann's production crawled into the prompter's box – into 'prompters' who step into the box immediately before Kaspar enters and feed him lines from it, as well as using the clowning and choreographed movement (which Handke had protested against in Peymann's staging of the earlier play as detracting from its verbal impact) to form the climax of the action and to characterise Kaspar's initial state.

In *Kaspar* Handke has selected a well-known historical situation, which has been re-used so frequently by German authors because of its obvious archetypal implications that it has become a literary cliché. The story of Kaspar Hauser, a retarded sixteen-year-old, struck the public imagination when he appeared in Nuremberg in 1828, having apparently been kept totally isolated from all human contact since birth. He died in suspicious circumstances shortly afterwards, and the bare facts of his life, which left more than enough room for speculation, formed the basis for several melodramatic renderings of the imprisoned prince motif. Then at the turn of the century the figure of Kaspar became the epitome of childlike innocence destroyed by institutional malice and stupidity, the progressive deformation of this 'beautiful soul' by education being a measure of the evil of society (Jacob Wasserman, *Kaspar Hauser, oder die Trägheit des Herzens*, 1908). He reappeared in Georg Trakl's 'Kaspar Hauser Song' ('Kaspar Hauser Lied', 1913), or in Hans Arp's poem 'Kaspar is dead' ('Kaspar is tot', 1920) as a divine being in the shape of a clown, the holy fool, whose murder symbolises the breaking of man's natural relation to the universe. More recently in Werner Herzog's film *The Enigma of Kaspar Hauser* he becomes a solitary but ordinary man whose social alienation is expressed in obsessive behaviour. Picking up on these familiar twentieth-century treatments – social conditioning from Wasserman, the murder of a clown from Arp, alienation and obsession from Herzog – Handke can not only leave plot details for the audience to fill in, concentrating on a general image of the human situation which might appear too abstract without the substructure of associations; he can also make his point clearly as a variation on a known theme. Thus in transforming the historical Kaspar's 'I want to be a horseman like my father once was', the only thing he was able to say when found, into 'I want to be someone like somebody else was once' (p. 16) Handke has no need to give the original sentence. The difference in meaning defines the theme of personal identity, while the verbal similarity establishes the psychological drama in a social context. The literary associations of the Kaspar image are equally significant since they reinforce the focus on words.

In his foreword Handke emphasises that the play is a demonstration of what can be done with a human being, not a representation of an actual situation; a theoretical model comparable to Brecht's *Man is Man*, except that here the test is the breaking point of personality under the impact of language instead of the remoulding of an individual by social forces. The merging of Brecht's Galy Gay into a collective gives him superhuman powers; Kaspar's integration destroys him. Handke reduces concepts to words, dramatic conflict to a clash of sentences. Since perception is a question of vocabulary, and control over one's environment is therefore proportionate to the ability to make grammatical connections, self-expression goes together with self-awareness. This is the basic definition of personality, and Kaspar's character changes as his command of words develops. (A sophisticated restatement of fundamentals – the Bible, where Adam's first act was to name the animals, or Descartes' 'I think therefore I am'.) At the same time words do not simply express a person's nature, or create a context which determines how one acts – the point of Handke's novel *The Peddlar* (*Der Hausierer*, 1968) – but have an independent pre-history and so condition what we are as well as what we can do. Language, the primary way an individual defines his uniqueness and controls his situation, imposes uniformity and predetermines action. It is therefore the ultimate form of social oppression, and Handke describes his play as 'speech-torture' (*Sprechfolterung*), implying that personal development is simultaneously a form of brainwashing. Hence the term used for the 'prompters' who educate Kaspar is literally 'indoctrinators' (*Einsager*, rather than *Vorsager* or *Soufflier*). The paradox – and its negative implications – is summed up in Kaspar's initial sentence, where the anarchic and presocial personal statement actually signifies a desire for assimilation, 'to be someone like somebody else'.

The sixty-five short scenes of the play illustrate and develop sixteen 'phases' or 'propositions' which Handke outlines in his notes. In the first stage Kaspar's personal sentence is broken down by a continual commentary on its value and application from the prompters. As he becomes aware of it as a sentence it becomes fragmented to 'I be I...I want to be else...Be. Somebody...' (pp. 24–5), to single letters, to sounds. Until Kaspar is reduced to dumbness and the prompters can begin to 'stuff' his mind with standard sentence structures. Kaspar learns to classify, differentiate and to accept. Conformity brings automatic obedience, and a desire for socially acceptable order comes with the ability to speak normally. Shoelaces are correctly tied, the furniture which he disarranged in his initial exploration is tidied; 'every sentence ...which doesn't disturb, doesn't threaten, doesn't aim, doesn't question, doesn't choke, doesn't want, doesn't assert is a picture of a sentence' (pp. 35–6). Every gain in outward order is accompanied by increasing inner tension. Having disciplined Kaspar into a well-adjusted nonentity who describes all as being for the best in the best of all possible words, the prompters' sentences reveal the other side of society in images of violence, so that his affirmation becomes contingent, a progressively more difficult effort of will: 'Everything that I say to myself is in order because I say to myself that everything that I say to myself is in order' (p. 44).

This syllogistic logic is typical of the dialogue. The sentences have sense, but only rarely meaning, since they are out of context, out of synchronisation with the actions they accompany, or fail to correspond to the emotions they are used to express. Many of the statements are formed from the detritus of verbal mass-production, slogans, advertising catchwords, newsclippings – a dadaistic effect equivalent to Kurt Schwitters' 'Merz' (from the centre syllable of '*Kommerzial*') montages. But in fact they are analogies, not linguistic *objets trouvés*, and the words are subtly shifted to show the reality the grammar conceals: for instance, 'All suffering is natural', and 'Every working man must be given leisure time in accordance with his need to replenish the energy expended while working' (p. 37), or 'Everything that appears to harm you is only in your best interest' (p. 39). The concentration on verbal forms and grammatical structures exposes the questionable nature of daily assumptions, but as in the earlier 'speaking plays' there can be no dialogue. Sentences can be varied, repeated, parodied; but not answered since their function disappears behind grammatical forms and the typical structure is circular so that statements cancel themselves out. Again, as in the 'speaking plays', patterns of sound replace intellectual content, and in Peymann's production these became increasingly complex, ranging from single voices, or the simple dialogue pattern of Kaspar's solo versus the prompters in unison, to syncopated rhythms, the counterpoint of loudspeaker against natural voice, or descants playing off one prompter's words against the beat of the group, and ending with an orchestrated motet of voices set against the harshly contrasting, anarchic, knife-edge noise of saws, files, scraping.

The prompters represent the unremitting use of language to direct individuals in modern urban society, the mechanical systems of mass-communication. They are the voice of technology, and Handke's notes compare their tone to public announcers, police spokesmen with megaphones, automatic answering services. The conditional clauses and the abstraction of sentences designed to cover every conceivable eventuality, which make reality appear hypothetical, also have an authoritarian reference, being modelled on the impersonality of legal language. Handke's earliest literary exercise was based on quotations from the penal code, and similarly here the effect is intended to be 'totally threatening and oppressive'.[11] On this level the final picture of monstrous, senseless autonomism stands for Kaspar's total integration, so that the multiplication of identical Kaspars, their struggle for a microphone (entangling themselves with its cord in a confusion of anonymous limbs as an ironic *Laocoon* in contemporary terms) and the grotesque mechanical noises they produce make a powerful statement about the alienating pressures of modern economic and political exploitation.

On another level this is an interior, psychological drama. The table, chair and cupboard are the furniture of Kaspar's mind, the prompters are the stream of sense data that impinges on the consciousness, and the verbal forms represent mental states. 'He becomes...a perfect man, a proper "human being" who finally even speaks in verse and, when the most extreme possible stage-order is achieved, in beautifully ringing rhymes. The world is factually rhymed for him.'[12] The second act then becomes a projection of complete schizophrenia following Kaspar's sudden awareness of what he has been saying. The linguistic order is compulsive, and the audience is confronted with the disastrous psychological effect of the imbalance in a civilisation which has traditionally separated intellect from emotion, and now increasingly ignores man's instinctive side as technology advances. Kaspar's education is thus a process of developing rationalism, which becomes more repressive and rigid until the emotional strain is intolerable, the primitive, regressive side of the mind reasserts itself, and his mirror images appear with their 'ululations, roaring, laughter, humming, purring, warbling, and a single sharp scream' (p. 86).

At the same time this behavioural model is more than a representation of psychological or political pressures. The stage represents the stage. Kaspar is not a specific individual but the traditional *Kasperl* of the puppet show (see Illustration 19), and the opening where he breaks through the backdrop in a parody of birth, his elaborately laboured attempt at walking and struggle with the furniture are pure slapstick. His costume with its harlequin patches and the half-mask that expresses exaggerated astonishment in the first act, incongruous contentment in the second, comes from the *Commedia dell' Arte*. He is a theatre figure, and spotlights direct his actions. The shovel is clearly labelled 'stage', the tables and chairs have to be instantly recognisable as props, and when he pushes them into conventional positions he creates the imaginary three walls of naturalistic drama. This follows Handke's basic principle that since any element of performance automatically ritualises reality, the only way drama can make a true statement or reveal reality is to represent actions as rituals. On the stage the only object which does not automatically symbolise something other than itself is a theatre object, and the only action which is not pretence is the open artifice of playing. As a result political commitment can never be directly expressed. As Handke put it in his essay on 'Street theatre and Theatre-theatre':

I personally would support Marxism every time as the only possible solution for the prevailing...contradictions: but not its proclamation in a theatrical performance...the theatre is so pre-emptive in its scope for signification that everything, which outside of the theatre is full of seriousness, concern, unequivocalness, finality, becomes *play*.[13]

The argument may be questionable since in practice Handke has simply substituted a new set of conventions for old, but the result is a gain in theatrically effective images which avoid the dogmatic oversimplifications of Brechtian or documentary drama.

This theatricality also has a positive function comparable to Brecht's 'alienation effect', forcing us to see things with fresh eyes so that we question what we normally take for granted. On the simplest physical level the act of sitting down is lifted out of context by being divided into separate phases, or Kaspar (and the audience) is made aware of what movement means by figures shuffling at an almost imperceptible snail's pace across the stage. The same technique is applied to concepts by splitting Kaspar's speech, movement, and the sense impressions to which he reacts into independent components. Handke's intention is to transform theatre into

a playing space that opens up the spectator's as yet undiscovered internal playing spaces, a means to make the consciousness of the individual not broader but more precise, a means of sensitising, stimulating, provoking reaction, a means of touching the world;[14]

and the 'tri-sectioning' of the action also imposes Kaspar's schizophrenia on the audience, while the orchestrated noise in the final section is designed to produce the utmost discomfort, reducing our complacency as spectators to something approaching Kaspar's mental anguish. The rasping of files across cardboard is 'of the kind that drives one wild', the sound effects of chalk on slates, hobnails on a marble floor, fingernails scraping across glass are 'excruciating' (pp. 94f.). Pity, the vicarious feeling of empathy, is replaced by an assault on the senses which in reproducing the character's emotional state in the audience forces them to reject his – and thus their own – situation; and the relevance of the model to the individual spectator is underlined by an intermission text. The 'prompters', in the form of taped excerpts from politicians and public speakers, which are mangled into meaninglessness and interspersed with industrial noise, invade the auditorium, theatre lobbies and even the street. The aim throughout

19   Handke, *Kaspar*, 1968. Opening sequence: the anarchic clown.

is not just to present an abstract analysis of the human situation for rational consideration, but to subject the audience to the same pressures, breaking down our set behaviour patterns in a similar way to the intellectual assault in *Offending the Audience*. Handke describes *Kaspar* as 'a purely anarchistic play: it imparts no social utopia, it only negates everything it comes across'[15] – and it is precisely here that it paradoxically performs a positive function.

The approach of *Kaspar* may be rather too literal, but it is one of the major stylistic advances in contemporary theatre. Its theatrical as opposed to linguistic and philosophical value can be indicated by Peter Brook's Paris production, where the forms and structures of sound were even more strongly stressed without sacrificing Handke's intended effect, and the original 'austere and verbal play became a musical with very little dialogue'.[16] In this play Handke has worked his way back from anti-theatre to a traditional basis on his own terms. The original version ended with a bleak recognition – 'I am only I by chance' – but Handke changed this, making it not only emotional but literary. The repeated cry of 'goats and monkeys' is meaningless by itself, but as a direct quotation of Othello's revulsion at sexual incontinence (*Othello*, IV, i, 274) it becomes a graphic expression for Kaspar to curse his own birth, and the Shakespearean reference was extended in his next play, *My Foot, my Tutor* (*Der Mündel will Vormund sein*, 1969) where the situation plays on the Prospero/Caliban relationship.

Even in his 'speaking plays' Handke's attitude to language is ambivalent. Our self-image, concepts of reality and ability to communicate depend on words which are at the same time barriers to understanding, instruments of oppression. One theme of his Büchner-Prize speech was the inadequacy of language as a response to politics – 'what is political thinking?....Speechless single words ..."Crooks! Bandits! Murderers!"....Anything more would be part of the fiction of communicating' – and he summed up the basis of *Kaspar* as a demonstration of 'the impossibility of *expressing* something with speech: that is, saying something which reaches beyond the actual sentence into the significant and meaningful'.[17] Logically this must apply equally to his own work, and in one essay under the title of 'Literature is Romantic' he argued that literature as such was incompatible with political commitment since it transferred attention from the possibility of action to style. *My Foot, my Tutor* is an attempt to get round the problem. Words are avoided altogether and the whole action is an extended mime.

As in *Kaspar* the situation is one of dominance/repression worked through by clown figures in grotesque half-masks. The guardian, who carries chalk in one hand and swings a censer in the other in one scene and represents all the archetypes of authority, reapeatedly stares the ward into submission; while the ward's attempts to assert himself, or to win approval by copying the guardian's actions only end in his own humiliation. When the guardian reads a newspaper, for instance, the ward picks up a miniature book, becomes bored and scribbles on his arms in imitation of the guardian's tattoos, at which the guardian crumples his newspaper into a ball and bends forward in his chair. The ward's exaggerated mimicry reduces him, like the newspaper, to a ball on the floor, curled with his knees crossed over his head. In another sequence the ward follows his guardian around the room, but bumps into him whenever he halts, and when the guardian exits, slamming the door in his face, the ward has no choice except to crawl through a cat-flap set in the door.

Much of the description is phrased in sentences opening with 'we see...', and the emphasis in the text is on what is to be perceived rather than on what is to be presented: 'The ward eats the apple just as if no one watches. (If people watch, the apple is to be eaten very affectedly)...He cuts his nails so slowly, so long, until it no longer seems comic.'[18] On one level the action is slapstick with the big guy/little guy pair based on Laurel and Hardy (the guardian has a grotesquely fat false stomach), and some of the visual gags are taken from Buster Keaton films. But if we laugh, it demonstrates our own callous acquiescence in the system of domination. In one striking image blood runs down the ward's face from his nose while the guardian ignores his suffering, and the overtly comic situations are intrinsically cruel and vicious, as in the play's climax. Here the guardian demonstrates the use of a turnip-topping machine, an instrument like a guillotine which is used by a mentally retarded boy in one of Handke's earlier short stories, *Eye-Witness Account* (1965), to chop off his guardian's head. Here however the ward is conspicuously unsuccessful, the light dims on his flailing failure to decapitate even a turnip, and the final scene shows him laboriously carrying out meaningless actions. There are definite political overtones in the various scenes, but Hern's interpretation of *My Foot, My Tutor* as a specific

parable advocating worker and student participation in management (*Mitbestimmung*)[19] seems too narrow. Again the intention is
to provide a general model which can be applied by any spectator
to his own experience.

The use of silent-film comedy, the B-grade movie cliché of
menace in the deep breathing in darkness which divides each scene,
and the presentation of reality as an image in the *trompe l'oeil* vista
of the turnip field, recur in Handke's next major play, *The Ride
Across Lake Constance* (*Der Ritt über den Bodensee*, 1970). Here
the characters are actors and the setting is a theatre set. In
performance 'the actors are and play themselves at one and the
same time';[20] in the reading text they are named after well-known
silent-film actors, Emil Jannings, Elizabeth Bergner, Erich von
Stroheim. They are heavily made-up, bizarrely dressed to demonstrate that their clothes are costumes, and the maid is in black-face.
The setting has the symmetry and elaborate staircase of a 1930s
Hollywood extravaganza, now shabby and faded, and is given a
quality of stasis and artificial preservation by the dust-sheets
which cover everything. As in *Kaspar* this is the furniture of the
mind, but here it is built up of *objets trouvés* from the popular
imagination, and the opening words, 'as I said', underline this.
There are political implications behind these media images, corresponding to an earlier comment by Handke that 'world views are
actually nothing but cinema stereotypes...and conversely cinema
stereotypes condition world views'[21] – and in the original concept
the characters were to be the same social roles of bishop, general,
society lady as in *Quodlibet* (1970): 'figures from the world-
theatre'. The finished text extends this political attack on the
structures of authority as artificial and unnatural (literally
'staged') performances, to reveal the world as a subjective stage
on which only role-playing can give a shape to inner emptiness,
and the effect of the theatricality is hallucinatory. Normal actions
become surreal, lifted out of context as part of an overt performance. The characters move in trances, talk in their sleep and
continually refer to their experience as a dream. Like Strindberg's
Dream Play, the structure is that of the mind, not the logic of
events. Double characters appear, a monstrous doll parodies the
human actors, cause and effect are arbitrary, as when suitcases
thrown off-stage make no sound while gloves crash like suitcases.
Emotional reactions are reduced to slapstick routines corresponding to the earlier clown plays, as when Jannings kicks George but
it is Porten who has her feet knocked from under her, while

In fact, VON STROHEIM *had already lifted his knee to administer a kick. Pause. Startled, they all look at each other. Pause.*
BERGNER: It's nice to watch when something is beginning to function smoothly...(p. 28).

When the same illogic appears in the dialogue, the result is equivalent to a verbal Rorschach test:

> Let us pray to God.
> PORTEN: *Instantly.* My chocholate.
> BERGNER: *In her sleep.* There's a rat in the kitchen (p. 68).

Free association forms the structure of the play, and is intended to duplicate the characters' feelings of insecurity in the audience. The title, a proverbial expression, is itself an image from the collective consciousness. It refers to the legend of a horseman who, lost in a blizzard, rides across the frozen lake without realising his danger and dies of shock when congratulated on the narrowness of his escape. The irony, the stress on reality as a mental projection make this proverb particularly appropriate to Handke's vision, and he had already used it in a novel, *The Hornets* (*Die Hornissen*, 1966), where the memory of ice breaking under a man's feet submerges him in a stream of consciousness. Like this protagonist, the characters (and audience) of *The Ride Across Lake Constance* clutch at apparently objective details which lead only to ambiguities. They walk on the thin ice of rationality, and their assumptions about ordered existence are constantly breaking under the emotional weight of their insecurities to precipitate them into the surreal depths of the subconscious. Concepts, on a basic level words, are shown to determine our perception. What we think we see therefore fails to correspond to the actual world, and this gap makes the individual incapable of functioning. The sequence in which characters descend the staircase while others count the steps for them is a rather over-obvious illustration. The counters miss a number, leave out the last or add an extra one, and each time the person walking down stumbles or falls. Actions are defined by words, personalities by social roles – and all relationships, extending the themes of *Kaspar* and *My Foot, My Tutor*, are reduced to games of mental domination: 'People began to socialise with one another and it became the rule' (p. 47). The two preceding plays are models of linguistic and psychological exploitation. This is a picture of an alienated society. The theatricality, the stress on the characters as actors which establishes a distance between the figure and his role, symbolises this alienation; and this use of theatre as an image for social conventions, and for the individual attitudes and state of mind conditioned by these conventions, is the key-stone of Handke's dramaturgy as well as a metaphor which recurs in his recent essays:

I felt the existence of others in myself, but rather as actors' masks than people...within the compact globe of the skull I experienced the general misery in almost banal strangeness...

In operating with these predetermined materials, words, responses, at that moment when we appear to be defining ourselves we are actually only actors speaking strange lines.[22]

The Ride Across Lake Constance is, as Handke points out in his note to the play, a logical progression from *Kaspar*; but the development from analysing the causes of alienation to alienated drama has brought certain basic problems. As the psychological picture becomes more abnormal, it loses its visible relevance to everyday life and comes to seem a study of madness rather than being a state we recognise in ourselves. The irrationality also produces obscurity, which is effective in so far as it is disquieting, but forces Handke into simplistic demonstrations of his points to put them across. The result, particularly with the symbolic weight given to clichés, borders on pretentiousness; and this is a major failing in his most recent play, *They Are Dying Out*.

Here the themes of *Kaspar* and *The Ride Across Lake Constance* are illustrated in a figure epitomising capitalism, an industrialist whose success in driving his competitors out of business destroys the conditions in which he can exist. The economic reference, however, turns out to be no more than a metaphor, since Capital here represents the ego, the product which corners the market is the self (the pre-packaged, nineteenth-century idea of 'a personality'), and 'even the Freudian slip has...become a management method'.[23] With the industrialist's developing monomania the material world grows increasingly unreal to him and his personality breaks down. As propositions both the economic and psychological points are at least arguable, but merging them is only confusing, and explaining either in terms of the other, as Handke does, leads to gross oversimplification. In addition, the premises on which the play's action is based, that individuality is an illusion and that character is nothing more than an externally imposed mask or functionally determined disposable role, conflict with the deeper thematic level on which a particular politico-economic system is

condemned by depicting its destructive effect in terms of the inner
state of an individual. What the stage presents is reality as seen
through the eyes of the industrialist, and therefore empty because
his profession has supposedly destroyed his humanity. But the
mind whose vision we share is also necessarily empty since
individuals are assumed not to exist, so what we are left with
are symbols which appear autonomous since the levels of reality
they relate to are self-cancelling. The penthouse furnishings of the
first act become transformed into objects that gain symbolic
resonance only because they have no visible relevance. A balloon
is substituted for a punchbag, a large, slowly melting block of ice
for matching sofa and chairs; and when the industrialist strangles
a minority shareholder in a loving embrace, or beats his own brains
out against a boulder on which suggestively meaningless fragments of aphorisms continually appear – 'Our greatest sin...the
impatience of concepts...the worst is over...the last hope' (p.
36) – we cannot take these actions literally, yet on a symbolic level
they lack coherence. It is even unclear whether the second half of
the play is intended to be an extension of the first, showing what
happens as a consequence of the decisions taken there, or a
repetition of it, revealing the true psychological state beneath
apparently rational behaviour. In Handke's earlier work the
ambiguities are productive because the level of stage reality is
firmly established. Here the potential dangers of his approach are
only too clearly revealed. Incomprehensibility masquerades as
profundity.

Handke's style is so radical that it appears uniquely personal, but
the surrealist evocation of subconscious states, the analysis of
social exploitation in psychological and linguistic terms is representative of a whole trend in contemporary theatre. More directly,
the rejection of representational conventions in his 'speaking
plays' is the theatrical equivalent of 'minimal art' and has found
imitators both in Germany and outside. *Appeasing the Audience*
(*Publikumsbesänftigung*, Moritz Boerner, 1968) used the same
rhetorical principles, Martin Walser questioned dramatic conventions in a parody play (*We'll Act alright/Wir werden schon noch
handeln*, 1968), and a recent British play, *Loaded Questions* by
Neil Hornick (1977), shows the continuing vitality of this approach. Significantly Hornick – whose dialogue, constructed
solely of questions which range from cliché politenesses to quasi-

philosophical puzzles, ending with 'where has the evening gone to?' and 'shall we call it a day?', is accompanied by projected Rorschach blots – associates himself with the pataphysical ideas of Jarry, the forerunner of absurd theatre. Handke's development in fact shows the definite influence of the absurdists, in particular Samuel Beckett. *My Foot, My Tutor* contains references to Beckett's *Act Without Words* (first performed in Germany at the same Experimenta Festival as Handke's *Offending the Audience*), and Handke's *Radio Play 2* (*Hörspiel 2*, 1968) quotes from Beckett's *Eh Joe*, while *Kaspar* has been compared with Ionesco's *Jacques* and *The Lesson*, and *The Ride Across Lake Constance* with Pinter.[24]

Peymann, who established Handke's work on the German stage, has also been responsible for popularising the Austrian answer to the absurd, Thomas Bernhard, and his productions of *A Feast for Boris* (*Ein Fest für Boris*, 1970) and *The Ignoramus and the Madman* (*Der Ignorant und der Wahnsinnige*, 1972) clearly indicated the parallels between Bernhard's vision and Handke's later work. Where Handke's major theme is the death of the soul through social conditioning, Bernhard is obsessed by the total negation of physical death. The existential pessimism expressed by the legless cripples and wheelchair tyrant of *A Feast for Boris* is closer to Beckett than anything in Handke – indeed on some levels the play is merely a restatement of *Endgame* – but the structure of the dialogue shows a similar linguistic focus. As in Handke, speeches are based on the variation and repetition of clichés, words are carried forward from one sentence to the next to create an equivalent effect of ambiguity. The analysis of society through language is extended in *The Ignoramus and the Madman*, which also comes into Handke's category of a 'speaking play'. The figures, an opera singer and a surgeon, are not characters in any conventional sense, but examples of thought processes pre-determined by speech patterns. The conflict is between the precision of coloratura phrases and the cold rationality of anatomical dissection, fine art or pure feeling versus science or impersonal rationality, both being equally inhuman and mechanical. As an image of the self-destructive, schizophrenic separation of soul and body, emotion and intellect in western man, this is a variation on the underlying theme of *Kaspar*, while *Force of Habit* (*Macht der Gewohnheit*, 1974) uses comparable clown figures.

There is no question of direct influence, although Bernhard

shares Handke's concerns and the parallels are sometimes striking
– as in *The Hunting Party* (*Die Jagdgesellschaft*, 1974) which is so
close in theme to *They Are Dying Out* (also first staged in the same
year) that, as critics were quick to note, 'the figures...could
switch from one play to the other with hardly a jar'.[25] Like
Handke, Bernhard's aim is to arouse self-awareness, his plays use
stage conventions in an overtly artificial, non-illusory way, and his
approach to art is iconoclastic. As he remarked in one of his novels,
'I am...no storyteller, fundamentally I hate stories. I am a
destroyer of stories.'[26] Like Handke too he uses farce to express
the mechanical nature of socially conditioned behaviour so that,
as the juggler puts it in *Force of Habit*, 'It's a comedy/...A
comedy/is a vicious humiliation';[27] and the subtitle to one of his
early plays outlines the grotesque basis of his work: 'The
Mountain. A play for puppets as people or people as puppets' (*Der
Berg*, 1960).

Apart from Bernhard's nihilism which is summed up in the final
lines of *Force of Habit*, 'Life consists in eradicating questions', and
has led to attacks on his work as politically reactionary, the
qualities that define his approach are really extensions of elements
in Handke's plays. Where Handke, for instance, requires his
actors to study *A Hard Day's Night* and other Beatles' films, the
Rolling Stones and the hit parade, or uses a song like 'Colours
for Susan' by Country Joe and the Fish to accentuate points in
My Foot, My Tutor, and models verbal patterns on structures
from beat music, Bernhard specifically classifies his plays as
'musical theatre'. Trained as a concert musician before turning
to literature, he inserts passages from popular orchestral classics
as quotations to indicate the weight of cultural traditions on the
individual or as thematic motifs. Thus the imaginative centre of
Force of Habit is Schubert's *Trout Quintet*, which the unfortunate
circus performers have been rehearsing unsuccessfully for the past
twenty years. Here the music is not simply a counterpoint, as in
the ironic ending where a recording played over the radio mocks
the Ringmaster Garibaldi's obsessive failure. It is a metaphor for
the sacrifice of individuality to 'higher aims', for the ambivalence
of discipline (artistry, but also the basis of tyranny) and sublimation
(the ideal expression of art, which is also self-abnegation), with
Garibaldi as one of a long line of vampire teachers going back to
Svengali. It is also the structural principle of the play, with the
dialogue following the quintet's pattern of theme and variations.

In theory this sounds fine. In practice the effect is indigestible, sentences becoming disjointed and the repetition of a phrase like 'Augsburg tomorrow' leading to abstraction. In music restating a pattern of notes creates a theme; doing the same with language removes the meaning from words and substitutes empty forms for ideas – and though this may perhaps be Bernhard's point, the result seems monotonous and pretentious.

In *Force of Habit* and *The Ignoramus and the Madman* art is an image of life, performing represents living, and this theme is most fully worked out in *Minetti* (1976) which is also a clear example of the relationship and difference between Bernhard and Handke. Originally written as an operetta, with the melodramatic cliché title of *The Evil Omen* (*Das böse Omen*), the approach in certain scenes which are played to the accompaniment of jazz music over a radio, is directly comparable to Handke, while the characterisation of the protagonist as a compulsive talker whose garrulous volubility says absolutely nothing shows a conventionally dramatic use of Handke's 'speaking play' concept. At first glance too the basic idea is the same as *The Ride Across Lake Constance*, 'Minetti, a theatre-artist (*Schauspielkünstler*)' standing for the stereotype of the actor and the role-playing personality in the same way as Bergner or Von Stroheim. But here the theatricality becomes simultaneously illusionistic and ironically self-parodying since Bernhard Minetti is a real actor who has specialised in Thomas Bernhard's work, acting Garibaldi in *Force of Habit*, the general in *The Hunting Party*, and the title role was not only written for but (in Peymann's production) played by him. Handke's clowns are purely theatre figures. Minetti is King Lear as 'a bitter fool' (the motto for Bernhard's play) who has given away his kingdom, a symbol of the artist whose single-minded pursuit of the artistic ideal is an abdication from the world. But he is also a real artist, whose kingdom is the make-believe of the stage, and the mirror that has reflected his acting all his life is the audience. There is a complex and disquieting interpenetration of fiction and actuality, signification and object.

The deceptively simple action presents the alienation of the artist from society, and the consequent alienation of society, in a nightmare vision based on James Ensor's expressionistic pictures of men as puppets in grotesque masks. The fictitious Minetti condemned himself to artistic isolation by rejecting mimetic, 'classical literature' as 'shamelessness' because it served only escapism,[28] and was driven into an exile where for thirty years he acted the part of Lear to himself in front of a mirror. (*King Lear* epitomises subjective, anti-classical art because of the implication in the storm scene that the world is a projection of man's mind). Now Minetti has arrived at a hotel in Ostend in response to a telegram summoning him to perform the part he has made his own in a Shakespeare festival. Here over thirty years earlier he had engaged Ensor to create a mask of Lear which he has brought along, together with reviews of his bygone performances in a heavy trunk. The mask has become his persona, the trunk is the weight of the past that has trapped him in his role, the hotel with its faded Victorian furnishings and its porter who spends his time working through outdated guest-registers, stands for European civilisation. Like Godot, the theatre director never comes, and Minetti, whose dress is reminiscent of Beckett's tramps – 'an ankle-length old winter coat, black patent leather shoes with spats, a broad-brimmed hat and an umbrella...the cord of his underpants is undone and dangles out down to the floor' (p. 11) – has lost his telegram, which may be as illusory as the tramps' letter. It is New Year's Eve and the hotel is swarming with 'screaming youths in carnival masks', one of Bernhard's favourite symbols that he uses to represent a culture which in outliving its vitality has frozen into a rictus (in his novel *Distraction/Verstörung*), or the automatism of materialistic society (referred to as a 'death-masked ball' in *Frost*). The distorted dog and ape faces of the drunken revellers supersede Minetti's Lear, powerfully acting out the same image of despairing rejection as in Milton's 'detraction' –

> I did but prompt the age to quit their clogs,
> By the known rules of ancient liberty,
> When straight a barbarous noise environs me
> Of owls and cuckoos, asses, apes and dogs.

– a parallel which helps to explain why Bernhard has been so vituperously attacked by the radical left in Germany. And in an epilogue as the old year ends we see him stiffen under the mask into a dead statue, pointed at by the youths as 'the artist/the theatre artist', after he takes an overdose of sleeping pills and sits 'motionless, until the falling snow covers him completely' (p. 59) – a literal illustration of the point made earlier in his rambling monologue:

The actor
is on one hand the victim of his *idée fixe*
on the other completely the victim of his audience (p. 45).

In *Minetti* the themes of Bernhard's earlier plays – the equiv-
alence of apparent opposites like theatre and existence, art and
mathematics, the 'ever greater isolation' and 'misunderstanding'
of artists who

in reaching our goal
have...outdistanced our ideas
set ourselves outside all human society
outside Nature (p. 22)

– are made explicit by being outlined discursively, as well as
formulated in images. The questioning of theatrical conventions,
as radical as in Handke, has become a fundamental querying of
the value of art without sacrificing dramatic effectiveness. The
resonances of *King Lear*, in a world where order has been turned
upside down, give depth to the seemingly incoherent dialogue, and
the use of masks is an appropriate theatrical way of presenting the
theme of man as actor. The symbolism, which tends to abstraction
in this type of drama, is tied in to our sense of reality by the
character study of Minetti, so that the play works on several levels
– a demonstration of the actor's art (Minetti as Minetti), 'a
portrait of the artist as an old man' (Minetti as Thomas Bernhard),
as well as a general philosophical challenge (Minetti's situation as
the predicament of all individuals in our alienated society). The
isolation is not only the obsession of a symbolic figure but the
loneliness of age, and the cold in which he freezes like Horváth's
'child of our times' is natural (we are told that the municipal
authorities will have removed his body before the townspeople are
out on the streets again after their New Year celebration) as well
as metaphysical (the winter of our discontent).

The context of Handke's later plays is very different, but the
attempt to overcome the problems of abstraction by grounding
the symbolic representation of ideas in a psychological study
is basically the same, and Handke has acknowledged that his
approach and Bernhard's are comparable:

I am convinced of the power of poetic thought to disentangle concepts
and so influence the future. Thomas Bernhard said that if even the trace
of a story surfaced on the horizon while he was writing he would shoot
it down. I reply: if while writing even the trace of a truism surfaces I

diverge – if I still can – into a different direction, a different landscape in which there is no relief, no fake consensus through [accepted] ideas.[29]

Paradoxically this radical, insistently *avant garde* style of theatre has become rapidly accepted, and Handke at times seems to be straining after novelty simply in reaction to the way he has been received as an 'instant classic'. But the reasons for this partly unwelcome public adoption, in spite of the intellectual difficulty of these plays, are not hard to find. The linguistic concern is one of the constant factors, from Hans Werner Richter's *'Kahlschlag'* prose to Kroetz's folk plays, that distinguishes German literature in the post-war period. The attempt to find appropriate theatrical forms to encompass new perceptions of social and individual realities, which has been a common denominator in serious German drama, leads logically to this radical questioning or rejection of traditional theatre forms. The portrayal of character in terms of sociological role-theory mirrors contemporary intellectual preoccupations, while the grotesque images and surreal representation of psychological states relate to established figures like Kafka (as well as Beckett) and even to Horváth's later plays. In short the stylistic and thematic approach developed by Handke and Bernhard can be seen as the culmination or extension of various central trends.

10. *Conclusions*

The political beliefs expressed in their drama may vary widely, their different approaches to the stage are distinct, defined by contrast and in opposition to each other, but on a general level these playwrights have much in common. All share the same starting point, Nietzsche's position that 'no artist tolerates reality'; and each would agree with Günther Eich that the artist's task is actively to oppose traditional power structures, that any work which does not challenge authority is in effect 'decorating the slaughter-house with geraniums'.[1] Yet in spite of the strong ideological commitment of some of the pace-setting dramatists, there is surprisingly little straight propaganda or tendentious and simplistic thesis drama. In the best plays, and even in political diatribes like *Song of the Lusitanian Bogey*, though the author's standpoint or the expected audience reaction may be clear, the statement is made in dramatic rather than explicit, political terms. Even if Handke or Hacks, Weiss or Wallraff believe in programmatic solutions, their plays allow interpretation, lead the audience towards a conclusion rather than imposing one, in short obey the same thematic guide-line as a conventional dramatist like Zuckmayer: 'It cannot be the task [of drama] to give finished answers, but only to contribute to clarification and to indicate a path.'[2] Political opposition is expressed in stylistic non-conformity rather than messages, and even where there is literal flag waving (as in *Discourse on Vietnam*) it is transformed into aesthetic patterning. This is partly what makes postwar German drama potentially so fruitful for contemporary theatre as a whole.

At the same time each style is not just a stage technique but a mode of perception, conditioning as well as reflecting the public's view of society and of themselves. The aim is to challenge, change or articulate our awareness. Reality, whether in a 'reconstruction' of actual events like *The Havana Hearing* or in the abstract of Handke's linguistic plays, is seen not as something absolute and material, but as a concept. This means that even the most factual work has a utopian dimension. Conversely the most imagistic, like Grass' or Dorst's adaptation of absurd drama, has a specific social basis and reference. As Weiss put it in the mouth of his fictional *alter ego* (giving his ideals the problematic form characteristic of so much contemporary German writing since Hölderlin speaks of himself in the third person, a tragically divided personality): 'He doesn't want to separate dream from reality/fantasy and action must be in the same sphere/only thus will the poetic become universal' – and so politically effective.[3] On this broad level then, German drama in the postwar period has an identifiable consistency in spite of the diversity of theatre forms, and although each style to some extent sets up its own criteria by creating different expectations, what can be related can also be measured against the same general standards.

It is one of today's commonplaces that matter is energy. Form by contrast is assumed to be simply a framework, a stable structure which holds highly charged forces (whether physical or, for drama, political and emotional) in equilibrium. In fact, of course, it is the form which gives a play's material its direction and significance, and at the least one requires any style to have an intrinsic vitality, a theatrical life which comes from realism – not to be confused with an 'illusion of reality' or superficial accuracy to facts – that correlation to our sense of the world which in a very traditional, Coleridgean sense can 'strike out unexpected truth'. In these terms the factual base of the documentary is no more or less valid than Dürrenmatt's apparently arbitrary *reductio ad absurdum*. Along the same lines the terms of this particular study have set up an additional requirement: that if a theatrical approach is to be viable it should have general applicability rather than being an idiosyncratic, personal vision. At the same time a style, unlike any particular work of art, is not greater than the sum of its parts. It may have great theoretical potential, but in practice it is only as valid as the best of the plays that embody it. Harmony, unity – the classical criteria which are applicable only to Hacks' later poetic work – seem alien to the modern experience which finds expression in juxtaposed contrasts, chiaroscuro, paradox and deliberate imbalance. But even here one can demand coherence, that heterogeneous elements add up to a convincing whole, consistent with those expectations which the stylistic formulation itself creates. In addition the stage itself imposes certain criteria. Since the aim of each new style is to alter the theatre or extend its range, these criteria cannot be narrowly defined and are mainly concerned with the possible level of audience response as well as with such practical requirements as precision, immediacy, visual and verbal interest, not just intellectual significance.

Finally, the form should not obtrude in performance. It must seem the natural expression of a play's subject. As Hacks put it in a perceptive parody of modern theatrical attitudes which is also an ironic picture of the common man as audience:

BIRKENBIHL: How for example do you judge the state of affairs in contemporary drama? Are you for the socialist realists or the realistic socialists? (*Fidorra contemplates*). Another important question is that of didactic theatre. Didactic is as much as to say dialectic, in German that is 'unemotional'. I translate the foreign word for you, I don't despise the common people... The gates of art stand open to every aspirant.

FIDORRA: ...I know a thing or two about culture. Once they arranged a guided tour... You must go on that, they said. I went on it. Other people, they went too, and the whole thing was led by an expert. We moved so to say collectively through the German habitat and reached a place where everything grew, so greenly. The expert explained, it's sorrel, which is edible. He exhorted us to eat sorrel. Everyone ate sorrel. I ate sorrel... Listen, hardly thirty paces and there too something growing, greenly. Shepherd's purse. The expert... exhorted us to eat shepherd's purse. Everyone ate shepherd's purse. At that I pulled on my coat, turned my back on that tour and went home – to a beer. Culture, young man, I can just as well eat that out of my front garden.[4]

As manipulative modes of vision, stylistic techniques are most effective when they work on a subliminal level. In addition, as Hacks implies, it is the quality of insight a dramatic form gives that justifies it, not aesthetic theory or political approval.

As we have seen, Brecht has been the major theatrical catalyst, the standard against which almost all contemporary German dramatists measure themselves. Yet even those whose work is directly comparable distance themselves from his stylistic example. Where Dürrenmatt, for instance, is most derivative his plays are least successful, while Hacks, whose earlier approach was closely associated with Brecht's principles which he sees as 'a system of methods designed to grasp reality in its total dialectic', has commented that 'Brecht's reality was the first half of the twentieth century. Our reality is already different, so our methods must be different to Brecht's if they are to be Brechtian' – a point echoed by 'folk dramatists' such as Sperr, for whom Brecht's is 'a naïve theatre for a naïve audience... As long as the naïve audience is lacking, the theatre has to use the old unnaïve conventions.'[5] Of course, just as Shaw transformed Ibsen into a Shavian iconoclast in *The Quintessence of Ibsenism,* so these comments reveal more about the aims of the speakers than about Brecht, and his influence is rather different from his own example. As Frisch put it, looking back on the late 1940s and the 1950s, 'everyone who worked with him at that time was more Brechtian than Brecht himself, for he really always worked empirically'.[6] Indeed, depending on circumstances, Brecht was quite capable of producing work which directly contradicted his basic premises – a reminder, if one is needed, that theatrical theories are essentially concerned with the audience, with specific effects, not abstract principles:

The Berliner Ensemble has put my play *The Mother*. . . into rehearsal, because we wished to make the Soviet Union lovable to our workers, our petty bourgeoisie and our intellectuals. Indeed very few spectators could avoid this effect [of empathy], as many comments indicate.[7]

The various attempts to move beyond Brecht, whether by extending his epic or dialectical conventions, mixing his techniques with Kafkaesque or Artaudian approaches, or creating a deliberately anti-Brechtian theatre, all have positive qualities to offer. But each have corresponding flaws and disadvantages, as a brief comparison of the two most radically different forms of drama illustrates.

The documentary, in some ways a straight-line development from Brecht with its distillation of contemporary society to broad general patterns, its 'historicising' approach and multi-media presentation, its objective, rational appeal and its aim of inciting direct political action, is designed (in typically Brechtian terms) as 'a theatre of the scientific age. . . It is directed at an enlightened public. Or more accurately: against one, against the culinary public.'[8] In fact, however, only too frequently what the modernity and factuality of the surface covers is ideological melodrama. The abstraction (as in *Discourse on Vietnam*), the tendency to slogans (*The Havana Hearing/Song of the Lusitanian Bogey*) and the stress on information *per se* have the effect of reducing conflict to virtuous revolutionaries versus vicious establishments – 'culinary' to an extreme. Consequently documentary plays too frequently seem to be preaching to the converted. To some extent this is the inevitable result of the claim that art can have no function independent of politics, and although it is partly due to

263

this overstatement that they gain validity as documents in their own right, rather than being merely the 'reproduction' of documents for an ephemeral (and illusory) political effect, the aspiration to give a play the status of a 'revolutionary act' is counterproductive in terms of the theatre itself, which relies on distinctions between the stage and real life to create imaginative insights. It is the political equivalent of psychodrama that naïvely merges audience and actors in a 'therapeutic' re-enactment of traumatic events, reliving 'the problem' so that the origin of the disorder can be perceived and the destructive pattern of behaviour broken.[9]

By contrast, although Handke has basically the same starting point as Brecht or Weiss, to alter the world not to describe it, his approach to theatre provides a pattern for playwrights who do not share the fixed concepts of the world inherent in such forms as absurd, epic or documentary drama. For Handke any alteration in the complex structures of contemporary society can only come through an awareness of basic psychological conditioning factors, the most fundamental of which is language, and the level on which his drama works can offer 'no political alternative to what is here and elsewhere (at most an anarchistic one)'.[10] At the same time this non-committal analysis tends to an undramatic lack of felt passion – as in *Offending the Audience* where even abuse becomes mock antagonism, a linguistic game – and the limitation of subject matter to such a basic level has the effect of reducing significant social points to hermetic demonstrations so far removed from the average individual's experience that stage technique takes precedence over meaning. The result is a highly philosophical kind of abstraction which, without even the melodramatic reference points of political oversimplifications, runs the danger of losing its audience in vague imprecision. There is a certain truth in Walser's remark that Handke's work is an 'un-thought-out mish-mash of Vienna positivism *and* German phenomenology, of Wittgenstein *and* Heidegger'.[11] – although Wittgenstein cannot be as simply equated with the Vienna Circle as Walser implies. However these heterogeneous philosophical positions do have one major thing in common, which is that they treat man as an asocial figure totally divorced from the political context. And even in Handke's more developed plays, where the focus is overtly political, the characters are still presocial or faceless (*Kaspar*), celluloid images (*The Ride Across Lake Constance*), or subjective projections of psychoses (*They Are Dying Out*); and the level of abstraction is indicated by the way Kaspar is transformed from a historical individual into 'the prototype of a sort of linguistic myth...a prototype of people who do not get on with themselves and their environment, who feel isolated'.[12]

Where these two theatrical forms, indeed contemporary German drama as a whole, are most vulnerable is in the way they distort the delicate balance between intellectual profit and pleasure, and in their treatment of the human character. The sense of didactic purpose is undisguised, and attempting to gain popular appeal by purely aesthetic patterns of movement (Weiss), sound (Handke), or overt theatricality only creates a split between content and presentation, which becomes obvious as soon as the documentary topic is overtaken by events or the linguistic challenge to preconceived ideas becomes accepted. Their defence is of course the Shavian claim that plays which have done more 'work' in the world are 'better' than deceptive beauty such as Shakespeare. But plays seldom survive simply because of a morally irreproachable message, and utilitarian art tends to be shortlived – something that playwrights such as Enzensberger or Wallraff even turn into a positive criterion through a quasi-Maoist concept of permanent revolution in artistic vision: the speed with which a work becomes outdated being a test of its effectiveness in moulding public opinion. Learning may in itself be a significant form of pleasure, as Brecht (citing Aristotle) pointed out – though in Brecht's case this assertion was little more than an attempt to avoid the obvious criticism of over-intellectualised didacticism, which hardly applies to his own work anyway since, despite his theories, all his major plays provide the traditional dramatic interest of developing, individualised characters in situations where conflict with society creates emotional stress – but in most postwar German drama the individual is missing. In one sense his absence may be unavoidable. It corresponds to the modern shift of historical perspective in which events can no longer be accounted for as the expression of an individual's will (Irving's recent historical study of Hitler, which seeks to demonstrate that he had no control over the 'final solution', is a typical illustration). It also reflects the contemporary inversion of Descartes in which a person's thoughts are determined by external pressures, and hence the concept of 'the individual' itself is seen as an artificial product of social conditioning. As a result even Frisch, usually thought of as the defender of individuality, in fact tends to turn his work into a kind of controlled psychological experiment by consciously reducing the attributes of his protagonists (as in *Biography* or novels like *Stiller* and *Homo Faber*) to a limited range of stable – and interchangeable – behaviour patterns. It is hardly surprising then that in more didactic forms the single actor represents the masses, is a symbol for impersonal forces, becomes reduced to a stage puppet or a fixed image implanted in the public mind by the media. Nor that the idea of 'self' as a consistent and unique personality can only be expressed (as in *They Are Dying Out*) by nineteenth-century literary clichés – which would seem to be throwing the baby out with the bath-water. There is a certain truth in the justification for abstract or two-dimensional characterisation: that 'looking deep into the soul' has the effect 'not only of reducing political questions to a personal level but declaring them in general insoluble, [since then] their solution lies buried in the inaccessible subjectivity of the isolated individual'.[13] But at the same time theatre uses men as its primary means of communicating, so there is a correlation between dramatic effectiveness and the impression of individual significance which comes from adopting, at least as a working hypothesis, the classic proposition that 'man is the measure of all things'. Perhaps the new forms developed in German drama have been too direct in their attempts to mirror contemporary consciousness?

At least, however, the radical nature of these experiments clarifies the issues facing modern theatre, while despite their flaws the different styles have produced plays which are among the most relevant and powerful dramatic statements of our time. As for the documentary, the technique of reportage and media presentation, or Weiss' 'physical theatre' generate the immediacy, the performance-excitement that are the qualities of a vital drama, and they can be used apolitically, as in Dorst's *Toller*. This approach has made it possible to deal with a subject of global proportions without resorting to symbolism or poetic inflation. While the positive use of the perception that 'literature cannot mirror reality, only the dominating ideology'[14] in a play like *The Havana Hearing*, or Weiss' integration of factual detail and mythical structure to create meaning in *The Investigation* indicates the subtlety with which material can be handled in this style. Similarly the ability to represent complex or ambiguous experience gained by Handke's drama of language, with its use of associative images and its development of overtly theatrical techniques to undercut ideological simplifications or to explore unquestioned assumptions, are definite stylistic gains. Even more significant is the way Handke's experiments have made it possible to show on stage the relationship between political exploitation and linguistic manipulation, individual alienation and social expectations. This is perhaps the most important single contribution to contemporary theatre. Indeed as a theme it could be called the keynote of postwar German drama and forms a link between various stylistic approaches, having also been treated less directly by Kroetz in his dramas of 'speechlessness', by Walser in *Rabbit Race* where 'the substance of the figures' is intended (though this is hardly discernible in the dialogue) to be their speech-forms,[15] by Dürrenmatt in his attack on the spiritual connotations of linguistic and theatrical conventions (Plush X Infinity) in *Play Strindberg*.

Comparable failings and alternative advantages are equally obvious in the other major stylistic innovations, Dürrenmatt's 'models', the different versions of 'dialectical' theatre, Kroetz's development of the 'folk play', even the German variation on absurdist drama. As responses to the problem of creating a stage form capable of expressing modern consciousness they offer provisional and provocative solutions on which further advances can be based. In short, German theatre has acquired a remarkable richness and diversity over the last thirty years, and the ironic exit line of Hacks' utopian dreamer, Moritz Tassow, provide an appropriate summation:

> ...I'll find myself another field
> For my business, pulling up the meagre seed
> of the future with forceps from the soil.
> I'll be a writer.[16]

Notes

Since this study is intended for the general reader as well as students of German, quotations have normally been taken from translations where these are available and accurate, and in all such cases references are to the English texts, not to the originals.

1 Introduction

1 Karl Marx, *Critique of Hegel's Philosophy of Right*, trans. Annette Jolin and Joseph O'Malley, Cambridge, 1970, p. 137, and Friedrich Wolf, cit., Walter Hinderer, *Die Zeit*, 16 June 1970.
2 Friedrich Luft, *25 Jahre Theater in Berlin*, Berlin, 1972, p. 10. Cf. also Cecil W. Davies, *Theatre for the People*, Austin, Texas, 1977, pp. 117f.
3 Bertolt Brecht, *Schriften zum Theater*, Frankfurt, 1963–4, I, pp. 226, 91.
4 Cf., Brecht, *ibid.*, III, p. 84, and Friedrich Dürrenmatt, *Theater Heute*, September 1968, p. 7.
5 Cf., Georg Lukács, 'Zur Soziologie des modernen Dramas', *Schriften zur Literatursoziologie*, Neuwied, 1961, pp. 262f.
6 Hugo von Hofmannsthal, *Gesammelte Werke*, IV, *Lustspiele*, Frankfurt, 1956, p. 419.
7 Wilhelm Michel, 'Physiognomie der Zeit u. Theater der Zeit', *Masken* 22, 1928, pp. 6f.
8 Cf., Martin Walser, *Sinn und Form*, 1974, II, p. 425.
9 Charles Marowitz, in *Mobiler Spielraum – Theatre der Zukunft*, ed. Karlheinz Braun, Maurico Kagel, Frankfurt, 1970, p. 127.
10 Cf., Dürrenmatt, afterword to *Die Wiedertäufer*, Zürich, 1967, p. 101.
11 Walser, *Theater Heute*, Sonderheft 1963, p. 69.
12 Cf., Walter Hinck, *Das moderne Drama in Deutschland*, Göttingen, 1973, pp. 216f., or Joseph Strelka, *Brecht Horváth Dürrenmatt*, Wien, 1962, p. 159.
13 For an example of the first, cf., Ann Jellicoe, *Some Unconscious Influences in the Theatre*, Cambridge, 1967, pp. 7f. Dorst's *Grosse Schmährede an der Stadtmauer* illustrates the second case. (Cf. p. 91 in this volume).
14 Peter Handke, *Offending the Audience and Self-Accusation*, trans. Michael Roloff, London, 1971, p. 7.
15 Brecht, *Schriften zum Theater*, I, p. 225.
16 Cf., Henning Rischbieter/Ernst Wendt, *Deutsche Dramatik in West und Ost*, Velber, 1965, pp. 40f., and Rainer Lübbreu, 'Über die deutsche Gegenwartsdramatik', *Neue Rundschau*, LXXVI, 1965, p. 472.

2 The starting point

1 Gustaf Gründgens, cit., Curt Riess, *Gustaf Gründgens*, Hamburg, 1965, pp. 214–15.
2 Cit., Siegfried Melchinger, *Theater Heute*, November 1963, p. 9.
3 Cit., Riess, p. 374.
4 Cit., Hans Schwab-Felisch, *Theater Heute*, October 1970, p. 46.

5 Cf., Volker Canaris, in *The German Theatre*, ed. R. Hayman, London, 1975, p. 249, or Teo Otto, in Artur Joseph, *Theater unter vier Augen*, Köln, 1969, p. 165.

6 Examples are *Der Löwe auf dem Marktplatz* (1948) by Ilya Ehrenburg, a satiric attack on the Marshall Plan, or an adaptation of Wolf's *Tai Yang erwacht* (1949). A typical critical reaction was 'if Piscator in New York learnt how his directorial ideas of twenty long years earlier could be misunderstood and falsely copied today, he would renounce his whole life work'. (Friedrich Luft, *Stimme der Kritik – Berliner Theater 1945–61*, Hannover, 1965, p. 71.)

7 The closeness of the artistic relationship, which Hauptmann in turn acknowledged in 1932, can be indicated by Zuckmayer's completion of *Herbert Engelmann* (1952), which Hauptmann had left as a fragment.

8 Carl Zuckmayer, 'Persönliche Notizen', *Die Wandlung* III, 4 (1948), pp. 331, 332.

9 Zuckmayer, *Meisterdramen*, Frankfurt, 1966, p. 451.

10 Karl Kraus, *Die letzten Tage der Menschheit*, München, 1957, p. 5.

11 Zuckmayer, *Als wär's ein Stück von mir*, Wien, 1966, p. 534.

12 Zuckmayer, *Meisterdramen*, p. 420. The same elemental quality is intended to be revealed in Schmidt-Lausitz, 'the most evil thing in the world...the high-school teacher as Nero, the worm as President' (Zuckmayer, 'Blätter der Städtischen Bühnen Augsburg', 1948/9 Season).

13 *Ibid.*, pp. 454–5. Zuckmayer was well aware of the problem, and admitted that Oderbruch was 'the only abstract, not fully humanised figure...more a symbol of despair than an active figure' (*Als wär's ein Stück von mir*, p. 473).

14 Cf., Luft, *Stimme der Kritik*, p. 68 and Herbert Jhering, *Theater der produktiven Widersprüche, 1945–9*, Berlin, 1967, p. 163.

15 Cf., Luft, *Stimme der Kritik*, p. 294.

16 Zuckmayer, *Meisterdramen*, p. 465.

17 Zuckmayer, *Der Gesang im Feuerofen*, Frankfurt, 1960, p. 136. One might also note the typically expressionistic use of the word 'transformation' (*Verwandlung*).

18 For a full discussion of the philosophical roots of expressionism, see Walter H. Sokel, *The Writer in Extremis*, Stanford, Calif., 1959.

19 Paradoxically however expressionism can be seen to have developed out of naturalism. In the analysis of individual character the greatest dramatists came to a point where it was necessary to go beneath social determinants, finding that the psyche could only be explored through symbolism. Ibsen's last plays, like Strindberg's after the *Inferno* crisis, are expressionistic, and elements in *The Cherry Orchard* indicate that Chekhov might have transformed his naturalistic subject-matter in the same way had he lived.

20 Gottfried Benn, *Nach dem Nihilismus*, Berlin, 1932, p. 20.

21 Wolfgang Borchert, *Draussen vor der Tür und Ausgewählte Erzählungen*, Hamburg, 1956, pp. 24–5, 39, 44.

22 August Strindberg, *Six Plays*, trans. Elizabeth Sprigge, New York, 1960, p. 193.

23 *Ibid.*

24 Cf., Wassily Kandinsky, 'Reminiscences' in *Modern Artists on Art*, ed. Robert Herbert, Englewood Cliffs, N.J., 1964, pp. 31f.

25 Wilhelm Duwe, *Deutsche Dichtung des 20. Jahrhunderts*, Zürich, 1952, II, p. 430, Wilhelm Grenzmann, *Dichtung und Glaube*, Frankfurt, 1967, pp. 307f.; Joseph Mileck, 'Wolfgang Borchert, Draussen vor der Tür', *Monatshefte*, 1959, pp. 333–4; A. Leslie Willson, 'Beckmann der Ertrinkende', *Akzente* 19, 1972, pp. 467f.

26 Luft, *Stimme der Kritik*, p. 23.

27 Current Catholic practice counts 14 'Stations of the Cross', or even 15 counting the Resurrection, but the expressionist convention which limited the '*Stationen*' of their plays to 7 was probably derived by analogy from the '7 joys', '7 Sorrows' (of Mary), the '7 Gifts of the Holy Spirit', etc.

28 Stephen Spender, introduction to Borchert, *The Man Outside*, trans. David Porter, London, 1966, p. 3.

29 'Das ist unser Manifest', in *Draussen vor der Tür*, p. 116.

30 Max Frisch, *Stücke* I, Frankfurt, 1962, p. 394.

31 Frisch, *Tagebuch 1946–49*, Frankfurt, 1950, p. 150.

32 *Ibid.*, p. 326. See also *Öffentlichkeit als Partner*, Frankfurt, 1967, pp. 20–1, where Frisch discusses culture as the German alibi.

33 *Tagebuch 1946–49*, p. 141.

34 *Ibid.*, p. 144.

35 Ulrich Weisstein, *Max Frisch*, New York, 1967, p. 106.

36 Zuckmayer, interview in *Welt am Sonntag*, 22 January 1967, and Borchert, *Draussen vor der Tür*, p. 113.

37 *Tagebuch 1946–49*, pp. 118–19.

38 Peter Palitzsch, *Theater Heute*, Sonderheft 1964, p. 26.

3 Developments

1 Dürrenmatt, 'Theaterprobleme', in *Theater Schriften und Reden*, Zürich, 1966, p. 120.

2 Frisch, *Stücke*, I, pp. 140–1.

3 Brecht, *Schriften zum Theater*, I, p. 226.

4 *Ibid.*, and 'Theaterprobleme', p. 119.

5 'Theaterprobleme', pp. 123–4.

6 *Ibid.*, p. 118.

7 Brecht, 'Kann die heutige Welt durch Theater wiedergegeben werden?' in *Schriften Zum Theater*, VII, p. 301.

8 *Ibid.*, p. 300.

9 Frisch, interview in *Gespräche mit Schriftstellern*, ed. Heinz L. Arnold, München, 1975, p. 48. The major points were first made in Frisch's speech accepting the Büchner prize, 'Das Engagement des Schriftstellers' (*Frankfurter Allgemeine Zeitung*, 14 November 1958). Prize speeches form a valuable index to the way dramatic theories developed, providing a unique opportunity for writers such as Frisch (1958), Dürrenmatt (1959), Bernhard (1971), Handke (1973) to establish their viewpoints publicly.

10 Frisch, *Neue Rundschau*, 1965, p. 37.

11 Frisch, in Arnold, p. 67, and *Neue Rundschau*, 1965, pp. 38 and 43.

12 Dürrenmatt, interview in *Werkstattgespräche mit Schriftstellern*, ed. Horst Bieneck, München, 1969, p. 122.

13 Cf., Walser, *Erfahrungen und Leseerfahrungen*, Frankfurt, 1965, pp. 64, 127, and Günter Grass, interview in Arnold, pp. 100–1.

14 Tankred Dorst, 'Die Bühne ist der absolute Ort', in *Grosse Schmährede an*

der Stadtmauer, Köln, 1971, pp. 116 and 113; Wolfgang Hildesheimer, 'Über das absurde Theater', in *Deutsche Dramaturgie der sechziger Jahre*, ed. Helmut Kreuzer, Tübingen, 1974, p. 11.

15 Friedrich Wolf, *Aufsätze über Theater*, Berlin, 1957, p. 17.

16 Günter Wallraff, interview in Arnold, pp. 203–4.

17 Cf., Arnold, pp. 37, 208, and Joseph, p. 66.

18 Wolf, *op. cit.*, p. 57, and Brecht, *Schriften zum Theater*, VII, p. 153.

19 Cf., Hans Magnus Enzensberger, 'Europäische Peripherie' and 'Peter Weiss und andere', *Kursbuch* 2, 1965, pp. 156f. and 6, 1966, pp. 172f., and Weiss, *Rapporte 2*, Frankfurt, 1971, p. 83.

20 Handke, *Prosa Gedichte Theaterstücke Hörspiel Aufsätze*, Frankfurt, 1969, pp. 305–6.

21 *Ibid.*, p. 306. See also p. 270.

22 Frisch, *Akzente*, 1955, p. 391.

23 Frisch, *Four Plays*, trans. Michael Bullock, London, 1969, p. 47.

24 *Tagebuch 1946–49*, p. 306.

25 Dürrenmatt, *Theater Heute*, February 1966, p. 12.

26 Dürrenmatt, *Dramaturgisches und Kritisches*, Zürich, 1972, p. 160.

27 Dürrenmatt, Programme Note to *Der Meteor*, Schauspielhaus Zürich, 1966.

28 Dürrenmatt, *Komödien* III, Zürich, 1966, p. 74.

29 *Theaterschriften und Reden*, p. 193.

30 Grass, *Über meinen Lehrer Döblin und andere Vorträge*, Berlin, 1968, p. 55.

31 Cf., Martin Esslin, *Brecht, a Choice of Evils*, London, 1959 (translated into German in 1962).

32 Cf., Grass, interview by Thomas K. Brown, in *Monatshefte* LXV, 1, 1973, pp. 12 and 6–7.

33 Dorst, *Toller*, Frankfurt, 1968, pp. 77 and 36.

34 Dorst, interview in *Theater Heute*, September 1968, p. 21.

35 Grass, *The Plebeians Rehearse the Uprising*, trans. Ralph Manheim, New York 1966, p. 25.

36 Dorst, *Theater Heute*, December 1968, p. 9, and *Spectaculum* 11, 1968, p. 329.

37 Rosa Leviné in *Die Münchener Räterepublik Zeugnisse und Kommentar*, ed. Dorst, Frankfurt, 1967, p. 138.

38 Dorst, *Spectaculum*, 11, 1968, p. 329.

39 Maurice Nadeau, *The History of Surrealism*, tr. R. Howard, Harmondsworth, 1973, p. 227.

40 Peter Weiss, *Trotsky in Exile*, trans. Geoffrey Skelton, London, 1971, pp. 47, 49.

41 Weiss, interview in *Der Spiegel*, 13 September 1971, p. 166.

42 Weiss, *Hölderlin*, Frankfurt, 1971, p. 11. It is difficult to find an equivalent for the archaic vocabulary and terse idioms of Weiss' rhyming verse, and translations from this play are only intended to be faithful to the sense.

43 Maria Eibach (psuedonym), in *Die Gruppe 47*, ed. Reinhard Lettau, Berlin, 1967, p. 22.

44 Cf., interviews in Arnold; Grass, pp. 75, 86, 87, and Frisch, p. 31. Dramatists who participated in *Group 47* readings included Enzensberger, Grass, Handke, Hildesheimer, Hartmut Lange, Siegfried Lenz, Walser, Günther Weisenborn and Weiss. Critics were also invited, among them Joachim Kaiser, Walter Mehring and Peter Szondi.

45 Manfred Wekwerth, *Theater Heute*, February 1968, p. 17.

46 Wolfdietrich Schnurre, in Lettau, p. 170.
47 *Aus der Welt der Arbeit. Almanach der Gruppe 61*, ed. Fritz Hüser, Berlin, 1966, p. 25.
48 Wallraff, *Von einem der auszog, und das Fürchten lernte*, München 1970, pp. 43–4.
49 *Ibid.*, p. 44.
50 Wallraff, in Arnold, p. 204.
51 *Ein Baukran stürzt um*, ed. Röhrer, München, 1970, p. 11.
52 *Gruppe 61, Arbeiterliteratur – Literatur der Arbeitswelt*, ed. H. L. Arnold, München, 1971, p. 194.
53 Wolf Vostell, *Theater Heute*, May 1965, p. 29.
54 Paul Pörtner, *Theater Heute*, May 1965, p. 35.
55 Siegfried Wagner (director of the Abteilung Kultur of the Central Committee) cit., Heinz Kersten, *Theater hinter dem Eisenen Vorhang*, 1964, p. 37.
56 Manfred Wekwerth, *Weimarer Beiträge*, 1973, 2, p. 31.
57 Heinar Kipphardt, *Stücke I*, Frankfurt, 1973, p. 9.
58 Wolfgang Joho, *Sonntag*, 26 March 1961.
59 Professor Erhard John, *Zum Problem der Beziehung zwischen Kunst und Wirklichkeit*, Leipzig, 1960, pp. 9f.
60 Cf., Helmut Baierl, *Sinn und Form*, 1966 Sonderheft 1, p. 742.
61 Professor Armin-Gerd Kuckhoff, 1959. Cit., Marcel Reich-Raniki, *Deutsche Literatur in West und Ost*, München, 1963, p. 462.
62 Cf., Manfred Starke, *Sinn und Form*, 1975, 1, p. 197.
63 Wagner, *Theater der Zeit*, 1959, 2 (Beilage), also cit., Kersten, p. 36.
64 Professor Kurt Hager, 'Parteilichkeit und Volksverbundenheit unserer Literatur und Kunst', *Neues Deutschland*, 25 March 1962.
65 Cf., Klaus Jarmatz, *Sinn und Form*, 1974, 1, p. 220.
66 Rainer Kerndl, *Neue deutsche Literatur*, 1976, 1, p. 43.
67 Cf., Hager (1962), and 'Bemerkungen zur DDR-Literatur nach den VII. Parteitag', *Neue deutsche Literatur*, 1976, 1, p. 24.
68 Cf., Baierl, *Theater Heute*, December 1970, p. 36, and *Sinn und Form*, 1966 Sonderheft 1, p. 737.
69 Hacks, cit., Rischbieter, *Theater Heute*, October 1969, p. 25. See also Heiner Müller, *Theater Heute*, Sonderheft 1975, p. 122.
70 Cf., Michael Krüger, *Akzente*, 1973, pp. 461f., and Starke, p. 198.
71 Wekwerth, *Notate. Zur Arbeit des Berliner Ensembles 1956–66*, Berlin 1967, pp. 153, 155.
72 Kurt Blatt, *Neue Deutsche Literatur*, 1974, 7, p. 138.
73 Hans Michael Richter, *Theater der Zeit*, 1964, 3 (also cit., Kersten, p. 52).

4 Images

1 Albert Camus, *The Myth of Sisyphus*, trans. Justin O'Brien, New York, 1955. Cf. pp. 4, 31.
2 Eugène Ionesco, *Notes and Counter Notes*, trans. Donald Watson, New York, 1964, p. 201.
3 *Ibid.*, p. 183.
4 Samuel Beckett, *Cascando and Other Short Dramatic Pieces*, New York, 1968, p. 54.
5 *Notes and Counter Notes*, p. 229.
6 *Materialien zu Becketts 'Endspiel'*, Frankfurt, 1968, p. 54.
7 Beckett, *Endgame*, New York, 1958, pp. 2, 84.

8 *Materialien zu Becketts 'Endspiel'*, p. 83.
9 *Ibid.*, pp. 38, 49, 65, 90–1.
10 Ionesco, 'ein paar Bemerkungen zur Inszenierung', *Theater Heute*, November 1968, pp. 8–9.
11 *Ibid.*
12 Hildesheimer (1960), in Kreuzer, pp. 2–3.
13 *Notes and Counter Notes*, pp. 256–7.
14 Luft, *Stimme der Kritik*, p. 149.
15 Grass, *Four Plays*, trans. Ralph Manheim and A. L. Willson, London, 1967, p. 38.
16 *Grosse Schmährede*, p. 42.
17 Grass, *Die Blechtrommel*, Berlin, 1965, p. 50. The images in Grass' novels are inherently theatrical and sections of *Die Blechtrommel* and *Hundejahre* (under the titles of *Beton Besichtigen* and *Goldmäulchen*) have been transferred straight to the stage.
18 Grass, *Münchner Merkur*, 24 October 1968, p. 9.
19 Grass, *Four Plays*, pp. 162–3.
20 Joachim Kaiser, in Lettau, p. 124.
21 Cf., Esslin, Introduction, Grass, *Four Plays*, p. ix.
22 Lothar Blumenhagen (the Count in the 1961 Schiller Theater production), interview 8 February 1977.
23 *Grosse Schmährede*, p. 13.
24 'Die Bühne ist der absolute Ort', in *Grosse Schmährede*, p. 119.
25 *Ibid*, pp. 115, 113, 116–17.
26 Dorst, *Theater Heute*, January 1962, p. 8.
27 'Die Bühne ist der absolute Ort', p. 114.
28 Walser, *Die Zeit*, 23 November 1962. (Also in Kreuzer, p. 19.)
29 Grass, in Arnold, p. 103.
30 Dorst, *Spectaculum*, 1968, 11, p. 331.
31 Erich Engel, *Schriften über Theater und Film*, Berlin, 1971, pp. 112f.
32 Grass, interview in *Monatshefte* LXV, 1, 1973, p. 9.
33 Dorst, *Spectaculum*, 1968, 11, p. 333.
34 *The Plebians Rehearse the Uprising*, p. xvi.
35 Grass, *Monatshefte* LXV, 1, 1973, p. 10.
36 Brecht, *Schriften zum Theater*, III, p. 158.
37 *The Plebeians Rehearse the Uprising*, pp. 60, 104. This emphasis on 'theatre in itself' and life as theatre is the reason for the one major alteration of history in *The Plebeians*, the substitution of *Coriolanus* for Brecht's actual (and equally ironic) occupation on 17 June 1953 – vainly attempting to persuade the state radio to broadcast a programme of revolutionary songs.
38 Grass, *Theater Heute*, April 1969, p. 31.
39 *Toller*, pp. 100f.
40 For a description of this production of *Hoppla, wir leben!* see either my book, *Erwin Piscator's Political Theatre*, Cambridge, 1972, pp. 94–5, 99–102, 127–30, or Jeanne Lorang, 'Toller/Piscator', *Travail Théâtral*, 13, October–December 1973, pp. 57f.
41 Dorst, *Spectaculum*, 1968, 11, p. 330.
42 Ernst Toller, *Prosa – Briefe – Dramen – Gedichte*, Reinbek, 1961, p. 114.
43 Pamphlet distributed by an APO group studying 'Culture and Revolution' in Berlin, 1968.
44 Dorst, cit., *Theater Heute*, February 1969, p. 17.

5 Models

1 *Theaterarbeit*, ed. Helene Weigel, Berlin, 1967, p. 54.
2 Brecht, *Schriften zum Theater*, 1, p. 273.
3 Frisch, *Die Zeit*, 22 December 1967. Cf., also Arnold, pp. 35, 38.
4 Frisch, *Theater Heute*, June 1967, p. 7. This 'drama of permutations' reached its fullest expression as the theme of *Biografie : ein Spiel*, produced in the same year.
5 *Tagebuch 1946–49*, pp. 148, 243.
6 Frisch, *Three Plays*, trans. Michael Bullock, London, 1962, p. 87.
7 In Arnold, p. 35, and *Tagebuch 1946–49*, pp. 125, 72.
8 Cf., Arnold, p. 34.
9 Cf., Frisch, Programmheft, Schauspielhaus Zürich, 14, 1957–8, pp. 5f.
10 *Theaterschriften und Reden*, pp. 102, 63, 233.
11 *Ibid*, pp. 184–5, 153, 187–8.
12 Dürrenmatt, *Theater Heute*, September 1968, p. 8.
13 *Theaterschriften und Reden*, pp. 89, 193, 73.
14 *Ibid.*, p. 122.
15 Cf., Erich Kühne, *Weimarer Beiträge*, 1966, p. 56; Rainer Taëni, *Drama nach Brecht*, Basel, 1968, p. 17; or Michael Patterson, *German Theatre Today*, London, 1976, pp. 21–2.
16 *Theaterschriften und Reden*, pp. 128, 49, 45.
17 Dürrenmatt, *Herkules und der Stall des Augias*, Zürich, 1963, pp. 86, 88.
18 *Theaterschriften und Reden*, p. 108.
19 See Ann Jellicoe's analysis of the way her play *The Knack* changed from a sophisticated comedy (for a student audience) to obscenity (an elderly audience in bath) to 'childlike' and 'innocent' (London). *Some Unconscious Influences in the Theatre*, pp. 7–10.
20 Afterword, *Die Wiedertäufer*, p. 107.
21 Dürrenmatt, *The Marriage of Mr Mississippi*, trans. Gerhard Nellhaus, New York, 1964, p. 45.
22 *Selected Works of Alfred Jarry*, ed. Roger Shattuck and Simon Watson Taylor, London, 1969, pp. 77–9.
23 Cf., Guillaume Apollinaire, *Il y a*, Paris, 1949, p. 176.
24 Alfred Jarry, *The Ubu Plays*, trans. Cyril Connolly and Simon Watson Taylor, London, 1968, pp. 143, 96.
25 *Selected Works of Alfred Jarry*, pp. 192–3.
26 *Theaterschriften und Reden*, p. 105.
27 Dürrenmatt, Programme Notes to *Die Ehe des Herrn Mississippi*, Schauspielhaus Zürich, 1952.
28 *Schweizer Journal*, May/June 1952.
29 Dürrenmatt, *The Visit*, trans. Patrick Bowles, London, 1962, pp. 53, 89.
30 Dürrenmatt, *Gesammelte Hörspiele*, Zürich, 1960, p. 253.
31 Dürrenmatt, *Komödien* I, pp. 52, 88.
32 Dürrenmatt, *Theater Heute*, February 1966, p. 11; *Theaterschriften und Reden*, p. 128; *Die Wiedertäufer*, p. 102.
33 *Theaterschriften und Reden*, pp. 123, 182.
34 Dürrenmatt, cit., Urs Jenny, *Friedrich Dürrenmatt*, Velber, 1968, p. 55.
35 *Theaterschriften und Reden*, p. 92.
36 *Ibid.*, pp. 176, 180. (Notes to *Romulus* and *Der Besuch*.)
37 *Ibid.*, cf., pp. 175, 245, 182.

38 Dürrenmatt, Programme Notes to *Frank V*, Schauspielhaus Zürich 1958–9. See also *Theaterschriften und Reden*, pp. 87, 118.
39 Dürrenmatt, cit. Urs Jenny, p. 58.
40 Kipphardt, *In the Matter of J. Robert Oppenheimer*, trans. Ruth Speirs, London 1967, p. 106.
41 *Theaterschriften und Reden*, p. 194.
42 Dürrenmatt, Programme Notes to *Die Physiker*, Schauspielhaus Zürich, 1961–2.
43 Dürrenmatt, *The Physicists*, trans. James Kirkup, London, 1963, p. 18.
44 Dürrenmatt, *Theater Heute*, February 1966, p. 10.
45 Dürrenmatt, *Play Strindberg*, trans. James Kirkup, London, 1972, p. 8.
46 *The Marriage of Mr Mississippi*, p. 78.
47 Cf., Walser, *Theater Heute*, November 1967, p. 20; Joseph, pp. 59–60.
48 Walser, *Theater Heute*, November 1962, p. 1.
49 Walser, *Der Schwarze Schwan*, Frankfurt, 1964, p. 48.
50 Walser, *Weimarer Beiträge*, 1975, 7, pp. 72, 79.
51 Walser, *Theater Heute*, January 1965, p. 2.
52 *Ibid.*, p. 1.
53 Walser, 'Der Realismus X', in Kreuzer, p. 30.

6 Dialectics

1 Cf., Ronald Hayman, *Techniques of Acting*, London, 1969, and *The German Theatre*, ed. Hayman, London, 1975, pp. 204–5.
2 Hartmut Lange, *Theater Heute*, September 1969, p. 37.
3 Brecht, *Schriften zum Theater*, II, pp. 116–17.
4 Brecht, *The Jewish Wife and other Plays*, trans. Eric Bentley, New York, 1965, p. 111; Baierl, *Stücke*, Berlin, 1969, p. 7.
5 Cf., Friedrich Wolf, in Brecht, *Über Realismus*, Frankfurt, 1971, pp. 142–3. Brecht's defence was that (a) the play was written in 1938 and therefore 'realistic', and (b) 'although Courage learns nothing – the audience can, in my opinion, still learn something by observing her'.
6 Brecht, *The Threepenny Opera*, trans. Hugh MacDiarmid, London, 1973, p. 47; and *Dreigroschenbuch*, Frankfurt, 1960, p. 131. Brecht himself extended his theme of bankers as criminals in *Die Beule* (1931) in which Macheath's band take over the National Deposit Bank.
7 Dürrenmatt, *Komödien* II, Zürich, 1966, p. 278.
8 Cf., Brecht, Notes to *The Threepenny Opera* in *Dreigroschenbuch*, p. 69.
9 Programme Notes to *Frank V*, Schauspielhaus Zürich, p. 9.
10 Dürrenmatt, interview in *Die Tat*, 18 March 1959.
11 *The Threepenny Opera*, p. 25. *Frank V* also contains a direct copy of this song in the bank employees chorus: 'Möchten Gutes tun. Doch eben!/Wollen wir in Wohlstand Leben/Müssen wir Geschäfte machen', *Komödien* II, p. 211.
12 For analyses of the productive uses of Brecht's techniques in *Die Ehe des Herrn Mississippi* and *Die Physiker* see Hans Mayer, in *Der Unbequeme Dürrenmatt*, ed. Reinhold Grimm, Basel, 1962, and Jacob Steiner, 'Die Komödie Dürrenmatts', *Deutschunterricht*, 15/6, 1963.
13 Cf., *Theaterschriften und Reden*, pp. 45, 97, 124, 207–8, 224.
14 Wekwerth, *Theater Heute*, February 1968, p. 18; *Weimarer Beiträge*, 1973, 2, pp. 39, 41.

15 Peter Palitzsch, *Theater Heute*, Sonderheft 1964, pp. 24, 26.
16 Brecht, '*Katzgraben*-Notate', *Schriften zum Theater*, VII, p. 105.
17 *Ibid.*, p. 140.
18 *Schriften zum Theater* VII, pp. 31, 34.
19 *Ibid.*, VII, p. 263.
20 Handke, *Prosa Gedichte Theaterstücke Hörspiel*, p. 303.
21 Palitzsch, in *Deutsche Dramaturgie der sechziger Jahre*, ed. Gotthard Wunberg and Max Niemeyer, Tübingen, 1974, p. 141. Compare Brecht, *The Messingkauf Dialogues*, trans. John Willett, London, 1965, pp. 63–4.
22 Brecht, *Schriften zum Theater* III, p. 101 and *The Messingkauf Dialogues*, p. 59. (Cf. also pp. 62, 88.)
23 The notes and text for *Der Rosenkrieg* are unpublished, in the possession of Palitzsch.
24 Palitzsch, in Joseph, p. 178.
25 *Sommergäste* (Programmheft der Schaubühne am Halleschen Ufer 1974/75, u. Textfassung), introduction, p. 1.
26 *Ibid.*, p. 10.
27 *Ibid.*, p. 68.
28 *Ibid.*, p. 69.
29 Dürrenmatt, *König Johann*, Zürich, 1968, p. 101.
30 Müller, *Theater der Zeit*, 1975, 8, p. 59.
31 Müller, interview with Horst Laube, *Theater Heute*, Sonderheft, 1975, p. 121.
32 *Ibid.*, p. 120.
33 Müller, *Theater der Zeit*, 1975, 8, pp. 58, 59.
34 'Projection 1975', *Schauspiel Frankfurt*, 30 (September 1975), p. 17.
35 Karl Marx, *Die deutsche Ideologie*, cit. David McLellan, *The Young Hegelians and Karl Marx*, New York, 1969, p. 132.
36 Jan Kott, cit., Richard C. Clark, 'Shakespeare's Contemporary Relevance – From Klein to Kott to Knight', *Shakespeare and England* (*Review of National Literatures*), vol. III, 2, pp. 186–7.
37 Müller, *Macbeth*, in *Theater Heute*, June 1972, p. 40.
38 Müller, in *Theater Heute*, Sonderheft, 1975, p. 120.
39 Müller, *Die Schlacht*, in *Theater Heute*, Sonderheft 1975, p. 130.
40 Weiss, in *Materialien zu Peter Weiss' Marat/Sade*, ed. K. H. Braun, Frankfurt, 1967, p. 98 (cf., Brecht's almost identical wording: 'So darf man es nicht machen – Das ist höchst auffällig, fast nicht zu glauben – Das muss aufhören', *Schriften zum Theater*, III, p. 55) and *The Times*, 19 August 1964.
41 Weiss, in *Materialien zu Marat/Sade*, pp. 98, 92.
42 *Ibid.*, p. 92.
43 *Ibid.*, p. 99. Cf., Weiss' definition of contemporary existence by opposites, p. 91.
44 Weiss, *Dramen* I, Frankfurt, 1968, cf., pp. 202, 169, 197, 207.
45 Weiss, in *Materialien zu Marat/Sade*, p. 112.
46 *Ibid.*, pp. 70–1 (Swinarski).
47 *Ibid.*, p. 112 (Weiss).
48 For a more detailed description of Perten's production cf., Heinz Klunker, *Zeitstücke–Zeitgenossen. Gegenwartstheater in der DDR*, Hannover, 1972.
49 Weiss, *Encore* 12, July/August 1965, pp. 19f., and *Materialien zu Marat/Sade*, p. 113.
50 Weiss, *Die Zeit*, 17 September 1971.

7 Documents

1 Erwin Piscator, *Schriften*, Berlin, 1968, II, pp. 203–4. By 1966 the technical capacity of the stage was more equal to the mechanical demands of the moving 'globe', but there were still unfortunate visual associations. Forty years earlier Alfred Kerr had attacked the *Rasputin* 'globe' as 'a creepy-crawly tortoise of grey tent-cloth' – a description which Piscator admitted was justified.
2 Cit., Piscator, *Bühnentechnische Rundschau*, October 1959. For a detailed analysis of Piscator's aims and achievements see my book, *Erwin Piscator's Political Theatre*.
3 Piscator, foreword to Rolf Hochhuth, *Der Stellvertreter*, Reinbek, 1963, pp. 7, 9.
4 Kipphardt, 'Wahrheit wichtiger als Wirkung', *Die Welt*, 11 November 1964, and *In The Matter of J. Robert Oppenheimer*, p. 5.
5 Kipphardt, *Spectaculum*, 1964, 7, p. 363.
6 Piscator, Regiebuch and notes, in the Akademie der Künste, West Berlin.
7 Cf., Karl Jaspers, *Man in the Modern Age*, trans. Eden and Cedar Paul, London, 1933.
8 Weiss, *Die Ermittlung*, Frankfurt, 1965, p. 210.
9 *Ibid.*, pp. 206–7. This is one of the passages cut in the American translation of the play, where the general social relevance which would be as applicable to the USA as the Bundesrepublik is consistently weakened.
10 Horst Niendorf, *Blätter der Freien Volksbühne*, 6, 1965.
11 *Die Ermittlung*, p. 89. One of Weiss' central additions to the transcript, this is an objectified rendering of his personal reaction to Auschwitz: 'as a survivor do I really belong with those who stared at me with their huge eyes whom I long since betrayed? Don't I rather belong with the murderers and hangmen?' (*Fluchtpunkt*, Frankfurt, 1962, p. 211.)
12 Weiss, *Dramen 2*, Frankfurt, 1968, p. 465.
13 Piscator, *Blätter der Freien Volksbühne*, 6, 1965.
14 Weiss, *Rapport 1*, Frankfurt, 1971, p. 142.
15 Weiss, *Discourse on Vietnam*, trans. Geoffrey Skelton, London, 1970, pp. 70, 172.
16 Weiss, *Dramen 2*, p. 470, and *Rapport 2*, Frankfurt, 1971, p. 63.
17 Piscator, *Blätter der Freien Volksbühne*, 6, 1965.
18 Weiss, *Dramen 2*, pp. 202, 270–1.
19 *Ibid.*, p. 469.
20 *Ibid.*, pp. 270, 269.
21 *Ibid.*, pp. 468, 469.
22 Weiss in Joseph, p. 65 – not a totally inaccurate judgement: *Gesang der lusitanischen Popanz* provoked an official protest from the Portuguese government.
23 *Rapport 2*, p. 22.
24 Cf., Joseph, p. 68.
25 Weiss, *Dramen 2*, pp. 470–1.
26 Cf., Brecht, *Schriften zum Theater*, V, pp. 235f.
27 Cf., T. S. Eliot, *The Use of Poetry and the Use of Criticism*, London, 1933, p. 151.
28 Cf., Weiss, *Dramen 1*, Frankfurt, 1968, p. 169.
29 Weiss, in Joseph, p. 66.

30 Weiss, *Kursbuch*, 1966, 6, p. 168.
31 Weiss, *Dramen 2*, pp. 263–4.
32 Cf., Weiss, *Theater Heute*, March 1967, p. 6.
33 Weiss, *Dramen 2*, p. 221.
34 Weiss, *New York Times*, 9 April 1967, and in Joseph, p. 64.
35 Cf., *Discourse on Vietnam*, pp. 71, 166.
36 Cf., Horst Gebhardt, *Theater der Zeit*, 10, 1965, p. 20, and Heinz Plavius, *Zwischen Protest und Anpassung*, Halle, 1970, p. 51.
37 Cf., *Kursbuch*, 6, 1966, p. 176.
38 Weiss, *Sonntag*, 15 August 1966.
39 Lange, Programme Note to *Trotzki in Cocoayan*, Deutsches Schauspielhaus Hamburg, 1972.
40 Weiss, *Dramen 2*, p. 465.
41 *Ibid.*, pp. 204, 253f.
42 'Offener Brief an die *Literaturnaja Gaseta*', in *Über Peter Weiss* ed. Volker Canaris, Frankfurt, 1970, pp. 143, 141.
43 *Sinn und Form*, XVII, 5, p. 685 and *The Times*, 21 June 1969. Weiss has also directed several films, notably in his early surrealist period. For a more detailed discussion of this aspect of his work cf., Ian Hilton, *Peter Weiss. A Search for Affinities*, London, 1970, pp. 14f.
44 Hans Magnus Enzensberger, *Das Verhör von Habana*, Frankfurt, 1970, p. 60.
45 *Trotzki im Exil*, Frankfurt, 1970, p. 9. (Inexplicably this sentence is omitted in the English translation.)
46 Cf., *Das Verhör von Habana*, p. 54.
47 *Ibid.*, p. 34. For Enzensberger's (undramatised) views on Cuba as an ideal socialist state, cf., *Kursbuch*, 18, 1969, pp. 192f.
48 Wallraff, in Arnold, pp. 233, 220, 231.
49 *Ibid.*, pp. 220, 202, 223–4.
50 Dieter Forte, Programme note to *Luther und Münzer*, Basler Theater, 6, 1971, reprinted in Kreuzer, pp. 84f.
51 *Ibid.*, p. 84, and *Theater Heute*, January 1972, p. 42.
52 Forte, *Theater Heute*, January 1972, p. 42.
53 Forte, *Martin Luther und Thomas Münzer*, Berlin, 1971, p. 125.
54 Forte, *Theater Heute*, January 1972, p. 42.
55 Patterson, p. 85.
56 Forte, *Theater Heute*, January 1972, p. 42.

8 Traditions

1 Cf., Interview with Hochhuth, *Partisan Review*, vol. XXXI, 3, reprinted in *The Storm Over the Deputy*, ed. Eric Bentley, New York, 1964, p. 55.
2 *Ibid.*, p. 56, and interview with Hochhuth, *Ramparts*, Spring 1964, also in Bentley, p. 43.
3 Cf., *Der Stellvertreter*, p. 182, where this inherent contradiction is obvious even from the stage-directions.
4 Hochhuth, in Kreuzer, p. 38.
5 Cf., Walter Muschg, 'Hochhuth und Lessing', reprinted as a programme note to the Frankfurt production, Städtische Bühnen, 5/1964.
6 Piscator, Regiebuch, in the Akademie der Künste, West Berlin.
7 Hochhuth, in Bentley, p. 53.
8 The historian Trevor-Roper brough an action against Hochhuth for mis-

representing his views on Sikorski's death in an article in *Der Spiegel* (December 1967) intended to substantiate the accusation against Churchill.

9 Hochhuth, *Soldaten*, Reinbek, 1967, p. 191.
10 Cf., Joseph, pp. 47, 53.
11 Hans Mayer, *Die Zeit*, 13 October 1967.
12 Hochhuth, in Joseph, p. 55.
13 Hochhuth, *Die Guerillas*, Reinbek, 1970, pp. 19–20.
14 Cf., Adorno, *Theater Heute*, July 1967, pp. 1–2.
15 Fritz Hochwälder, ' Über mein Theater', in *German Life and Letters*, 1958–9, p. 103.
16 *Ibid.*, pp. 111, 104.
17 *Ibid.*, pp. 103–4.
18 Hochwälder, *Dramen* 1, München, 1959, pp. 93–4.
19 Hochwälder, in *German Life and Letters*, 1958–9, p. 107.
20 Peter Hacks, *Theater Heute*, September 1961, p. 56.
21 Hacks, Programme note to the DDR première, Volksbühne 1973.
22 Hacks, *Theater Heute*, March 1968, p. 29.
23 Hacks, *Das Poetische, Ansätze zu einer postrevolutionären Dramaturgie*, Frankfurt, 1972, pp. 36, 78.
24 *Ibid.*, pp. 34, 76, 90, 118.
25 Cf., Hacks, *Vier Komödien*, Frankfurt, 1971, p. 277.
26 Cf., Günther Rühle, *Theater Heute*, Sonderheft, 1975, p. 110.
27 Ödön von Horváth, cit., *Theater Heute*, Sonderheft, 1971, p. 73.
28 Horváth, *Stücke*, Hamburg, 1961, pp. 168, 280, and *Sladek oder die schwarze Armee* in *Gesammelte Werke* 1, Frankfurt, 1970, p. 474.
29 Horváth, cit., *Theater Heute*, Sonderheft, 1971, p. 75.
30 Martin Sperr, *Theater Heute*, Sonderheft, 1967, p. 74.
31 Peter Stein, *ibid.*
32 Franz Xaver Kroetz, *Theater Heute*, December 1971, pp. 13–14, and *Süddeutsche Zeitung*, 20/21 November 1971, p. 4 (reprinted in Kreuzer, pp. 78f.).
33 Kroetz, *Suddeutsche Zeitung*, 20/21 November 1971, p. 4.
34 Kroetz, *Gesammelte Stücke*, Frankfurt, 1975, pp. 69, 156, 72, 126, 80, 172.
35 Sperr, *Theater Heute*, Sonderheft, 1967, p. 53.
36 *Ibid.*
37 Reported in *Tageszeitung*, 23 March 1971.
38 Horst Siede, Regiebuch, in the Kammerspiele München.
39 Kroetz, Programme Note to *Heimarbeit/Hartnäckig*, Kammerspiele München, 1971.
40 Kroetz, *Gesammelte Stücke*, pp. 189–94.
41 Kroetz, *Vaterland*, 22 April 1971.
42 Cf., Emile Durkheim, *Suicide*, trans. John Spaulding and George Simpson, New York, 1951, pp. 246, 254, 356–7.
43 Kroetz, *Tageszeitung*, 23 March 1971.
44 Kroetz, *Gesammelte Stücke*, pp. 400, 411. This media element is so intrinsic to the dialogue that in the DDR production (Deutsches Theater, 1974) the proscenium was turned into the frame of a TV screen as the only way of 'locating' the play for an audience who were not exposed to the same advertising slogans.
45 Cf., Kroetz, 'ich entscheide selber was ich mache', and *Das Nest*, in *Theater Heute*, May 1975, pp. 42, 49.
46 Kroetz, *Gesammelte Stücke*, pp. 426, 452, 455, 473.

9 Dialogues

1 Cf., Handke, *Prosa Gedichte Theaterstücke Hörspiel Aufsätze*, p. 303.
2 Handke, *Theater Heute*, March 1968, p. 28.
3 Handke, *Kaspar*, trans. Michael Roloff, London, 1972, p. 58.
4 Handke, *Offending the Audience and Self-Accusation*, pp. 34, 26.
5 Nicholas Hern, *Peter Handke*, London, 1971, pp. 35f.
6 Handke, in Joseph, pp. 28, 27.
7 *Offending the Audience*, pp. 12–13; also repeated in the only other stage direction, pp. 38–9.
8 Handke, in Joseph, p. 32.
9 Handke, *Stücke* I, Frankfurt, 1972, p. 91.
10 Handke, in Joseph, pp. 28, 30.
11 Cf., *Prosa Gedichte Theaterstücke Hörspiel Aufsätze*, p. 266.
12 Handke, in Joseph, pp. 37–8.
13 *Prosa Gedichte Theaterstücke Hörspiel Aufsätze*, p. 305.
14 *Ibid.*, p. 306.
15 Handke, in Joseph, p. 39.
16 Peter Brook, in Judith Cook, *Directors' Theatre*, London, 1974, p. 27.
17 Handke, 'Die Geborgenheit unter der Schädeldecke', *Theater Heute*, December 1973, p. 1, and in Joseph, p. 38.
18 *Prosa Gedichte Theaterstücke Hörspiel Aufsätze*, pp. 158–9, 170.
19 Cf., Hern, p. 82.
20 Handke, *The Ride Across Lake Constance*, trans. Michael Roloff, London, 1973, p. 8.
21 Handke (1969), in Kreuzer, p. 113.
22 Handke, *Theater Heute*, December 1973, p. 2; Sonderheft, 1975, p. 114.
23 Handke, *They Are Dying Out*, trans. Michael Roloff, London, 1975, p. 60.
24 Cf., Hern, pp. 70f., and Patterson, p. 32.
25 Peter Iden, *Theater Heute*, June 1974, p. 58.
26 Thomas Bernhard, *Der Italiener*, Salzburg, 1971, p. 152.
27 Bernhard, *Die Macht der Gewohnheit*, Frankfurt, 1974, p. 34.
28 Bernhard, *Minetti*, published in Programmbuch 21, Würtembergische Staatstheater Stuttgart, 1976, p. 51.
29 Handke, *Theater Heute*, December 1973, p. 2.

10 Conclusions

1 This was the theme of Günter Eich's Büchner Prize speech in 1959, cit., Susanne Müller-Hanpft, *Über Günter Eich*, Frankfurt, 1970, p. 37.
2 Zuckmayer, foreword to *Des Teufels General*, ed. Johnson, London, 1962, p. 34.
3 *Hölderlin*, p. 181.
4 Hacks, *Die Sorgen und die Macht*, in *Fünf Stücke*, Frankfurt, 1965, pp. 341–2.
5 Sperr and Hacks, *Theater Heute*, March 1968, pp. 28–9. Similarly Walser has called Brecht's plays 'at best interpretable as evidence of an out-dated battle' (*Erfahrungen und Leseerfahrungen*, p. 83).
6 Frisch, in Arnold, p. 29.
7 Brecht, *Schriften zum Theater* VI, p. 296.
8 Weiss, in Joseph, p. 66.
9 For an interesting comparison between psychodrama and stage performance

cf. Eric Bentley, 'Theatre and Therapy' in *Theatre of War*, New York, 1972, pp. 385f.

10 Handke, *Die Zeit*, 11 July 1969.
11 Walser, *Kursbuch* 20, 1970, p. 31.
12 Handke, in Joseph, p. 35.
13 *Das Verhör von Habana*, p. 45.
14 Enzensberger, cit., Klaus Konjetzsky, *Weimarer Beiträge*, 7, 1975, p. 70.
15 Walser, 'Arbeitsnotizen', printed as a Programme Note to *Eiche und Angora*, Schiller Theater, 1962/3 Heft 124.
16 Hacks, *Vier Komödien*, p. 115.

Chronology

Chronology	Major world premières	Traditional forms	Epic theatre and derivatives	Images (Absurdist)	Documentary drama	Linguistic theatre
1944 All theatres in Germany and Austria closed	Wilder, *The Skin of Our Teeth*					
1945 Reopening of Deutsches Th. (Berlin), Schlosspark Th. (Berlin), Burgth. (Vienna)		Frisch, *Nun singen sie wieder* (Requiem)				
1946 Nuremberg War Criminals trial		Zuckmayer, *Des Teufels General* (Naturalism)				
1947 Brecht leaves USA for Switzerland	Williams, *Streetcar Named Desire*	Borchert, *Draussen vor der Tür* (Expressionism)	Brecht, *Antigone* (Zürich production)			
1948 Brecht writes *Kleines Organon für das Theater*		Hochwälder, *Der öffentliche Ankläger* (historical problem play)	Brecht, *Puntila* (Zürich production)			
1949 Brecht founds Berliner Ensemble in East Berlin	Miller, *Death of a Salesman*		Brecht, *Mutter Courage* (B.E. production)			
1950	Ionesco, *La Cantatrice Chauve*	Zuckmayer, *Gesang im Feuerofen* (Expressionism & Requiem)				

Chronology	Major world premières	Traditional forms	Epic theatre and derivatives	Images (Absurdist)	Documentary drama	Linguistic theatre
1951 Wekwerth and Palitzsch join B.E. Piscator returns to Germany						
1952			Dürrenmatt, *Die Ehe des Herrn Mississippi*			
1953 Uprising of East Berlin workers crushed by Soviets	Miller, *The Crucible*. Beckett, *Waiting for Godot* (Directed by Beckett, Berlin 1975)		Strittmatter, *Katz-graben*. (Hacks, *Volksbuch v. Herzog Ernst* – premiere 1967). Dürrenmatt, *Engel kommt nach Babylon*			
1954			Brecht, *kauk. Kreidekreis* (B.E. production)			
1955 Dürrenmatt publishes *Theaterprobleme*	Williams, *Cat on a Hot Tin Roof*	Zuckmayer, *Das kalte Licht* (Naturalism)				
1956 Brecht dies. Hungarian uprising crushed by Soviets	Osborne, *Look Back in Anger*		Dürrenmatt, *Besuch der alten Dame*. Hacks, *Schlacht bei Lobositz*			
1957 Mao: 'Hundred Flowers' speech	Beckett, *Endgame* (directed by Beckett, Berlin 1967)					

Chronology	Major world premières	Traditional forms	Epic theatre and derivatives	Images (Absurdist)	Documentary drama	Linguistic theatre
1958	Pinter, *The Birthday Party*		Frisch, *Biedermann u. die Brandstifter*	Hildesheimer, *Pastorale.* Grass, *Onkel Onkel*		
1959 DDR 'Bitterfeld Line' proclaimed. Kipphardt dismissed from Deutsches Th., leaves DDR	Arden, *Serjeant Musgrave's Dance.* Wesker, *Roots*					
1960 Palitzsch leaves DDR. Eichmann trial				Dorst, *Die Kurve, Freiheit für Clemens*		
1961 Jaspers publishes *Die Atombombe und die Zukunft des Menschen.* Berlin Wall erected	Osborne, *Luther*		Baierl, *Frau Flinz* (Dialectical)	Dorst, *Grosse Schmährede.* Grass, *Die bösen Köche.* Walser, *Der Abstecher*		
1962 Piscator appointed 1st *Intendant* of Freie Volksbühne (West Berlin). Bay of Pigs invasion, Cuba	Albee, *Who's Afraid of Virginia Woolf?*		Dürrenmatt, *Die Physiker.* Walser, *Eiche u. Angora*	Weiss, *Nacht mit Gästen*		
1963 Gründgens dies. Frankfurt Auschwitz trials (1963–5)	Ionesco, *Victimes du devoir* (directed by Ionesco, Zürich 1968)	Hochhuth, *Der Stellvertreter* (Schillerian drama of ideas)	Dürrenmatt, *Herkules*			

Chronology	Major world premières	Traditional forms	Epic theatre and derivatives	(Absurdist)	drama	theatre
1964 Peking Opera announced as spearhead of Cultural Revolution	Brook, 'Theatre of Cruelty' season	(Horváth revival, *Kasimir u. Karoline*)	Brecht/Wekwerth, *Coriolan*. Weiss, *Marat/Sade*. Walser, *Der schwarze Schwan*		Kipphardt, *Oppenheimer*	
1965	Bond, *Saved* (German première, 1967)				Weiss, *Die Ermittlung*. Kipphardt, *Joel Brand*	
1966 Piscator dies. Princeton meeting of Group 47. Angolan war of liberation intensifies	Brook, *US*. Grotowski, *Akropolis* (Paris performance)	(Horváth revival, *Geschichten aus dem Wienerwald*) Sperr, *Jagdszenen* (folkplay)	Dürrenmatt, *Der Meteor*	Grass, *Die Plebeier*	Kirst/Piscator, *Aufstand der Offiziere*	Handke, *Publikumsbeschimpfung, Selbstbezichtigung*
1967 Vietnam protest intensifies		Hochhuth, *Soldaten* (Schillerian heroic tragedy). Sperr, *Landshuter Erzählungen* (folkplay). Ziem, *Nachrichten aus der Provinz* (folkplay)	Palitzsch/Shakespeare, *Der Rosenkrieg* (Dialectical)		Weiss, *Gesang der l. Popanz*	
1968 DDR army participates with Soviets in invasion of Czechoslovakia. French students take over Comédie Française	Living Theatre, *Paradise Now* (performed in Berlin, 1970)	Hacks, *Amphitryon* (new classicism). Bauer, *Magic Afternoon* (corrupt folkplay)		Dorst, *Toller*	Weiss, *Vietnam Diskurs*. Wallraff, *Nachspiele*	Handke, *Kaspar*
1969			Dürrenmatt, *Play Strindberg*. Frisch, *Biographie: Ein Spiel*			Handke, *Mündel will Vormund sein*

285

Chronology	Major world premières	Traditional forms	Epic theatre and derivatives	Images (Absurdist)	Documentary drama	Linguistic theatre
1970	Brook/Shakespeare, *Midsummer Night's Dream*	Hochhuth, *Guerillas* (heroic symbolism)		Bernhard, *Ein Fest für Boris*	Weiss, *Trotzki im Exil.* Forte, *Martin Luther.* Enzensberger, *Verhör von Habana*	Handke, *Ritt über den Bodensee*
1971 Eighth Party Congress of SED	Brook, *Orghast*	Kroetz, *Heimarbeit* (folkplay). Fassbinder, *Bremer Freiheit* (popularised folkplay)			Weiss, *Hölderlin*	
1972 Helene Weigel dies		Kroetz, *Stallerhof, Oberösterreich* (folk plays). Hochhuth, *Die Hebamme* (Aristotelian farce)	Müller, *Macbeth*		Lange, *Trotzki in Coyoacan*	Bernhard, *Ignorant u. der Wahnsinnige*
1973 US withdrawal from Vietnam		Hacks, *Adam u. Eva* (poetic transcendence). Kroetz, *Maria Magdelena* (updating the classics)		Dorst, *Eiszeit*		
1974			Stein/Gorki, *Sommergäste*			Bernhard, *Macht der Gewohnheit.* Handke, *Die Unvernünftigen*

Chronology	Major world premières	Traditional forms	Epic theatre and derivatives	Images (Absurdist)	Documentary drama	Linguistic theatre
1975		Kroetz, *Das Nest* (developed folkplay)		Kafka/Weiss, *Der Prozess*		
1976 Wolf Biermann exiled from DDR			Stein, *Shakespeare's Memory*			
1977	Bolt, *State of Revolution*				Forte, *Jean-Henri Dunant*	Bernhard, *Minetti*

Selected bibliography

The Plays: Major Translations in English

Bauer, Wolfgang. *All Change and Other Plays* (*Magic afternoon*; *All Change*; *Party for Six*), tr. Martin and Renate Esslin, London, 1973.

Bernhard, Thomas. *The Force of Habit*, tr. Neville & Stephen Place, London, 1976.

Borchert, Wolfgang. *The Man Outside*, tr. David Porter, Foreword, Kaye Boyle, intro. Stephen Spender, New York, 1971.

Outside the Door, Engl. version by Erwin Piscator & Zoe Lund-Schiller, Paris, 1949.

Dorst, Tankred. *The Curve*, tr. Henry Beissel, Montreal, 1963.

Freedom for Clemens, tr. George Wellwarth, *Postwar German Theatre*, New York, 1967.

Grand Tirade at the Town-Wall, tr. Henry Beissel, Montreal, 1961.

A Trumpet for Nap, a play for marionettes. In a free tr. and with original lyrics by Henry Beissel, Montreal, 1968.

Dürrenmatt, Friedrich. *Four Plays* (*Romulus the Great*; *The Marriage of Mr Mississippi*; *An Angel Comes to Babylon*; *The Physicists*) tr. Gerhard Nellhaus and others, London, 1964.

Hercules and the Augean Stables, tr. Agnes Hamilton, Chicago, 1963.

Incident at Twilight, tr. George Wellwarth, in *Postwar German Theatre*, New York, 1967.

The Marriage of Mr Mississippi & *Problems of the Theatre*, tr. Michael Bullock, New York, 1964.

The Meteor, tr. James Kirkup, London, 1973.

Play Strindberg, tr. James Kirkup, London, 1972.

The Visit, adapt. by Maurice Valency, New York, 1958.

The Visit, tr. Patrick Bowles, London, 1973.

Writings on Theatre and Drama, tr. H. M. Waidson, London, 1976.

Eich, Günter, *Journeys*: two radio plays tr. Michael Hamburger, London, 1968.

Enzensberger, Hans Magnus. *The Havana Inquiry*, tr. Peter Mayer, intro. Martin Duberman, New York, 1974.

Forte, Dieter. *Luther, Münzer, and the Bookkeepers of the Reformation*, tr. Christopher Holme, New York, 1973.

Frisch, Max, *Andorra*, tr. Michael Bullock, New York, 1964.

Biography : a Game, tr. Michael Bullock, New York, 1969.

The Chinese Wall, tr. James L. Rosenberg, intro. by Harold Clurman, New York, 1961.

The Firebugs, tr. Mordecai Gorelik, New York, 1963.

The Fireraisers, tr. Michael Bullock, London, 1973.

Four Plays (*The Great Wall of China*; *Don Juan or The Love of Geometry*; *Philipp Hotz's Fury*; *Biography : a Game*), tr. Michael Bullock, London, 1969.

Now They Sing Again, tr. Michael Roloff, in *The Contemporary German Theatre*, New York, 1972.

Three Plays (*Don Juan or the Love of Geometry*; *The Great Rage of Philip Hotz*; *When the War was Over*), tr. James L. Rosenberg, New York, 1967.

Three Plays (*The Fireraisers*; *Graf Öderland*; *Andorra*), tr. Michael Bullock, London, 1962.

Grass, Günter. *Four Plays* (*Flood*; *Mister-Mister*; *Only Ten Minutes to Buffalo*; *The Wicked Cooks*), tr. Ralph Manheim & A. Leslie Willson, intro. Martin Esslin, London, 1968.

Max : a Play, (German title: *Davor*), tr. A. Leslie Willson & Ralph Manheim, New York, 1972.

The Plebians Rehearse the Uprising, tr. Ralph Manheim, London, 1967.

Rocking Back and Forth, tr. George Wellwarth, in *Postwar German Theatre*, New York, 1967.

Handke, Peter. *Kaspar*, tr. Michael Roloff, London, 1972.

Offending the Audience; and *Self-Accusation*, tr. Michael Roloff, London, 1971.

The Ride Across Lake Constance, tr. Michael Roloff, London, 1973.

They Are Dying Out, tr. Michael Roloff, London, 1975.

Hildesheimer, Wolfgang. *Nightpiece*, tr. Hildesheimer in *Postwar German Theatre*, New York, 1967.

The Sacrifice of Helen, tr. Jacques-Jean Rose, Philadelphia, Pennsylvania, 1968.

Hochhuth, Rolf. *The Deputy*, tr. Richard & Clara Winston, New York, 1964.

The Representative, tr. with a preface: Robert Macdonald, Harmondsworth, 1969.

Soldiers, tr. Robert Macdonald, London, 1968.

Hochwälder, Fritz. *The Public Prosecutor*, tr. Kitty Black, London, 1958.

The Strong are Lonely, adapted by Eva Le Gallienne from the French version by J. Mercure & R. Thieberger, London, 1968.

Kipphardt, Heinar. *In the Matter of J. Robert Oppenheimer*, tr. Ruth Speirs, London, 1967.

Kroetz, Franz Xaver. *Farmyard and Four Other Plays*, (*Request Concert*; *Farmyard*; *Michi's Blood*; *Men's Business*; *A Man, a Dictionary*), tr. Jack Gelber, Michael Roloff, Peter Sander, Carl Weber, New York, 1976.

Sperr, Martin. *Hunting Scenes from Lower Bavaria*, tr. Michael Roloff, in *The Contemporary German Theatre*, New York, 1972.

Tales from Landshut, tr. Anthony Vivis, London, 1969.

Walser, Martin. *Home Front*, tr. Michael Roloff, in *The Contemporary German Theatre*, New York, 1972.

The Rabbit Race and The Detour, tr. R. Duncan & R. Grunberger, London, 1963.

Weiss, Peter. *Discourse on Vietnam*, tr. Geoffrey Skelton, London, 1970.

How Mr Mockinpott was Cured of his Sufferings, tr. Michael Roloff, in *The Contemporary German Theatre*, New York, 1972.

The Investigation : Oratorio in 11 Cantos, tr. Alexander Gross, London, 1966.

The Persecution and Assassination of Jean-Paul Marat, Engl. version Geoffrey Skelton; verse adaptation by Adrian Mitchell, intro. Peter Brook, London, 1965.

The Tower, tr. Michael Benedickt in *Postwar German Theatre*, New York, 1967.

Trotsky in Exile, tr. Geoffrey Skelton, London, 1971.

Two Plays (*The Song of the Lusitanian Bogey* and *Discourse on Vietnam*), tr. Lee Baxandall & Geoffrey Skelton, New York, 1970.

Secondary literature in English

Bauland, Peter. *The Hooded Eagle : Modern German Drama on the New York Stage*, New York 1968.

Bentley, Eric (ed.) *The Storm Over the Deputy*, New York, 1964.

Best, Otto F. *Peter Weiss*, New York, 1967.

Cunliffe, Gordon W. *Günter Grass*, New York, 1969.

Davies, Cecil W. *Theatre for the People, The Story of the Volksbühne*, Austin, Texas, 1977.

Demetz, Peter. *Postwar German Literature : A Critical Survey*, New York, 1970.

Esslin, Martin. *The Theatre of the Absurd*, Harmondsworth, 1968.

Garten, H. F. *Modern German Drama*, London, 1964.

Hayman, Ronald (ed.) *The German Theatre*, London, 1975.

Hern, Nicholas. *Peter Handke – Theatre and Anti-theatre* (Modern German Authors Series, vol. 5), London, 1971.

Hilton, Ian. *Peter Weiss – A Search for Affinities* (Modern German Authors Series, vol. 3), London, 1970.

Innes, Christopher D. *Erwin Piscator's Political Theatre*, Cambridge, 1972.

Jenny, Urs. *Dürrenmatt, A Study of his Plays*, London, 1973.

Leonard, Irene. *Günter Grass*, Edinburgh, 1974.

Mason, Ann L. *The Sképtical Muse : A Study of Günter Grass' Conception of the Artist*, Bern, 1974.

Patterson, Michael. *German Theatre Today*, London, 1976.

Schmidt, Dolores & Earl (eds.) *The Deputy Reader : Studies in Moral Responsibility*, Chicago, 1965.

Shaw, Leroy R. (ed.) *The German Theatre Today. A Symposium*, Austin, Texas, 1963.

Sokel, Walter H. *The Writer in Extremis – Expressionism in 20th Century German Literature*, Stanford, Calif., 1959.

Subiotto, Arrigo V. *German Documentary Theatre*, Birmingham, 1972.

Tank, Curt L. *Günter Grass*, New York, 1969.

Thomas, R. H. & Bullivant, K. *Literature in Upheaval, West German Writers and the Challenge of the 1960s*, Manchester, 1974.

Weisstein, Ulrich. *Max Frisch*, New York, 1967.

Index

Index

Capote, Truman, 64
Castle, The (Das Schloss – Kafka, Franz), 84
Caucasian Chalk Circle, The (Die Kaukasische Kreidekreis – Brecht, Bertolt), 283
Chaikin, Joseph, 167
Change of Residence . . .(Die Umsiedlerin oder das Leben auf dem Land – Müller, Heiner), 72
Chapbook of Duke Ernest, The (Das Volksbuch vom Herzog Ernst – Hacks, Peter), 215, 283
Chekhov, Anton, 22, 269
Clair, René, 96
Cold Light, The (Zuckmayer, Karl), 120, 199, 283
Congreve, William, 9
Conspiracy, The (Die Verschwörung – Schäfer, Walter), 26
Coriolan (Brecht, Bertolt), 16, 18, 52, 56, 75, 94, 140, 285
Coriolanus (Shakespeare, William), 7, 16, 199
Craig, Edward Gordon, 142
Cries for Help (Hilferufe – Handke, Peter), 240–1

Dairy Farm (Stallerhof – Kroetz, Franz Xaver), **224–6**, 229–30, 286
Dallas 22 November (Jens, Walter), 171
Dance of Death, The (Strindberg, August), 124, 139, 187
Danton's Death (Dantons Tod – Büchner, Georg), 167
Days of the Commune (Die Tage der Kommune – Brecht, Bertolt), 70
Death of a Salesman, (Miller, Arthur), 1
Derschaus, Christoph, 69
Detour, The (Der Abstecher – Walser, Martin), 131, 284
Devil's General, The (Des Teufels General – Zuckmayer, Karl), 20, **22–6**, 39, 208, 282
Dialectical theatre, 5, 16, 101, **135f.**
Diechsel, Wolfgang, 235
Dirty Hands (Sartre, Jean-Paul), 208
Discourse on Vietnam (Vietnam–Diskurs – Weiss, Peter), 165, 167, 173, **178–88**, 260, 263, 285
Distraction (Verstörung – Bernhard, Thomas), 257
Documentary theatre, 5, 11, 13, 46, **165f.**, 263–6
Doll's House, A (Ibsen, Henrik), 187, 200

Don Carlos (Schiller, Friedrich), 203–4
Don Juan or The Love of Geometry (Don Juan oder die Liebe der Geometrie – Frisch, Max), 79
Dorst, Tankred, 1, 3, 7, 45, 48, 52–4, **57–9**, 78, 82, 84–5, **88–92**, 93–4, 97, 100, 260, 266
Dream Play (Strindberg, August), 29, 32, 250
Drums in the Night (Trommeln in der Nacht – Brecht, Bertolt), 33
Dürrenmatt, Friedrich, 1, 2, 3, 7, 12, 13, 15, 40, **41–5**, 48, 51, 63, 78, 101, **106–19**, **120–4**, 126, 130–1, 137–9, 152, 202–17, 261–2, 267

Eh Joe (Beckett, Samuel), 254
Ehrenburg, Ilya, 269
Eich, Günther, 260
Einen Jux will er sich machen (Nestroy, Johann Nepomuk), 219
Eisenstein, Sergei, 56
Eisler, Hanns, 218
Eiszeit (Dorst, Tankred), 286
El Gran Teatro del Mundo (Calderón, Pedro), 210
Eliot, T. S., 78, 184
Empedokles (Hölderlin, Johann), 62
Endgame (Beckett, Samuel), 79, **80–1**, 82, 254, 283
Engel, Erich, 52, 93, 94
Entertainer, The (Osborne, John), 137
Enzensberger, Hans Magnus, 47, 68, 187, **189–95**, 265
Epic theatre, 5, 7, 10, 13, 16, 73, **101f.**, 263
Esther (Hochwälder, Fritz), 213
Everyman, 105, 208–10
Evil Omen, The (Das böse Omen – Bernhard, Thomas), 256
Exception and the Rule, The (Die Ausnahme und die Regel – Brecht, Bertolt), 108, 135
Expressionism, 5, 6, 15, **28–35**, 39, 108, 269

Faith, Love and Hope (Glaube, Liebe, Hoffnung – Horváth, Ödön von), 236
Family Favourites (Wunschkonzert – Kroetz, Franz Xaver), 230–1
Fassbinder, Werner, 68, 222, 227, 235
Faust (Goethe, Johann Wolfgang), 18, 233
Feast for Boris, A (Ein Fest für Boris – Bernhard, Thomas), 254, 286
Felsenstein, Walter, 75

292